The Hidden War

(The Desecration of the Promise of America)

By Richard Otto

Critical Acclaim for "The Paradox of our National Security Complex" and "Rethinking America"

The Paradox...
"Richard Otto has produced a powerful overview of our dangerous, gargantuan national security state...I highly recommend this book."
Donald Jeffries, author of Hidden History and Survival of the Richest

"Don't just read it—STUDY it."
David R. Wayne, co-author of Dead Wrong and Hit List

"Highly recommended."
Vincent Palamara, author of Survivor's Guilt and The Not-So-Secret Service

"This is a chilling and well-informed book. I regard it as a moral imperative to articulate such thoughts."
David Lorimar, Paradigm Explorer

"This meticulously researched and referenced work is masterfully written and leaves nothing to the imagination. It is a must-read for researchers and anyone questioning why the United States seems to have entered an era where war and destruction seem to be a never-ending cycle."
Robert Kirkconnell, author of American Heart of Darkness

Rethinking America...

"Reading "Rethinking America" is absolutely one of the most therapeutic exercises I've had in many years. Reading it answered so many questions and connected so many dots that it brings our current era into sharp focus. Richard Otto's summary of American history and his ability to identify the many underlying social forces that have maneuvered America's ship of state into the present era, allows one to make sense of today's America. Otto brings all the pieces of America's political and historical puzzle together into a crystal-clear whole. This is an instant classic that should be read by every thinking person who craves a comprehensive understanding of America's complex trajectory into the present."
Carl Williams, Vietnam veteran and courageous political activist

"In author Rick Otto's latest book, Rethinking America, you may not agree with every point he makes, but you will find that his grasp of US History is quite expansive. Interestingly, you'll also learn about the author's own background, and that of his family, and in particular, about his father's wartime experiences in Vietnam. But, throughout, what is most noticeable, is his depth of research, from the Indian Wars to today. To give one example, many may not understand that Senator Robert F. Kennedy was clearly killed because he was planning to bring to justice those who were behind the conspiracy to kill his brother, President John F. Kennedy. The book's historical details on the administration of JFK are especially poignant -- from his war with the mob, to civil rights, the environment, to his valiant work in international diplomacy, and his unique support for the arts and education. Not surprisingly, the author joins the call for Nancy Pelosi to reopen all of the 1960s assassination conspiracy cases. Finally, with the Trump impeachment hearings in progress and the next presidential election less than a year away, this book offers a timely warning: Beware of lies masquerading as truth!"
Patrick Nolan, author of "CIA Rogues and the Killing of the Kennedys"

The pathological liars who have stained and torn what the American flag is supposed to stand for have nowhere to hide once you read this explosive book! With the precision of a surgeon's scalpel, Richard has exposed the fundamental lies that have corrupted the American republic and the traitors who have conjured them up. This wonderfully talented and experienced writer has put a face on what most Americans, more and more, know is outright deception. He has shined a flashlight on the outrageous assassinations of the 1960s, coming up with dark, hidden secrets never before exposed. Add to this that this book exposes how these lies have festered for years and poisoned the present. We must rethink America because we do not know where we are and how we got here, until now. From beginner to seasoned researcher, you will not be able to put this book down without saying -- "No wonder we are in the mess we are in!" And thanking Richard Otto for exposing America's darkest secrets!
Robert Kirkconnell, author of "American Heart of Darkness Vol. I & II"

I dedicate this book to my loving father who died on March 4, 2015, and his twin – my beloved uncle Dick who passed away in 2008.

"I have a foreboding of an America in my children's and grandchildren's time – when the United States is a service and information economy; when nearly all the key manufacturing industries have slipped away to other countries; when awesome technological powers are in the hands of a very few, and no one representing the public interest can even grasp the issues; when people have lost the ability to set their own agendas or knowledgeably question those in authority; when, clutching our crystals and nervously consulting our horoscopes, our critical faculties in decline, unable to distinguish between what feels good and what's true, we slide, almost without noticing, back into superstition and darkness. The dumbing down of America is most evident in the slow decay of substantive content in the enormously influential media, the 30-second soundbites (now down to 10 seconds or less), lowest common denominator programming, credulous presentations on pseudoscience and superstition, but especially a kind of celebration of ignorance."

Carl Sagan (astronomer, astrophysicist, astrobiologist, and author) as quoted in his co-authored book "The Demon-Haunted World" published in 1997

Kindle Direct Publishing, 2020

Text copyright: Richard A. Otto

ISBN: 9798564476980

All rights reserved. Except for brief quotations in critical articles or reviews, no part of this book may be reproduced in any manner without written permission from Richard A. Otto.

The rights of Richard A. Otto as author have been asserted in accordance with the Copyright, Designs and Patents Act 1988.

Design: April Bowles/Jonathan Lewis (front cover)

Table of Contents

Preface	1-11
CHAPTER 1 - Where are the Journalists?	12-23
CHAPTER 2 - The Forgotten Snow	24-27
CHAPTER 3 - Knocking on Hell's Gate	28-33
CHAPTER 4 - The Secret Government and its threat to our Democratic Republic	34-37
CHAPTER 5 - Murder Incorporated (The 1954 Guatemalan Training Documents)	38-56
CHAPTER 6 - A Horrifying Discovery by the Green Onion	57-69
CHAPTER 7 - A House of Cards	70-74
CHAPTER 8 - A Coup in Dallas (The CIA's Consciousness of Guilt)	75-94
CHAPTER 9 - The Devil Collects his Price for Dealey Plaza (Remembering 1968)	95-103
CHAPTER 10 - The Urgency of Now (The Words of Jesus Inspire a Non-violent Crusade for Justice)	104-108
CHAPTER 11 - The Case for Conspiracy (The RFK Assassination)	109-122
CHAPTER 12 - The Looking Glass (Rethinking America)	123-136
CHAPTER 13 - A Bitter Harvest	137-163
CHAPTER 14 - Has Capitalism revealed its Innate Flaw?	164-167
CHAPTER 15 - It is a Sin to Silence a Mockingbird	168-176
CHAPTER 16 - Why Not?	177-184
CHAPTER 17 - The Enemy Within	185-191
CHAPTER 18 - The Shaming of our Discontent	192-201
CHAPTER 19 - Specifying the Targets of Hatred	202-208
CHAPTER 20 - Death of Russiagate	209-219
CHAPTER 21 - Water Most Foul	220-229
CHAPTER 22 - Broken Windows	230-241
CHAPTER 23 – The Need for Public Financial Banks and the Hazards of Incrementalism	242-244
Conclusion – Where are the leaders?	245-251
Epilogue	252-257
Bibliography and Sources	258-269

Preface

My prior volumes were entitled "The Paradox of our National Security Complex" and "RETHINKING AMERICA: Lies Masquerading as Truth." This new book is fundamentally a sequel to my prior volumes. It is essentially my final thoughts on how the politics of this nation have descended into its present perverted state and how the rise of our national security complex rose to such heights that it dominates our domestic priorities and dictates the objectives of our foreign policy, regardless of which party occupies the White House. It has become such a behemoth in our nation and so intimately enmeshed in our daily lives that it has become impervious to criticism. Consequently, this complex with all its alliances, most particularly with the mainstream media, can capriciously dismiss, disparage, persecute and even murder those who muster the courage to attempt to critique, reveal its secrets and reform it.

This tome includes essential essays that have been augmented and amended in some cases from my prior books to lay the foundation of my analysis that buttress the revelations elicited in the new articles. This was done so that if a reader just wanted to read this volume the contextual framework of my prior writings would not be omitted.

These volumes, most particularly my second book, are about the America I thought existed when I was a child in the 1960s and 1970s sheltered within the enclaves of the white middle class and that America I discovered in my research. The real America that I reveal refutes the common narrative we are taught in school or is perpetuated by the corporate media, the intelligence community, the entertainment industry and the advertising of products that is accepted by many without critical deliberation. Most of this narrative is constructed on a foundation of lies, myths and half-truths that appeals to our pride and patriotism.

The real history of our nation is dismissed reflexively by most as unpatriotic or too disturbing for many to accept. The reality that I examine goes back to our founding, but I focus on those influences that were dominant after our victories over Nazi Germany, fascist Italy, and Japan. Ever since World War II ended, the aristocracy have committed their vast resources to reclaiming that power that the New Deal transferred to the people which culminated in a civil war in the 1960s that most of our citizens are not even aware of.

The power struggles that were waged within this war were not held on battlefields but were covert actions that were classified such as the FBI's COINTELPRO and the CIA's Operation Chaos, Mockingbird and MKULTRA. As

The Hidden War

such, the quest for power over our past, present, and future were virtually unknown to most of America. And while some of this turbulence and violence percolated into the streets and onto the front pages of many newspapers, there was effectively no palpable comprehension of the dynamics of this unconventional war of ideological visions in which the people's republic and their American dream ended up on the losing side.

Robert Kennedy in his presidential campaign for the Democratic nomination at Kansas State University on March 18, 1968, alluded to this conflict when he warned, "I urge you to learn the harsh facts that lurk behind the mask of official illusion with which we have concealed our true circumstances, even from ourselves.

Our country is in danger: not just from foreign enemies, but above all, from our own misguided policies – and what they can do to the nation that Thomas Jefferson once told us was the last, best, hope of man.

There is a contest on, not for the rule of America, but for the heart of America."

These remarks become more ominous with the knowledge that Senator Kennedy had been secretly investigating the assassination of his brother in Dallas ever since the shots rang out in Dealey Plaza and had become familiar with those powers hidden in the shadows, in the bowels of government and by the "mask" he referred to that were determined to impose their vision of America by covert action and by violence, if necessary, upon all the rest of us. Thus, he knew as he admitted to some during his campaign that there were guns between him and the White House.

Their eventual triumph led us on a path towards building an empire not a democratic republic that benefits the establishment and their corporate manifestations. The consequence is that we now reside within a corporate Oligarchy aligned with our national security complex with a new generation of rapacious robber barons that have created a modern Gilded Age.

The American experiment has been a tale of contradictions ever since we achieved our independence from Great Britain. The foundation of our separation was to ensure that the governed were never "taxed without representation" and that enshrined in our founding documents were that government power was limited and balanced while protecting our fundamental constitutional rights. A government whose primary fiduciary obligation was to respond to the interests of the governed.

And yet, the Constitution that was enlightened further by the attachment of the Bill of Rights that buttressed our liberty paradoxically tolerated the institution of slavery which was the antithesis of freedom. Although the government was intended to represent the people, only white male property owners were legally permitted to vote for their representatives and leaders.

The founders were not oblivious to these conflicting concepts incorporated within our founding documents and were justly concerned how these paradoxes could undermine our liberty, our solidarity, our national integrity and ultimately the viability of our republic's survival. They felt impotent in particular cases to confront these contradictions, some of which they believed were in the interest of the country, but, in any event, created a Constitution that was malleable, so that each generation could limit or expand its mandates or make the privileges contained therein more inclusive through amendments approved by the governed.

Others provoked such intense passion that they surmised that if they attempted to confront these flaws entrenched within the framework of their young republic that its fragile connections could be ripped apart before the nation had a chance to consolidate the bonds that connected them. This certainly was true of slavery.

George Washington and Thomas Jefferson that ironically benefited from slave labor, knowing it was morally wrong, for example, held on to the delusion that slavery would over time fade away and die a natural death. Washington even in his last Will and Testament upon his wife's death freed his slaves and bequest small parcels of land and money to help educate their children, so they could be literate. He hoped that because of his stature within our nation that this act would encourage others to do the same. Unfortunately, it had no impact. Even his wife Martha bequest her personal slaves to other family members.

Most of the South of course was determined to not let that foretold eventuality of a "natural death" be realized. The southern aristocracy that had become dependent on slave labor to maintain its status and permitted their ostentatious lifestyle, and clearly had been its sole beneficiary, used their influence to promote its expansion beyond the Mississippi River as western territories that were acquired by the Jefferson administration from France, known as the Louisiana Purchase, were reconfigured into new states.

They knew that if slavery remained only where it had been established that overtime they would be outnumbered by free states and would eventually lose

The Hidden War

its majority in Congress as their opponents multiplied. Thus, they zealously fought for its perpetuation in the Missouri Compromise of 1820 which regulated the expansion of slavery for the next three decades. This agreement authorized the admission of Missouri as a slave state and Maine as a free state into the Union. It further prohibited slave states north of Missouri's southern border. Although the South had made concessions, the overall thrust of the compromise fell far short of what abolitionist groups had envisioned.

The catalyst that reignited the smoldering derisive tensions between abolitionists and slave enthusiasts was the Mexican-American War (1846-1848) which resulted in the acquisition of vast new territories during the administration of James K. Polk. The war had been instigated by the annexation of Texas that Mexico refused to accept.

Lincoln was elected to the House of Representatives as a Whig from Illinois in the fall of 1846, taking control of that seat in March of the following year. He served only one term and left office in March of 1849. During his brief congressional experience, the war was winding down and was in the negotiation stage. Lincoln had vehemently opposed this conflict on the ground that he believed President Polk had provoked an unnecessary war with a neighbor and that the pretext used to justify it was false. He never accepted the administration's assertion that Mexico deliberately without provocation had crossed the Rio Grande and attacked our troops commanded by Zachary Taylor that was the catalyst for the war. More significantly, he considered this a ruse to expand slavery into these newly acquired territories that resulted from Mexico's defeat.

The reviving of these old contentions culminated in 5 separate bills that originated in the Senate that became known as the Compromise of 1850. These bills were mediated by Whig Senator Henry Clay, a hero of Abraham Lincoln, and Democratic Senator Stephen Douglas which was supported by President Millard Fillmore. The compromise settled Texas' borders and admitted California as a free state. The New Mexico and Utah territories were governed by the concept of "popular sovereignty" which essentially granted the people the power who resided within these territories to decide if slavery was legally permitted. Most of the residents were opposed to Slavery. Many historians have contended that this accord had sufficiently diffused the issue to the extent that its enactment postponed the inevitable calamitous confrontation that would be known as the Civil War.

Preface

These accords that averted war and reduced tensions would be disturbed again when Senator Douglas sponsored the Kansas-Nebraska Act of 1854. This bill's passage not only disrupted the delicate balances of 1850 but is also accredited with repealing the Compromise of 1820. The main thrust of the bill was based on popular sovereignty which permitted each territory or newly admitted state the right to decide for themselves if slavery would be allowed not the Congress. This led to conflicts known as "Kansas bleeding" which were violent confrontations between anti and pro-slavery militias. It also gave rise to the anti-slavery Republican Party.

Lincoln, as mentioned above, was a former Whig congressman who at the time was a country lawyer traveling around the state of Illinois representing clients in court. He was infuriated that Douglas had overturned Senator Clay's monumental achievement while opening the flood gates for slavery's expansion north of Missouri's southern border and further west, prolonging its viability into the future.

He initiated his campaign to repeal Douglas' bill by joining the fledgling Republican Party in 1856 which gave him the platform to oppose Douglas in 1858. The Democratic senator felt compelled to debate his rival that had shadowed him all over the State. This resulted in the famous Lincoln-Douglas debates. Although Lincoln lost his bid for Douglas's senate seat, he had created a name for himself in the mid-west that planted the seed that would germinate into his triumph at the Republican convention in May of 1860. It was, however, his speech at the Cooper Union in New York City on February 27, 1860, that quelled any notion that he was not intellectually qualified to manage the awesome duties of the presidency at a time of national peril. The objective of Lincoln's analysis was to prove that it was not in our national interest to permit the expansion of slavery and that in fact the founding generation agreed with him.

This speech had a profound effect on those who were present to hear it. One prominent New York writer penned "No man ever before made such an impression on his first appeal to a New York audience." An audience that was not only situated in William F. Seward's backyard, a former governor and senator from New York that would become one of Lincoln's adversaries when nominated by the Whig Party for the presidency, but was composed of much of the eastern elite that had tremendous influence on the politics of their day.

Lincoln concluded his oratory by elucidating, "...Nor can we justifiably withhold this, on any ground save our conviction that slavery is wrong. If

The Hidden War

slavery is right, all words, acts, laws, and constitutions against it, are themselves wrong, and should be silenced, and swept away. If it is right, we cannot justly object to its nationality – its universality: if it is wrong, they cannot justly insist upon its extension – its enlargement. All they ask, we could readily grant, if we thought slavery right: all we ask, they could as readily grant, if they thought it wrong. Their thinking it right, and our thinking it wrong, is the precise fact upon which depends the whole controversy. Thinking it right, as they do, they are not to blame for desiring its full recognition, as being right; but, thinking it wrong, as we do, can we yield to them? Can we cast our votes with their view, and against our own? In view of our moral, social, and political responsibilities, can we do this?

Wrong as we think slavery is, we can yet afford to let it alone where it is, because that much is due to the necessity arising from its actual presence in the nation; but can we, while our votes will prevent it, allow it to spread into the National Territories, and to overrun us here in these Free States? If our sense of duty forbids this, then let us stand by our duty, fearlessly and effectively. Let us be diverted by none of those sophistical contrivances wherewith we are so industriously plied and belabored – contrivances such as groping for some middle ground between the right and the wrong, vain as the search for a man who should be neither a living man nor a dead man – such as a policy of 'don't care' on a question about which all true men do care – such as Union appeals beseeching true Union men to yield to Disunionists, reversing the divine rule, and calling, not the sinners, but the righteous to repentance – such as invocations to Washington, imploring men to unsay what Washington said, and undo what Washington did.

Neither let us be slandered from our duty by false accusations against us, nor frightened from it by menaces of destruction to the Government nor of dungeons to ourselves. Let us have faith that right makes might, and in that faith, let us, to the end, dare to do our duty as we understand it."

As 1860 unfolded, this gangly figure who endured much ridicule by the southern press and his opponents' rhetoric would persevere as his message echoed around the nation. The Cooper Union speech would be reprinted in many newspapers throughout the fall. When all was said and done, this man stood at the precipice of destiny as he stared into the abyss that threatened to ruin his presidency and abolish this nation.

He had never been a religious man and in fact in his youth had rejected his father's Calvinist beliefs, but he never abandoned his faith in a just God. And when he faced this momentous challenge, he wrote, "I know there is a God, and that he hates injustice and slavery. I see the storm coming, and I know that his hand is in it. If he has a place and work for me - and I think he has – I believe I am ready."

Although he understood that slavery was morally wrong, his views on race were not as charitable as he assumed his duty to do what was right as he understood it. Over time his views would be enlightened by the courage of "negro" soldiers fighting for freedom, black communities he visited in his travels to and from the White House and his summer retreat at the Old Soldier's Home, but most prominently by his meeting of Frederick Douglass. A man he believed in every sense was his equal. A man who had been a former slave. When he began preparing what would become his Emancipation Proclamation, he solicited Douglass' advice who had become a trusted advisor and a friend.

The nation would survive the Civil War, but the institution of slavery would not. Lincoln as he savored his victory while preparing for reconstruction would be assassinated by John Wilkes Booth as part of a larger conspiracy in Ford's Theatre on April 14, 1865. He at that moment, as lamented by Secretary of War Stanton while witnessing his last breath observed, "Now he belongs to the ages." Without his presence and guidance, reconstruction never achieved its ambitious goals and consequently the nation's original sin would continue to haunt the people.

A century later a young president who admired Lincoln was on the night of June 5, 1961, returning to Washington from his somber meeting with Nikita Khrushchev in Vienne. President Kennedy had hoped that his conference with the Soviet Premier would initiate an understanding that might lay the foundation for peace. Instead, his concerns had been heightened by Khrushchev's belligerent rants about western imperialism, the righteousness of communism and his determination to remove the allied presence in West Berlin.

During the flight, a weary president asked his secretary Evelyn Lincoln to gather his documents that he had been reviewing and file them. As she began to clear the table, she noted a small slip of paper that had inadvertently fallen on the floor. Written on that paper by Kennedy was a quote from Lincoln now commonly referred to as Lincoln's prayer. She read "I know there is a God – and I see a storm coming; If he has a place for me, I believe that I am ready."

The Hidden War

Just like Lincoln, Kennedy was the leader of a nation that still was not completely free and because of the tensions between two superpowers was facing the possibility of another war. However, this war would not just determine the fate of the nation but of humanity. As Kennedy attempted to navigate through these treacherous waters, making mistakes along the way, and while combatting with enemies from within his government that were determined to frustrate his objectives of unifying the nation and ending the Cold War, he courageously pressed forward to confront the storm and avert Armageddon. This included his prevention of proxy wars in Cuba, Laos, and Vietnam that the generals and the echelon of the CIA's clandestine services zealously advocated for in their obsession to confront and defeat the communists. His assassination in Dallas on November 22, 1963, just like Lincoln's 100 years before left the nation vulnerable to further civil unrest and conflict.

The forces that opposed him were now in control over the direction this nation would take. A path that Kennedy had so valiantly resisted that earned him the wrath of rogue zealots within the national security apparatus that viewed him as a treacherous impediment to our national security. Just 48 hours after his death, President Johnson and the generals prepared for war in Vietnam. And although the Civil Rights Act of 1964 and the Voting Rights Act of 1965 were magnanimous achievements, institutional and structural racism would remain until the present.

Kennedy's murder was the tragic culmination of an internal struggle over the division of power in our society and how that power was to be used that led us into another civil war. His death essentially was the spark that ignited this conflict just as the siege of Fort Sumter (4/12/1861) by the newly formed Confederacy initiated the war between the North and the South.

A clandestine conflict over the heart of America that would determine our destiny as either a militarized superpower whose primary purpose was to obtain total defeat of the communists and hegemonic control over the world's resources, or an exemplary nation that complied with international law in its laudable quest for a peaceful conclusion to the Cold War, making the world safe for diversity. A world, as stated in Kennedy's inaugural, in which the strong were just, the poor were secure, and the peace preserved by international commitments that recognized our common humanity and interests.

This would be significantly dissimilar to the first war that was waged on battlefields that now stand as historical monuments of that conflagration. This time the chaos and the turmoil enhanced by the constant churning of dark events because of their camouflaged perversion would not be understood as such until many decades later when the historical tides that connected them could be unmasked by researchers and historians.

The social movements, the war in Vietnam, the overthrowing of legitimately elected governments, repressive tactics by police to squash dissent, and the assassinations of our sagacious and charismatic progressive voices within this milieu of revelation unequivocally were not random isolated events but rather were all tethered by injustice, racism, greed, and militarism. All of which were blatant contradictions to the principles that had given birth to this nation.

President Kennedy addressed the nation on June 11, 1963, to confront these contradictions in our society that threatened to tear asunder the bonds that united us as a people. While looking at the network cameras from his desk in the Oval Office orated, "…This nation was founded by men of many nations and backgrounds. It was founded on the principle that all men are created equal, and that the rights of every man are diminished when the rights of one man are threatened…This is not a sectional issue. Difficulties over segregation and discrimination exist in every city, in every State of the Union, producing in many cities a rising tide of discontent that threatens the public safety. Nor is this a partisan issue. In a time of domestic crisis men of good will and generosity should be able to unite regardless of party or politics. This is not even a legal or legislative issue alone. It is better to settle these matters in the courts than on the streets, and new laws are needed at every level, but law alone cannot make men see right. We are confronted primarily with a moral issue. It is as old as the Scriptures and is as clear as the American Constitution… One hundred years of delay have passed since President Lincoln freed the slaves, yet their heirs, their grandsons, are not fully free. They are not yet freed from the bonds of injustice. They are not yet freed from social and economic oppression. And this nation, for all its hopes and all its boasts, will not be fully free until all its citizens are free…We face, therefore, a moral crisis as a country and a people. It cannot be met by repressive police action. It cannot be left to increased demonstrations in the streets. It cannot be quieted by token moves or talk. It is a time to act in the Congress, in your State and local legislative body and, above all, in all our daily lives…A great change is at hand, and our task, our obligation, is to make that revolution, that change, peaceful and constructive for all. Those who do nothing are inviting shame, as well as violence. Those who act boldly are recognizing right, as well as reality…This is

The Hidden War

what we're talking about and this is a matter which concerns this country and what it stands for, and in meeting it I ask the support of all our citizens."

We currently have oppressive police tactics to squash dissent and people marching in the streets, sometimes reverting to violence, seeking social justice and progress. Because we as a people lost that civil war in the 1960s, we are still residing in a nation that is not fully free, reliving the ghosts of the past.

Where are the leaders asking us to rise to the challenge and do what we know is right? That moral crisis that we know in our hearts requires that we fulfill our ideals at home by progressive structural changes that eviscerate the prejudices that divide us and by demanding an end to our endless wars abroad. To reverse the interests of empire by rebuilding a democratic republic. To essentially address the three major evils of our society that Dr. King referred to as racism, extreme materialism, and militarism.

This book examines our country's hypocrisies and contradictions that have prevented us from achieving the ideals that founded this nation. Those forces that shame our discontent as unpatriotic or even the reverberations of utopian seekers who naïvely criticize what they do not understand.

The essays are a combination of new and old to provide the reader with a cohesive analysis of those powers within our society that have diverted our nation from fulfilling its potential.

A nation that in my youth was summoned by a young president in 1961 to go to the moon by the end of the decade, not only accepted that challenge but landed men on the moon ahead of schedule while bringing them safely back to earth. Who that witnessed it on July 20, 1969, can forget that moment of triumph? That moment when Neil Armstrong stepped down off the Apollo Lunar Module's ladder onto the surface of the moon announcing to the world, "One small step for a man and one giant leap for mankind." A dazzling example of the capacity of this nation for great achievement when its resources were mobilized to advance humankinds' quest for knowledge and progress in a turbulent decade of relentless tragedy.

This is the same nation that in 2020 when COVID-19 hit us like a tidal wave had to purchase masks, as caustically described by satirist Lee Camp, in "international flea markets" because we were unable to manufacture them in the quantities needed here at home. This volume explains what happened to the ingenuity and spirit of this country and why we are in the mess that we find ourselves today.

And finally, the reason progressive leadership has not risen to the presidency and occupied the White House since President Kennedy is that the powers that opposed him learned their lesson. It is much more effective to prevent that kind of leadership than to confront it while in positions of power.

Terry Turchie, a former director of FBI's counterintelligence, admitted several years ago on the Tucker Carlson Show that when he started his career in the Bureau the primary objective of his unit was preventing the election of "progressives and self-described socialists" from rising to power. The mission of FBI's counterintelligence was "to keep these people out of government" because they create massive dysfunction and disinformation as perceived by the FBI hierarchy. These tactics utilized to achieve their objective ironically included the dissemination of misinformation and propaganda to smear their integrity and credibility to undermine their support. Could this be why we are left with two visionless, war mongering and uninspiring candidates running in 2020?

CHAPTER 1
Where are the Journalists?

I want everyone to maintain an open mind while considering this well-founded quote that has been over the years attributed to Mark Twain. "It's easier to fool the people than to convince them that they have been fooled."

This certainly can be applied to a whole spectrum of events that became seminal moments in our history or even mendacious narratives that justify oppression, inequality, racial injustice, poverty, greed, and war. This dissemination of propaganda, sometimes coupled with half-truths, becomes entrenched in our national psyche, so much so that to surgically remove it requires evidence that is tantamount to what is commonly referred to as a "smoking gun", ignoring a mountain of circumstantial evidence, witness testimonials and forensic examinations that reveal a different reality.

In most cases, especially if clandestine intelligence agents are involved, rarely - if ever - does this type of evidence exist because of the basic protocols bred into their amoral cultures to never write anything down for posterity that recounts illegal activities or operations that may include reprehensible crimes against humanity. And if on those rare occasions documentary evidence by necessity is created and its contents are threatened by prying investigators, whether sought by government officials or private researchers, these documents are shredded or incinerated down what Orwell described as the "memory hole" in his dystopian novel "1984."

Hence, the difficulty that meticulous researchers have confronted in their earnest attempts to convince their fellow citizens that Lee Harvey Oswald was not in that 6th floor window, shooting at the President through a tree that partially obstructed his view with an antiquated bolt action rifle with a defective scope. A weapon that the Italian Army in WWII referred to as the "humane weapon" in that it spared many lives as the bullets missed their intended targets. And yet, he allegedly was able to accomplish what experts in simulations could not achieve.

He, therefore, as asserted by these meticulous researchers was not responsible for what transpired in Dealey Plaza on November 22, 1963. In fact, Dallas Police Chief Jesse Curry, who oversaw the investigation at the time of Kennedy's assassination, in a 1969 interview with the Dallas Morning News conceded, "We don't have any proof that Oswald fired the rifle, and never did." He added, "Nobody's yet been able to put him in that building with a gun in his hand."

Another astonishing admission by our leaders was contained in a secret recorded telephone conference between President Lyndon Johnson and Senator Richard Russell of Georgia in 1964 that was released in the last few years. In that brief conversation, Russell who had been a member of the Warren Commission when referring to the single bullet theory told Johnson that, "I don't believe a word of it." Johnson's laconic reply was "Neither do I."

Even J. Edgar Hoover, the infamous FBI Director, responded to a question posed to him in the summer of 1964 by Billy Byars' (Texas oil man and close friend of Hoover) teenage son Bill, Jr. who wanted to know if he thought Oswald had acted alone. Hoover was silent for a moment and then replied, "If I told you what I really know, it would be very dangerous to this country. Our whole political system could be disrupted."[1]

Even many of the FBI agents in the field knew the Warren Commission was wrong. For instance, FBI agent Don Adams was transferred to Dallas in mid-1964. He decided to view a copy of the Zapruder film with two of his colleagues in their screening room. After viewing the film, he immediately turned to the other agents and said, "Well, he was obviously hit from two directions." The other two agents agreed.[2] You will never read or hear these types of statements by the corporate media that have consistently reported to the public that there was overwhelming evidence of Oswald's guilt.

The millions of pages of declassified documents and witness testimonials that were released pursuant to the 1992 JFK Records Act supports the proposition that not only did he not act alone, but also verifies the fact that he did not fire a single shot on that dark day when the candle of the New Frontier went out. He was simply reading a paper on the first floor and eating his sandwich in the lunchroom on the second floor of the Texas School Depository Building as recounted by all the witnesses to the Warren Commission in 1964 and the Assassination Records Review Board (ARRB) that was formed in the 1990s.

The ARRB was designed to enforce the objectives of the JFK Records Act which was to declassify all the relevant documents, recordings, and videos. When viewing all this evidence dispassionately, it becomes apparent to the objective researcher that Oswald was clearly what he exclaimed to the press while in custody, "I'm just a patsy."

Thus, it was major segments of the mainstream media aligned with our intelligence agencies - in accordance with a top-secret operation called

The Hidden War

Mockingbird - that promulgated the lie of Oswald's culpability for this heinous crime that has become the accepted narrative of our society. Therefore, I have chosen to focus on this powerful institution, often referred to as the fourth estate, whose purpose according to our founding fathers was to educate the citizenry on government policy, as well as to hold it accountable to the people by unveiling its lies and corruption. As I will demonstrate, they clearly have failed that mission with few exceptions.

The mainstream media, frequently referred to as corporate media, that is currently controlled by 6 corporations that have formed alliances with Wallstreet, the Pentagon and our intelligence community are spewing out more propaganda and lies than even Trump and his cohorts can claim. They arbitrarily dismiss researchers that write about subjects, such as Syria, Venezuela, Bolivia and the assassinations of the 1960s, in which new evidence has inspired fresh perspectives on all these topics that are more consistent with the witness testimonials, forensic evidence and all the tapes and documents that have been declassified over the last three decades, as paranoid lunatics and conspiracy theorists. They disparage these well documented investigations, and reports written by investigative journalists that travelled to these countries, that are buttressed by a plethora of facts while contemporaneously blaming all our democratic electoral problems on the biggest conspiracy theory of them all with little to no evidence to support it. This theory we all know and love, or perhaps despise, as Russiagate.

This belief that Vladimir Putin and President Trump colluded to hack into the Democratic National Committee's computer servers to steal their communications so that WikiLeaks could publish them with the hope that this would derail Hillary Clinton's preordained victory on election day. This hysteria over Russia coupled with this intense hatred for Trump has caused much of our media to throw reason and logic aside in their myopic pursuit to destroy Trump's presidency by undermining his legitimacy.

They are so brazen in their approach to foment suspicion on Russia that they present wild accusations as substantiated facts by connecting dots – no matter how distant from each other – as though they naturally were intimately linked, similar to the contorted inferences Glen Beck asserted years ago on the Fox Network. For instance, NBC recently claimed that sources such as New Knowledge and an individual that CNN described as a "cyber security buff" had discovered Russian bots on social media platforms that indicated Russia was supporting Tulsi Gabbard's presidential campaign.[3] This was unequivocally done to disparage a peace candidate that was building momentum with her popular positions that threatened the status quo. This of course was debunked not only because of the lack of evidence but also because their sources had been discredited.

Another example was Susan Rice's bizarre assertion on CNN (this past summer) - who was President Obama's UN Ambassador and later his National Security Advisor - that Russian infiltrators had instigated the protests utilizing bots on social media to "spread misinformation." These protests that in actuality were inspired by groups such as Black Lives Matter were marching in the streets in response to George Floyd's death caused by Minneapolis police officer Derek Chauvin that placed his knee on the back of his neck for 9 minutes while three other officers failed to intervene on Floyd's behalf even while he cried out "I cannot breathe", evoking the memory of Eric Garner's death. A death that was the result of a chokehold administered by Staten Island police officer Daniel Pantaleo in 2014 who was assisting several colleagues as they wrestled the large black man to the ground for allegedly peddling cigarettes without a stamp tax mandated by the city of New York.[4] Both deaths were attributed by the medical examiners as asphyxiation and were determined to be homicides.

Rachel Maddow, demonstrating the insanity of her obsession with Russia, on her MSNBC show began a segment that was describing the polar vortex phenomenon in the mid-west that had plummeted temperatures to 70 degrees below zero when the wind chill effects were included in the calculations. This event as you remember occurred in early 2019. She described this deep freeze and how it had caused many deaths. She then with all seriousness stared into the camera and asked her viewers to contemplate what could have happened if Russia had hacked into our power grid and turned it off. This is a classic example of fear mongering. I could not believe it when I viewed her comments on the Jimmy Dore Show. Former Senator Joseph McCarthy would have been proud that she was emulating his tactics on her nationally televised newscast.

I used to watch her newscast several years ago and had thought at the time that some of her commentary was quite astute. Although she is the number one rated news show on that network, primarily because of her obsession with Russiagate, I must say that I think she has lost her connection to reality as she delves deep into this anti-Putin and anti- Russian narrative clearly supported by the corporate structure above her and our national security state. She is no longer a journalist but rather a propagandist that is espousing stories approved by the establishment within the power sectors of our society to keep her $30,000 a day job.

My views on Maddow are buttressed by what happened to Ed Shultz who was fired by MSNBC because of his dogged determination to do stories on Bernie Sanders' campaign in the 2016 Democratic primaries. He at the time was unaware that his superiors at that network were close friends of Hillary Clinton and were part of a deliberate effort to minimize coverage of her surging opponent. One of the primary examples of this is the exclusive interview Ed had negotiated with Bernie's campaign to question the Senator just prior to New Hampshire voters casting their votes. As Shultz prepared to meet the Senator and go on the air, management contacted him and instructed him not to follow through with the scheduled interview just 5 minutes prior to greeting his viewers. They incredulously told him to replace Bernie with an old story in Texas that had been bantered about in other newscasts for 3 weeks. Shultz was furious and had a heated argument with the executive producer of his show. Shultz eventually calmed down and went with the Texas story.

When he went to RT America, he gave an interview that described what he had confronted at MSNBC and how impressed he was with his new employer. He indicated that the management at MSNBC wanted to know all about his top stories he planned to present on the air each evening. If you recall, Shultz came from a working-class family and was a big supporter of labor. On many occasions, they blocked him from presenting his chosen news items on his highly rated show, especially if they were about Sanders' policies or the growing success of his grassroots campaign. Shultz compared this with RT management by stating that they never interfered with his chosen topics for his nightly show. And yet, the mainstream media consistently disparage RT America as a propaganda arm of Putin. The point in all this is that to keep your high paying job at MSNBC you must peddle the establishment's narrative, compromising your journalistic integrity.

As you know, WikiLeaks disclosed the collusion that occurred between the media, DNC management and Hillary's campaign staff when they published the DNC emails. The chairperson of the DNC, Debbie Wasserman Shultz, was required to resign over these disclosures. Donna Brazile, a high-ranking DNC member who was also part of this scandal, in her tell all book even admitted that she was providing Clinton with the questions prior to each nationally televised debate. The publicized emails also revealed that contributions that were being collected by DNC for lower tier candidates were all being funneled into the Clinton campaign. In fact, the environment was so toxic at the DNC during the primaries that Tulsi Gabbard resigned as vice-chair to be free to advocate for and join Bernie's campaign.

Another prominent example is how Phil Donahue was treated by MSNBC management during the build up to the Iraq War in 2002 and 2003. He was staunchly opposed to the Bush administration's push for war. He was skeptical of the claims by our intelligence community that Saddam Hussein had weapons of mass destruction and had colluded with Al Qaeda in their plans to attack the U.S. on 9/11. His views were clearly not shared by MSNBC's management, or with corporate media in general, who continued to parrot the administration's narrative that justified the invasion.

MSNBC management attempted in 2003 to blame Donahue's firing on a downward trend in ratings for his show that had been gradually emerging over the previous 3 years. This was contradicted by a secret internal MSNBC memo that was leaked to the public that described the real impetus for discharging Donahue. The memo essentially warns that Donahue was "a difficult public face for NBC in a time of war." It further explains that his show was "a home front for the liberal antiwar agenda at the same time that our competitors are waving the flag at every opportunity."[5] To translate in clearer language, the network and the corporate authority above them despised Donahue's hippie peacenik message that they perceived as an intolerable indignity to their company and, more importantly, was interfering with their desire to patriotically join the flag waving to cheer on the war effort just as the other networks were doing. Why should they get all the glory?

Donahue told Amy Goodman and Juan Gonzalez of Democracy Now in an interview he did with them in 2013 that the decision to fire him clearly came from above his immediate supervisors. He shared that in his opinion the owners of MSNBC and its parent company NBC which was General Electric at that time were "terrified of the antiwar voice." It simply was not good for business. As Donahue explained, "Donald Rumsfeld and the Defense Department were their biggest customers." So, he naturally had to go even though the real numbers for his show clearly verified his assertion that he had the largest viewing audience of all their newscasts on their network at the time of his dismissal.

Other examples of those who were tenaciously opposed to the war in Iraq were Jesse Ventura, a former Navy Seal in Vietnam and Governor of Minnesota, who was also discharged by MSNBC, as well as Chris Hedges who

The Hidden War

was a Pulitzer Prize winning investigative journalist that was forced to leave The New York Times. Of course, we all know now who was on the right side of history and who was manipulating public opinion to support a perfidious narrative promulgated by the Bush administration and all 17 intelligence agencies.

Another more subtle tactic by the media to control public opinion is to promote obfuscation to confuse their audience. The objective of this tactic is to make the political elite's view, no matter how much evidence exists that debunk their argument, a credible debate. For instance, The PBS News Hour unwittingly does this almost every newscast. Of course, I must concede that I have not watched the PBS News Hour in years. For instance, when I was a viewer, they would invite two experts to debate a subject such as the merits of supply-side economics. The interviewer remains neutral in this format as each present their views even though there are numerous objective studies by the Congressional Budget Office and universities that have concluded that this economic theory did not trickle down to the middle class, did not create jobs, did not lower the deficit but rather was a major drag on the economy and created the largest deficits in U.S. history. The two administrations that promoted and signed the largest tax cuts in our history based on this fallacious economic theory are Presidents Ronald Reagan and George W. Bush. It is not a coincidence that their tax cuts contributed to the largest deficits since the founding of this nation.

Studies have unequivocally demonstrated that tax cuts that primarily benefit the working and middle class create the largest upsurge in economic growth because of the multiplier effect. Instead, the tax cuts as enacted by the above administrations resulted in the transfer of trillions of dollars to the fortune 500 and the top 1% income earners. Subsequently, 3 families in our current economy have as much wealth as the bottom 50% of the American population. In 2017 for example, 82% of new wealth generated in the U.S. went to the top 1%. In the 1960s, which was the height of the middle class, only 10% went to this superclass of capitalists. 90% went to the middle class and the poor.

Thus, it should not be a shock that Trump's tax cut of 2017 - justified by this flawed model - has also exacerbated the nation's debts which are currently assessed at over $22 trillion. In addition, the beneficiaries of these tax cuts such as General Motors who received $514 million in tax relief during this period decided to close 5 plants and transfer these operations to Mexico. This single act by one corporate giant who has been bailed out by the taxpayers to the tune of $50 billion since 2008 was projected to eliminate almost 15,000 high wage jobs with excellent benefits. Consequently, the communities in which these plants were located were bracing for this inevitable financial disaster. Fortunately, GM was shamed into preserving some of these jobs.

As the journalist refers to these historical facts while soliciting commentary from their two distinguished guests, their self-imposed neutrality makes it exceedingly difficult for the average viewer to discern the truth. This is because the impartiality of the interviewer insidiously impresses upon the viewer that each argument is of equal weight. This approach reinforces the concept that whether you support one side, or the other, is a matter of perspective or your political ideology. This is in my opinion consistent with George Orwell's concept of "doublethink" in which 2 + 2 can equal 5. Anything is possible. Under this concept, truth mirrors the ideology of power and not reality.

After watching many of these discussions, unless you were well versed in the subject matter, you leave the interview more confused than before the debate.

This is also true in other issues such as fracking or climate change. Those of us who have researched these matters know there is an answer to these complex issues and as a result can recognize who is closer to the truth. Those that enter the debate with preconceived biases will naturally favor the expert that espouses their views unless they are challenged to consider facts that contradict their conclusions. As a result, the primary purpose of the media which is to educate the citizenry is lost in this absurd concept that the media's primary role is to preserve its neutrality while protecting our established institutions and agencies. This clearly was not the tact that Edward R. Murrow took in the 1950s when he confronted the treachery of McCarthyism and the threat it presented to our liberty and to our republic. Ironically, these delicate balances that are applied to many issues do not seem to be in play when the media does reports on our build up to war or on Russiagate.

Another example of a journalist taking a stand and was willing to confront those in power is Cenk Uygur who is often referred to as The Young Turk. He had a news show on MSNBC several years ago for a brief period that was as provocative as Ed Schultz's newscast when he was employed by that network. On occasion, Uygur would be combative with his guests when he perceived them to be disingenuous or attempting to misinform his audience. MSNBC must have received formal complaints for his behavior, for his network supervisors did instruct him to tone down his demeanor and to be more conciliatory to his guests. Uygur responded that he was not going to enable

The Hidden War

these establishment figures to use his media platform to deceive his viewers. To Uygur's astonishment, MSNBC management, as recounted by Jimmy Dore on his YouTube show, retorted, "I don't think you understand. We are the establishment!" He then voluntarily resigned shortly after that session to focus on his successful on-line media outlet called The Young Turks (TYT).

As an aside, the MS in MSNBC is the acronym for Microsoft which purchased that network after the passage of the 1996 Telecommunication Act signed by President Bill Clinton – currently that network is owned by Comcast - which represents another disturbing threat to free speech which are the alliances of national media outlets with high-tech conglomerates and social media platforms. Facebook while enforcing its secret algorithms that allegedly can detect "fake news" has contracted with CNN, ABC and other corporate media to censor smaller alternative independent media outlets that are attracting most of the young people of which these media giants naturally view as a threat to their long-term viability. For example, the age of the average CNN viewer is almost 70 years old.

The reason I have focused on MSNBC is not because their network is the only example of media bias and corporate control, but rather that this network is supposed to be a progressive media outlet that promotes freedom of the press and freedom of speech. A network that originally was dedicated to educating its viewers not indoctrinating them. A counter to the growing popularity of Fox News which endorsed conservative ideas and was considered by many as the propaganda arm for the Republican Party. I could just as easily point out many similar examples on CNN, Fox News, or the other networks. For instance, William M. Arkin resigned on January 4th of 2019 from NBC. He is an award-winning investigative journalist that had been employed by NBC, off and on, for 30 years. He elucidated his reasons for doing so in a cogent email he disseminated to the public.

"My expertise, though seemingly to be all the more central to the challenges and dangers we face, also seems to be less valued at the moment. And I find myself completely out of synch with the network, being neither a day-to-day reporter nor interested in the Trump circus.

I thought that the mission was to break through the machine of perpetual war acceptance and conventional wisdom to challenge Hillary Clinton's hawkishness. It was also an interesting moment at NBC because everyone was looking over their shoulder at VICE and other upstarts creeping up on the mainstream. But then Trump got elected and investigations got sucked into the tweeting vortex, increasingly lost in a directionless adrenaline rush, the national security and political version of leading the broadcast with every snowstorm. And I would assert that in many ways NBC just began emulating the national security state itself – busy and profitable. No wars won but the ball is kept in play.

I'd argue that under Trump, the national security establishment not only hasn't missed a beat but indeed has gained dangerous strength. Now it is even more autonomous and practically impervious to criticism. I'd also argue, ever more gingerly, that NBC has become somewhat lost in its own verve, proxies of boring moderation and conventional wisdom, defender of the government against Trump, cheerleader for open and subtle threat mongering, in love with procedure and protocol over all else (including results). I accept that there's a lot to report here, but I'm more worried about how much we are missing. Hence my desire to take a step back and think why so little changes with regard to America's wars."

He then prefaced his subsequent comments by asserting that he is not a Trump supporter, "I'm alarmed at how quick NBC is to mechanically argue the contrary, to be in favor of policies that just spell more conflict and more war. Really? We shouldn't get out of Syria? We shouldn't go for the bold move to denuclearizing the Korean peninsula? Even on Russia, though we should be concerned about the brittleness of our democracy that is so vulnerable to manipulation, do we really yearn for a new Cold War? And don't even get me started with the FBI: What? We now lionize this historically destructive institution."

Essentially, his employer had become an echo chamber that parroted the war machine's justifications for further military spending in support of their wars. There was minimal, if any, attempt to question these rationalizations or independently investigate their validity. NBC was not alone in this in that CNN would have generals discussing the viability of using our military to overthrow the governments in Iran and Venezuela without informing their viewers that these experts had been hired as consultants, and even as lobbyists, by companies like Lockheed Martin and Raytheon. Arkin corroborated this in his email when he acknowledged that, "There's a saying about consultants, that organizations hire them to hear exactly what they want them to say."

This clearly illuminates why MSNBC, NBC, CNN, ABC, CBS, Fox News, and others have hired former generals and intelligence people to be their experts such as James Clapper and John Brennan to keep their war narrative on track.

The Hidden War

This is why you will rarely, if ever, see Ray McGovern, William Binney, Phil Donahue, Chris Hedges, Dylan Jason Ratigan or Professors Stephen F. Cohen, Noam Chomsky and Jeffrey D. Sachs, among others, on their panels, for they know they will not support their sponsor's message, nor the interests of the corporate structures that cast shadows on their newscasts. More importantly, they would tell the truth about Russiagate and our perpetual wars that would discredit everything they had been propagating to manipulate their viewers, revealing to their audience, their hidden bias, as well as their malfeasance.

There are two powerful quotes by Malcolm X that compellingly illustrate the power of the media and how they can promote a false narrative that not only masquerades a lie as truth but can manufacture our consent to endorse absurdities. And by doing so, as pointed out by Voltaire, can make us all vulnerable to commit atrocities, such as the sanctions imposed on Iraq after Gulf War 1 that contributed to the deaths of 500,000 Iraqi children; the support of Saudi Arabia's war on Yemen that has caused the deaths of 85,000 Yemini children and Wounded Knee in which 153 unarmed Native Americans were murdered by the Army in 1890. All of these are examples from the present and past of propaganda that deliberately promoted a message that provoked our fears and encouraged our prejudices while specifying the targets of hatred. These same tactics today are being applied to Russia, illegal immigrants, and Muslims.

Malcolm X as a victim of their venomous lies stated, "The media's the most powerful entity on earth. They have the power to make the innocent guilty and to make the guilty innocent, and that's power." They can do this, "Because they control the minds of the masses." He also sagaciously observed that, "It (the media) will make the criminal look like he's the victim and make the victim look like he's the criminal. If you're not careful, the newspapers will have you hating the people who are oppressed and loving the people who are doing the oppressing."

Think about this as you reflect upon what is being done to Julian Assange or even the victims of police brutality and violence, protesting for justice.

Currently, Assange for instance is being held in a maximum-security prison in East London under the threat that if he is extradited to the U.S., he could face life imprisonment, if not be executed, simply because he told inconvenient truths that the power elite preferred to remain secret. The mainstream media that should be supporting Julian Assange and his defense of freedom of the press have joined the national security complex in their effort to psychologically destroy him and eradicate his media creation, WikiLeaks. So, I ask where are the journalists? For real journalists should know that it is power that operates in secrecy that is the biggest threat to a democratic republic, not the dissemination of truth.

CHAPTER 2
The Forgotten Snow

I included this essay not only because I dedicated this book to my father, but also in recognition of all those that lost their fathers and loved ones to COVID-19. Even though my dad died several years ago, his memory remains in my daily thoughts.

I had no premonition or feelings of gloom and doom when my father died. I was in my office fulfilling my mundane obligations that day without any sense of the emotional pain and loss that loved ones in Connecticut were suffering. Instead, I had to be apprised by my brother over the phone of our father's unexpected passing by causes unknown to us at that moment. My father was physically fit and active, and his mind was lucid and sharp. He appeared healthier than those much younger and yet he had died by some mysterious natural cause. If he had been aware of subtle symptoms, they were never shared with anyone.

After my brother had spoken those dreaded words that I was not anticipating for another 10 years, I sat in stunned silence. My first question uttered in disbelief was "What Happened?" My brother carefully explained the events of that morning and retraced what our father may have been doing in the barn just prior to his death. We discussed these events in detail as though their resolution would end our despair and bring Dad back to life, triumphantly causing this tragedy to vanish as fast as it had appeared.

I glanced out the window and thought of how awful this winter had been and what was our mother going to do without him. They had been married for 56 years and had rarely been apart with exception to Dad's service in Vietnam assigned to the Repose. A floating hospital stationed off the coast of Da Nang operated by the Navy during the war.

My mind shifted again and wondered what would become of our father now that he was no longer among us. I hoped he was in a better place that allowed him to accept what had happened and to be reunited with his twin brother and his parents, as well as other loved ones that had gone before him. I then refocused on what my brother was painfully trying to explain as his voice would quiver from time to time. He said, "I knew once I turned his body over and could see his face that Dad was not there." We would eventually learn from the coroner that his death was the result of a massive heart attack due to the same defect that had caused the demise of his twin brother.

My interaction with my father in recent years was not as simple as when I was fighting the Battle of the Bulge with toy soldiers or constructing tree forts or even as a younger man. But I do not dwell on such things for I understood that I was extremely fortunate to have had a father as loving and accomplished as he was. And thus, I will remember for the most part his loving gestures and generous nature that was revealed to all who knew him. But most of all, I thought about how much I already missed him and was saddened that I never got the chance to hold him and say goodbye.

Because of circumstances beyond our control, my father died alone. The death scenes of historical figures that I read about where family gathered around the patriarch's bed to say goodbye and write down their last words for posterity was not to be for us or for Dad.

I hope the snow, as well as this season, will gracefully fade into the past as will – unfortunately – my father's presence. At some point, the snow will be forgotten, and we will welcome the spring and then the warmth of summer. This will all occur without our father and that is a reality we must learn to accept.

I looked out the window several nights after his death to observe the moon casting shadows upon the snow. My first thought was that Dad would have noticed this angelic scene and would have cherished it. In his memory, I paused to appreciate it before retiring to bed. I also thought of the epitaph I had read on a headstone years ago while visiting a local graveyard. It simply said, "Remember me."

When I think of my father, I will think of the woods, and the long hikes we had walked together. I will think of the rock walls he built, and the vegetable garden he tended. I will think of his boat and the afternoons we had spent drifting in Long Island Sound eating turkey sandwiches with tomatoes that my Uncle Dick made with such pride. This was our tradition that was an intricate part of our ritual when out on the boat. But most of all, I would tell my Dad if I could that unlike the fallen snow that soon will recede into the past that I shall always remember my loving father.

I located a poem by Henry David Thoreau who enjoyed nature as much as my father, and I believe he would have enjoyed the sentiments tendered in this brief verse if he had read them.

Every blade in the field-
Every leaf in the forest-

The Hidden War

Lays down its life in its season,
As beautifully as it was taken up.

Since I also dedicated this volume to my uncle Dick, I decided to include my father's eulogy. He was a gentle man to whom I shared many of my life's tribulations. He had this knack about him that when he listened to you it was as though nothing else mattered. He graduated from the University of Connecticut with a bachelor's degree in English and for a brief period was an English teacher while he worked on his Ph.D. in psychology. The last 27 years of his career was dedicated to the Old Lyme School District as their special education director. My father was a pathologist.

The oration below that my brother saved for posterity was my father's eulogy of his fallen brother who had unexpectedly died at the young age of 71 because of an undetected heart defect that would 7 years later take my father's life. It is my hope that they have rejoined each other in a better place.

He gave this eulogy to a large audience crammed into a local church in which many of the attendees were my uncle's colleagues, as well as close friends and family.

Thoughts of My Brother
"In case you haven't noticed I am Dick's twin brother.

I am not going to talk about Dick's profession, since you all know more about this than I do. I was not involved in his professional activities although at times I am sure he thought I could have benefitted from them. Instead, I thought you might be interested in knowing what it is like to be a twin.

My brother and I were like two buckets of water that you poured into one. We were symbiotic, sort of like psychological Siamese twins, but without the boundaries – we accepted each other unconditionally. We did not communicate in the usual ways.

My mother spoke of times when we were fed in a double highchair – when one of us liked something on the other's plate we could just look at each other and switch plates – and eat the part we liked. She also recalled, when we were beginning to walk, Dick and I would look at each other in a certain way and it was a signal that we were about to run in opposite directions – and Mom would not know which of us to go after.

My dear wife, after I had been on the boat with Dick for 6 or 7 hours, would ask, "Did you ask Dick about such and such?" And I would say, "No. I forgot." And she would reply (in frustration), "Don't you ever talk?" And I said, "No, not much." We never talked a lot. I never even told my brother (that) I loved him. I didn't have to, it was understood.

My brother and I resided within each other's souls – and a part of his will live in me until the day I die – but a part of me died with him the other day."

May they both rest in peace, as well as all those that died of COVID-19.

CHAPTER 3
Knocking on Hell's Gate

Thomas Jefferson wrote, "Experience hath shewn, that even under the best of governments, those entrusted with power, in time, and by slow operations, perverted into tyranny." This knowledge was the inspiration for the founders to create a government that was balanced, and responsibilities divided such that one branch of government would not become more powerful than the rest. They also imbued within the Constitution the concept that power was derived from the people and accordingly to be used to benefit the governed. The Bill of Rights for instance was a listing of civil liberties to protect the people from government abuses and transgressions, and thus imposed limits to its mandate and authority. Over time, these fundamental rights so wisely incorporated within our Constitution have been incrementally eroded to the extent that our democratic republic is no longer functioning as the founder's intended.

Since World War II, we have witnessed the unfettered growth of a secret government that is comprised by our national security complex. This complex consumes 57% of our discretionary budget and is significantly diverting our resources from other national priorities such as our dilapidated infrastructure. This emphasis on secrecy and security, whether based on fears of communism or terrorism, is subverting the foundation of our republic which is energized by the liberties that enrich our lives. All of this, the integrity of our democratic institutions and our fundamental liberty, is now under threat by these internal structural changes that have been stimulated by the deep state and implemented by our government officials to circumvent the checks and balances amalgamated within the Constitution. These political leaders that appear more interested in serving their perceived financial masters rather than the people. These subtle vicissitudes can be placed into a clearer perspective by examining a poignant example from the past in which a republic was transformed into a tyranny.

The Reichstag (German Parliament) on February 27, 1933, was destroyed by a fire that many immediately suspected was set by an arsonist. This occurred at a time when Germany was in the midst of a major transformation. The Reichstag had been established in 1871 when Germany was unified under the leadership of Otto Van Bismarck. The building was completed in 1894. Just like Britain, there was an upper and lower house. The Bundesrat was the Imperial Council of the Reigning Princes of German States. Thus, Germany became one of

Europe's Monarchies until the advent of WWI. After this atrocious example of the failure of human beings to resolve their differences civilly, the misguided Versailles Treaty of 1919 was signed five years after the assassination of Archduke Ferdinand and imposed upon the German's fledgling democracy known as the Weimar Republic. The reparations that were levied on Germany as retribution for that bloody war doomed this republic from its beginnings.

Adolf Hitler one month earlier had been sworn in as the Chancellor of Germany. He shared power with the President, Paul Van Hindenburg. The National Socialist Workers Party (Nazi Party) in the general election of 1932 had unexpectedly won a plurality of the seats in the Reichstag. The Nazi Party seated 196, and the Social Democratic Party that Hindenburg led held 121 seats. The Communist Party of Germany also added to their numbers of which totaled 100 seats, and the Centre Party held 70 seats. Hindenburg because of the election aligned his Social Democrats with the Nazi Party to prevent the Communists from forming coalitions with other parties that when combined could potentially elevate them as the majority party.

Hindenburg had been elected President of the Weimar Republic in 1925, during a period of tremendous economic stress that was fueled by inflationary influences that were significantly devaluing their currency. His administration consequently was not very popular. After the disastrous election, he – under tremendous pressure from Hitler – appointed him as Chancellor even though the Nazis were a minority in the cabinet.

Many believe the burning down of the Reichstag was orchestrated by Nazi supporters attempting to implant fear in the citizenry, so the party could take advantage of the chaos and terror that resulted from this ominous event to further its quest for power. Hitler before any evidence had been submitted accused communist agitators for the fire. A Dutch communist named Van Der Lubbe was arrested after a witness alleged that he was seen in the vicinity at the time of the blaze. He would eventually confess to the crime after being tortured by the Gestapo. The Nazis claimed this was proof that the communists were plotting to undermine the German government as part of a conspiracy to spur revolutionary embers throughout Europe.

These events culminated in the Reichstag Fire Decree. This decree that had been fomented by fear of communist subversion significantly suspended important civil liberties to augment national security. This decree nullified habeas corpus, freedom of expression, freedom of the press, the right to

The Hidden War

association and public assembly. In addition, it suspended the protections of personal communications, property, and activities within the home.

The decree also enhanced the power of the Nazi Party in that they now had members in powerful positions throughout the government. It established draconian penalties for offenses against the government and the imprisonment of anyone deemed to be an opponent of Hitler's party. It also suppressed publications that were not considered "friendly" to their cause. It eventually contributed to the formation of a one-party Nazi State.

While all this was occurring, dozens of communists were being rounded up and taken into custody as would be the fate of Jews later that decade. As the numbers increased, it became a public relations matter that Hermann Goring, the head of the Prussian Ministry of the Interior, felt compelled to develop policies to justify these arrests. The Chief of Prussian State Police, Ludwig Grauert, proffered that they could issue an emergency presidential decree under article 48 of the Weimar Constitution. This would authorize the president to take any measure necessary to protect public safety without involving the Reichstag. Several weeks later the Enabling Act of 1933 was passed. The government obtained arbitrary powers that it could implement without any authorization from the Reichstag. It passed both houses and was signed by Hitler.

Hindenburg died one year later which enabled Hitler to declare himself as the Fuhrer or supreme commander. This final act solidified his power and condemned the German people to a nightmare that would cause the deaths of millions in concentration camps and 50 million more in a world war.

Hitler defended the necessity for the implementation of the Enabling Act to the Reichstag in which he passionately orated, "The mobilization of the most primitive instincts leads to a link between the concepts of political theory and the actions of real criminals. Beginning with pillaging, arson, raids on railways, assassination attempts, and ... all things morally sanctioned by the communist theory." He continued, "The burning of the Reichstag was an unsuccessful attempt to foment civil war...this is only a taste of what Europe would have to expect from a triumph of this demonical doctrine."

After projecting these evil strategies onto his declared enemy that ironically became tactics that the Nazis would later become synonymous with, he then equated their political theory with demonic traits to elevate the threat they represented not only to Germany but to all of Europe. The Nazi Party as a result of their aggressive actions to confront this threat had become their savior. He then began to justify the Act's suppression of civil liberties and the responsibilities of the Reichstag to Germany's future. He argued, "Simultaneously with the political purification of our public life, the Reich Government intends to undertake a thorough moral cleansing of the German volkskarper (society?). The entire system of education, the theater, the cinema, literature, the press and radio…will be used as a means to this end and valued accordingly. They must all work to preserve the eternal values residing in the essential character of the volk (people)." This meant that all the sectors of German society must be redirected for the good of Germany and thereby purged of unpatriotic dissent. He concluded this speech by making it clear that there was only one choice, "…the government is just as determined as it is prepared to accept notice of rejection and thus a declaration of resistance. May you, gentlemen, now choose for yourselves between peace and war!"

This is how a democratic republic was declared irrelevant when confronted by a "demonical doctrine" that made it necessary to suppress civil liberties to reinforce national security. Once Hitler obtained the power of dictator, he would never relinquish it. After all, as pointed out by Orwell, "The object of power is power." By examining these events in Germany, we can begin to see correlations with what has been occurring in our country since World War II and most particularly since 9/11.

The Patriot Act of 2001 and the development of the Department of Homeland Security in 2002 were just the initial stages of the ordained orthodoxy that national security matters were supreme even when weighed against our civil liberties and our democratic institutions. More importantly, we have been incessantly told that liberty and security are mutually exclusive concepts. Thus, the political tenet of the neoconservatives that was set in concrete was as stated by President Bush, "You are either with us or against us." If you criticized the war in Iraq for instance, you were not supportive of the troops and in fact were accused of being unpatriotic. Journalists that spoke out against the war such as Phil Donahue was fired by MSNBC, and Christopher Hedges was forced off The New York Times editorial page. Hedges now writes for alternative media and is employed by RT America.

The more recent actions by our government are even more demonstrative of my point. The Trump administration has repealed net-neutrality, significantly increased our defense budgets with bi-partisan support, has proclaimed that methods such as torture are legitimate tools in our arsenal to combat terrorism, has double-down on his predecessors' wars, has vilified Muslims and

The Hidden War

immigrants and with Democratic support is seeking the augmentation of the 2001 Authorization for Use of Military Force (AUMF) enacted just after the traumatic event of 9/11. This gave President George W. Bush emergency powers that allowed him to suppress our rights and ignore the Constitution when he and his national security team deemed it essential to protect our national security.

The new and enhanced 2018 AUMF according to Professor Emerita at Thomas Jefferson School of Law Marjorie Cohn, as written in her article for Truthout.com, dated, May 10, 2018, indicated that "Under the guise of exercising power over the president's ability to use military force, congress is considering writing Donald Trump a blank check to indefinitely detain U.S. citizens with no criminal charges." This is a bi-partisan bill that was introduced by the Senate's Foreign Relation's chair Bob Corker (R-Tennessee) and committee member Tim Kaine (D-Virginia) with 4 additional sponsors. The 2001 bill permitted the president to use "all necessary and appropriate force" which is reaffirmed – if not expanded – in this updated legislation.

The 2001 version as pointed out by Cohn has been used to justify 37 military operations in 14 countries many of which had no relationship with 9/11. She further asserts that this new bill permits a president to "claim that a U.S. citizen who writes, speaks out or demonstrates against U.S. military action is a 'co-belligerent' and can lock him or her up indefinitely without a charge" as is being done to foreigners at the Guantanamo Detention Center or other victims of the extraordinary rendition program. She added that the International Covenant on Civil and Political Rights which was ratified by the U.S. and under the supremacy clause of the Constitution forbids this. She warns that this act may "enshrine the president's power to wage war" without congressional consent in addition to indefinitely holding U.S. citizens without criminal charges being levied against them. This is a chilling development that in many ways is reminiscent of Germany's Reichstag Fire Decree and the Enabling Act.

If you link this with Stellar Wind which is the massive surveillance program administered by the NSA that has essentially gutted our privacy protections and the designation of alternative media outlets as assets of foreign intrigue that need to be suppressed if not eliminated, such as WikiLeaks and RT America, you clearly have the foundational elements of a national security state as was established in Nazi Germany. I think this is self-evident when whistleblowers who are attempting to preserve and protect the Constitution and our liberties are smeared or sentenced to prison while government officials who violate every fundamental tenet of our republic every hour of every day are not held accountable and in fact, as in the case of "bloody Gina", are rewarded.

Gina Haspel was recently affirmed by the Senate (5/17/17) as the Director of the CIA; An agency that according to a study done in the 1990s by the Association of Responsible Dissent was culpable for the deaths of 6 million since its inception in 1947.[6] An agency that was labelled the "American Gestapo" by its founder President Harry S. Truman. He asserted further that their mission had been distorted in ways not consistent with his intentions. He made these ominous comments shortly after the assassination of President Kennedy.

Hitler stated, "By the skillful and sustained use of propaganda, one can make a people see even heaven as hell or an extremely wretched life as paradise." He also elatedly observed, "What good fortune for governments that the people do not think."

We cannot allow ourselves to be fooled any longer with narratives and explanations for events when no evidence is submitted to justify their allegations or their actions. We must re-assert and demand that our government fulfills its fiduciary obligation to uphold and to protect our sacred Constitution and those fundamental rights that enrich our lives. We now stand where the Germans did in 1932. We need not open and enter those gates as some wittingly curious victims of horror films. We all know what happens once you enter and ignore the warnings posted outside the gates of hell.

CHAPTER 4
The Secret Government and its Threat to our Democratic Republic

The creation of the CIA and the evolution of its "other powers" is very relevant to comprehending what our government is covertly doing in the war on terrorism and under the umbrella of national security in many nations around the globe. For instance, President Truman's editorial that he started composing several days after President Kennedy was assassinated with eloquent clarity described the damage the CIA's clandestine operations had done to our credibility and reputation as a supporter of liberty, international law and peace. He was concerned that these "strange activities" were the focus of much Cold War intrigue that was not consistent with its primary mission when he established it in 1947. His letter to the editor was submitted to the Washington Post and was published in the Sunday morning edition on December 22, 1963, only to be removed from the afternoon publication, presumably because of demands for its removal by former CIA Director Allen Dulles who was good friends with the owner of the paper. The timing of this piece was indisputably disconcerting and for the CIA potentially a public relations nightmare.

The CIA essentially operated under the principle that the end justified the means. And for the most part, it still does. Because of the doctrine of plausible deniability and the extensive classification protocol we have instituted since World War II, their clandestine activities remain classified and protected under the ambit of national security.

These nefarious operations that were supported by our military has transformed our nation as a beacon of hope and a champion of liberty to a nation that is feared for its military power. A nation that is enforcing a "Pax Americana" on the rest of the world by our weapons of war which is exactly what President Kennedy in his oration at American University astutely asserted should not be our objective.

The CIA's secret prisons, torture methods and the drone program are all part of our foreign policy. These programs are openly supported by Republican and Democratic administrations as legitimate tools to combat terrorists and achieve our security objectives. This has precipitated in the Agency's obsession with clandestine operations that is propelling it away from its primary purpose which was to collect and interpret foreign intelligence.

The origin of this obsession occurred under the stewardship of Dulles in the 1950s and early 1960s. The intelligence gathering aspect of the CIA during this period was neglected as more and more resources were poured into covert paramilitary operations, extraordinary rendition, assassination projects and the toppling of leftist governments that threatened corporate profits and were perceived as communist havens. In most cases, such as Iran, Guatemala, Indonesia, and Chile, they were socialist democracies that were sponsoring policies that were intended to improve the quality of life for their citizenry.

The conflict occurred when these governments tried to reign in western corporate exploitation of their labor and their natural resources, curtail government corruption and form alliances with radical political parties to consolidate their power. Because their mandate to rule had been given by their people, they were extremely sensitive to any appearance that could encourage allegations of collusion with former colonial or outside powers. Accordingly, these governments were very independent and, therefore, exceedingly difficult to manipulate and control. This was the impetus for the CIA and other intelligence agencies with military support to sponsor coups to overthrow their governments and replace them with malleable brutal regimes that oppressed their people while corporations reaped massive profits at their expense. This was permitted while much of their citizenry languished in misery as they struggled to feed their families. The dictators and their cohorts were rewarded for their cooperation by military aid packages that were negotiated by each administration and appropriated by congress to maintain their power and to assist in the war against the communists. Their continued political indifference to corporate plundering of their natural resources was also assured by corporate bribes.

As Truman pointed out in his editorial above, the CIA was never intended to be involved in policy formation or form shady alliances with organized crime or drug cartels to supplement its congressionally approved black budget or achieve its nefarious objectives cloaked in claims of advancing democracy while allegedly enhancing national security. By allowing it to morph into a secret policy making arm of the executive branch, we have formed an agency that threatens those institutions and values that it was originally created to protect. An agency that has more similarities with the ministries described in George Orwell's dystopian novel "1984" than an organization that is part of a democratic republic. A government that Lincoln cogently had reaffirmed at Gettysburg was "of the people, by the people, for the people."

The Hidden War

The assassinations of the 1960s are the ultimate examples of how our national security complex has become an insidious colossal power that has tremendous influence not only on our foreign policy, but also on our domestic priorities. It has perpetuated a global orthodoxy that is based on expanding our ordained prosperity while protecting an empire. To achieve these objectives, we are constantly intruding upon the national sovereignty of other nations while supporting programs that violate international law. This not only has created tremendous antipathy towards our nation but has significantly contributed to the suffering of humanity and has exacerbated the chasm between the rich and the poor. These strategies have also caused the displacement of millions who are fleeing these war zones and brutal governments in search of refuge from the violence. All this disruption and upheaval has aided our enemies who take advantage of the chaos as they infiltrate war ravaged cities and lawless territories abandoned by once powerful security forces. It has also made it easier to recruit replacements for those that were lost. Consequently, our security is diminished as we create more enemies than we can kill.

Those that were assassinated in that turbulent decade of the 1960s were opposed to this entrenched militaristic and corporatist orthodoxy and, thus, threatened powerful elements in our society that were immensely benefiting politically, financially, and ideologically from these doctrines. The idea of achieving peace and investing in programs that ameliorate the social ills of our society and the developing world was antithetical to what they were attempting to impose on the rest of us.

President John F. Kennedy, Malcom X, Dr. Martin Luther King, Jr., and Senator Robert F. Kennedy were essentially perceived as impediments to their power and ultimately the world they were determined to build. They were considered a treacherous threat and a Cold War liability that had the potential to undermine everything they had built and had planned for in the future. And ultimately, they were deemed expendable while in pursuit of their larger objectives. After all, the end would justify the means.

For those of us that lived through that future and now look upon the wreckage perpetrated by their policies and global orthodoxy, we can now appreciate how much the country lost by their tragic assassinations. We can genuinely appreciate the courage they exemplified as they challenged the status quo while asking us to envision a future in which the strong were just, the poor secure and the peace preserved. A world in which politics was a noble profession that encouraged a government that was worthy of our trust and was receptive to our demands. A nation that was admired for its compassion, wisdom, and grace in pursuit of man's greatest quest that of peace and goodwill to all humanity. As Albert Camus, the French dissident writer, wrote, "I should be able to love my country and still love justice."

CHAPTER 5
Murder Incorporated (The 1954 Guatemalan Training Documents)

We have seen the enemy, and it was within us all along.

President Lincoln observed that if you wanted to ascertain the character of a man just "give him power." And now consider that this power is unfettered by legal authority and is cloaked by the impenetrable shield of national security which is exactly what was wittingly given to the Central Intelligence Agency (CIA) in 1948 when its leadership was permitted to expand its mandate to include clandestine operations to its responsibilities in defense of the nation. A dark force had been let out of the bottle which we have been unable to control ever since. Much of their covert activities are so secret and sensitive that the Congress were not apprised of their existence and in some cases were conducted without presidential authority. Max Weber a German sociologist surmised that, "Power without legal authority is tyranny." The history of the CIA and the damaging ramifications to the United States (U.S.) and its moral integrity by its secret nefarious activities not only buttresses Weber's conclusion but in the judgment of history is undeniable.

The men that formulated the culture of the CIA since its founding in 1947, and those that dominated the development of its internal social structures, were liars whose duplicity was only surpassed by their desire for absolute power. The more proficient your deceptions the more likely you would be promoted. This is not my description of them but rather James Jesus Angleton's who was not just their friend and colleague but was also one of the most powerful members of their fraternity as the Counterintelligence Chief from 1954 until his forced resignation in 1975. Many CIA whistleblowers over the decades have reaffirmed this assessment of how the Agency operates and the arrogance manifested by many of its commanding officers. This is one of many reasons that has motivated Kevin Shipp, a former counterintelligence officer of the Agency, to publicly advocate for the formation of a modern-day Church Committee.

This is not to condemn all those who have been employed by this infamous agency. For many of its low-ranking members, especially in the intelligence gathering and analytical sector, they had applied to the Agency to defend our republic such as CIA officer Ray McGovern who was inspired by Kennedy's dynamic inaugural address to serve his country. This is rather an indictment of those who were attracted to the "cloak and dagger" nature of intelligence and relished the power they wielded in secret as they participated in covert activities under the auspices of the CIA's predecessor the Office of Strategic Services (OSS) in World War II. It was within this select group of Ivy-league elitists composed of staunch anticommunists and neo fascists that included Frank Wisner, Richard Helms, Allen Dulles and former Nazis of the Third Reich that were recruited under Operation Paperclip that advocated for an intelligence agency in peacetime that would counter the intelligence capabilities of our perceived adversaries and fill the void created by the termination of the OSS after the war had ended. Although William Donovan, aka "Wild Bill", is considered the founder of the CIA, his vision was partially usurped by Allen Dulles and his ilk in the 1950s.

It is essential to understand that the debate that occurred prior to its founding included concerns that a secret intelligence agency was antithetical to our republic and could pose a significant threat to our democratic institutions and eventually our individual liberty. The fear as observed by its critics was that it could become an "American Gestapo" as Truman later described it when he conceded that he regretted assenting to its creation. Many of his public criticisms of the Agency were included in an editorial he started composing only 7 days after President Kennedy's assassination that would be published on December 22, 1963, in the Sunday morning edition of The Washington Post.

The timing of his harsh condemnation of the Frankenstein monster he had authorized is not a coincidence. The former President had become fond of Kennedy and had supported his foreign and domestic agenda. President Kennedy and the First lady had invited Harry and Bess Truman to several White House functions and private dinners that included overnights. Truman had even entertained Kennedy's guests by playing the piano at one of the White House's auspicious galas. Because of their mutual respect and growing friendship, Kennedy had consulted with Truman on many occasions, and I am quite confident JFK discussed his concerns regarding the war mongering generals whose advice he was consistently dismissive of and the nefarious actions by rogue elements within the CIA to undermine his policies. The impetus for his writing his editorial in my opinion was partially derived from these candid discussions he had with the martyred President.

The governing tenets of all intelligence whether it be the former KGB, MI6 or the CIA are that the end justifies the means and that the enemy of my enemy is my friend. These agencies in their initial stages enhance national security but as

The Hidden War

their power grows the loyalty to country is transferred to the agency and its corporate allies. Consequently, many intelligence organizations digress into amoral institutional structures that not only threaten the Constitution it was sworn to protect but in fact undermine it. These governing doctrines precipitate the internal corruption that contaminates their institutional culture that eventually demoralize their original mission as outlined in their authorizing charter. Hence, you have the CIA supporting Al Qaeda forces in Syria that oppose Assad's regime who is backed by the Russian and Iranian governments. These principles are also prevalent in the CIA's torture programs in which its present Director was implicated up to her eyeballs.

This rationalization proclaims that the means by which we achieve our ultimate objective are essentially irrelevant as long as they obtain the desired outcome. These same reasonings are the foundational justifications for the development of the Agency's assassination protocols and programs that eventually were authorized such as Operation 40, Task Force W, MKULTRA and the Phoenix Program. The cryptonym used by the CIA for "executive action" in February of 1961 was ZR/RIFLE which was organized and supervised by an infamous and recklessly dangerous agent named William Harvey. This top-secret operation, however, was initiated in the final year of the Eisenhower administration to assassinate Cuban leaders not just Castro. Harvey decided to hide this secret assassination program in Staff D which was responsible for SIGNIT. Its primary duties were signal intelligence and electronic intercept. Staff D was so secret that it made it a good place for ZR/RIFLE to reside.[7]

The programs mentioned above utilized assassination as a significant tool to obtain their objectives. The Phoenix operation for instance as referenced in my book "The Paradox of our National Security Complex" murdered 26,000 civilians and suspected Viet Cong in South Vietnam during the war, generating a reign of terror among all the Vietnamese that resided within the hamlets and rural villages. The CIA was confident that these abhorrent tactics would coerce the Vietnamese that resided in these rural areas to oppose the Viet Cong and their allies. It of course had the opposite effect.

The Agency's covert operational sector was officially created by National Security Council 10/2. Within this document was the concept that all clandestine operations had to be developed such that the CIA and the federal government could maintain plausible deniability if any of these operations became public. As the Agency invested more resources to the operational side, it began to explore numerous options to support its corporate allies and to wage its covert war against the communists. The origins of the assassination protocols and procedures gained acceptance in this milieu of cloak and dagger tactics to achieve its objectives. After all, its Soviet and Chinese counterparts had already developed such a capacity to accomplish their goals as defined by their governments.

The use of what was referred to as "executive action" began to develop more acceptance within the CIA under the government sanctioned overthrow of Mohammad Mossadegh's government in Iran in 1953. According to an article written by Kate Doyle and Peter Kornbluh entitled "CIA and Assassinations: The Guatemala 1954 Documents", the idea of creating a formal procedure and policy for an assassination program was not developed until the implementation of operation PBSUCCESS which was authorized by President Eisenhower in August of 1954. If the operation to remove Jacobo Arbenz from power was not as successful as it became, the Agency was prepared to assassinate Arbenz and other key leaders in his government. As the essay pointed out, these classified documents on PBSUCCESS that were released in 1997 included an instructional guide on assassination among the training files of the operation.

The CIA has denied that they intended to assassinate anyone in Guatemala at that time. It has been difficult to determine the veracity of their assertion in that all the names of those listed as potential targets in Iran and in Guatemala were redacted from the documents. The present view is assassins sponsored by Rafael Trujillo of the Dominican Republic were to infiltrate and eliminate those on the list if this became necessary. Nevertheless, we know from other covert operations that the CIA has assassinated thousands of individuals up through the present most notably under the drone program initiated during the Clinton administration. This operation administered by the CIA in cooperation with the military expanded significantly during the war on terror initiated after 9/11 under the Bush, Obama, and Trump presidencies.

The assassination manual is essentially a 19-page instructional guide in the art of political killing which encompassed detailed descriptions of the procedures, instruments, and implementation of assassination. The manual underscores the fact that to maintain plausible deniability that "no assassination instructions should be ever written or recorded." Decisions and instructions should be shared on a need to know basis. The drafters of this guide also state that murder "is not morally justifiable" and that those "persons who are morally squeamish should not attempt it."

The Hidden War

This document lists every weapon imaginable, including, but not limited to, knives, screw drivers, axes, pistols, drugs, long range rifles and automatic weapons. It discusses further the optimum conditions for each weapon. The guide also asserts that if this action is designated "secret" than it is imperative "... to conceal the fact that the subject was actually the victim of assassination, rather than an accident or natural causes." Other types of assassination may not require this but in such cases the assassin must make sure that they do not fall into "enemy hands."

The assassin under what is designated a "safe" assassination (the assassin will survive after the task) can be a clandestine officer of the Agency. "He should be determined, courageous, intelligent, resourceful, and physically active. If special equipment is to be used, such as firearms or drugs, it is clear that he must have outstanding skill with such equipment." A fictional example of this was committed by Ian Fleming's protagonist James Bond as agent 007 of MI6 on many occasions.

The guide continues that in terrorist assassinations "it is desirable that the assassin be transient in the area. He should have an absolute minimum of contact with the rest of the organization and his instructions should be given orally by one person only." The assassin's safe evacuation is essential. "It is preferable that the person issuing the instructions also conduct any withdrawal or covering action which may be necessary." In "lost" assassinations (the assassin will die with the target), "the assassin must be a fanatic of some sort. Politics, religion or revenge are about the only feasible motives." Since the fanatic is usually psychologically unstable, he must not be privy to the other members of the organization because if he does not die in the act the plan must be confined to maintain its secrecy.

The techniques used must assure the death of the target. The guide indicated that the attempt on Hitler's life failed because the "conspiracy did not give this matter proper attention." For secrete assassinations, the "contrived accident" is most effective because it attracts minimal attention and "is only casually investigated." I would add that false suicides also have the same advantages over an overt murder or assassination. As legendary CIA asset Bill Corson chilling remarked, "Anybody can commit a murder, but it takes an expert to commit a suicide."

The manual asserts further that the most efficient accident is a fall from a height of at least 75' onto a hard service. The drafters wrote "an elevator shaft, stair wells, unscreened windows or a bridge will serve" this type of murder. In chase cases, it may be necessary to "stun or drug" the intended subject "before dropping him." This description certainly is indicative of what happened to special agent Frank Olson who was drugged before he allegedly committed suicide by jumping through a closed window and falling 13 floors to his death.

Special agent William Harvey supplemented this manual in 1961 in a memorandum he created for Staff D "cover material." The problem he was confronted with was how to provide cover for agents involved in ZR/RIFLE and Task force W. He considered the "creation of a false 201 file" for the assassins. He added that "... planning should include provision for blaming Sovs (Soviets), or Czechs in case blow (cover blown) ...should have phony 201 to back stop this, all documents therein forged or backdated." It should resemble a counterintelligence file. In another section of the memo, Harvey made it clear that if the plans included blaming Soviets and the Czechs than the use of "Americans" for "direct action" or anyone "tainted by use by American agency" would not be prudent especially if plan was detected. He also referred to "anesthesia" and "disposal" in the context of the assassin(s). It may be that Harvey was contemplating what to do with an assassin or a patsy after the task was completed. This is not clearly delineated within the memorandum. As asserted in my book "The Paradox of our National Security Complex", this certainly resembles what happened to Lee Harvey Oswald.

In the 1950s and early 1960s, many Americans trusted their government. They believed for the most part what they were told by their national leaders and clearly accepted that our adversaries were evil and that we represented those forces that were preventing these dark powers from enveloping the world in chaos, violence and lawlessness. The notion that the U.S. government was targeting foreign nationals - never mind heads of state or U.S. citizens – for assassination would have been considered unconscionable at the time. This is the innocence that pervaded the political and social constructs in which Allen Dulles and his intelligence cabal operated. Thus, it was imperative that all these nefarious activities, and most certainly their assassination program, be hidden from the courts, the Congress, the media, and the public. Because of the CIA's alliance with Wall Street and most of the mainstream media, their ability to maintain this curtain of deceit was made much easier than it should have been in a true republic. Consequently, Operation Mockingbird and other secret alliances enabled the Agency to successfully make these reprehensible programs invisible to those who were not part of the secret government. As we

The Hidden War

will discover, even Presidents were not privy to this information or were lied to.

The JFK assassination changed all the above and initiated a period in which many began to question our government and doubt the answers that were provided. The Vietnam War significantly contributed to this controlled anxiety and suspicion that eventually exploded into the streets of our cities and throughout our institutions as more Americans joined the protests in our communities and on our college campuses.

The anti-war movement by the late 1960s would coalesce with others such as civil rights, women rights, and the environmental movement.

By 1967, COINTELPRO which was a classified FBI operation that initially was created in the late 1950s to search for communists and undermine any group that was deemed supportive of their cause transferred its focus to the protestors. It began to infiltrate groups such as the Students for a Democratic Society and the Black Panther Party for Self Defense to foment discord within their ranks, as well as assassinate their leaders as was done to Fred Hampton in Chicago in 1969.

As for the CIA, President Johnson sanctioned Operation CHAOS which was devised to spy on these left-wing organizations that they believed were inspired by communist agitators. This would also be the view of the Nixon administration. During this turbulent year which would only get worse in 1968, the Garrison probe was out in the open which ignited further allegations levied at the Agency for its possible involvement in Kennedy's murder.

This is the context in which Drew Pearson and Jack Anderson wrote their article that was published on March 7, 1967, which revealed that the CIA had attempted to assassinate Fidel Castro in 1963. This revelation further complicated the CIA's public relation difficulties which caused many to doubt the Agency's denial of any involvement in what transpired in Dealey Plaza. The Warren Commission for instance was never apprised of these top-secret conspiracies. The Castro plots, however, were contained for another 7 years until the Rockefeller Commission and the Church Committee brought the issue into the forefront of national debate. President Johnson because of the article ordered that the CIA conduct an internal investigation that prompted this top-secret Inspector General's Report on CIA plots to assassinate the Cuban leader.

The IG Report was completed that same year. It was so sensitive according to Professor Peter Dale Scott that Presidents Johnson and Nixon were not permitted to read it by CIA Director Richard Helms. When he met with

President Johnson to brief him on the investigation, he verbally reported the conclusions from notes he had written down prior to their meeting. I am confident that Helms who was known as the keeper of the Agency's secrets never divulged the most salacious aspects of the IG Report. One might wonder who was in charge of our government and what level of security was necessary to read classified documents if the Commander-in-Chief by virtue of his office did not have the requisite security clearance. The report was essentially the culmination of dozens of interviews with CIA officers who were implicated in these CIA-Mafia plots against Castro.

These plots were initiated by the Eisenhower administration in August of 1960. There were essentially three phases as outlined in the report. Phase I ended in April or May of 1961. The second phase started in April 1962 and ended in February of 1963. The third phase ran from February of 1963 until sometime in 1965. Debra Conway who is the co-founder of the JFK Lancer website opined in her analysis that phase III continued much longer than acknowledged by the CIA.

The murder of Che Guevara in 1967 tends to support Conway's suspicion. In 1965, Che resigned from his position within the Cuban government to venture out on his own to foment what was considered by Dick Goodwin, a special assistant to JFK and LBJ, to lead "a ...non-existent revolution in the forsaken wretchedness of Bolivia."[8] Once Che left the protections afforded him by Cuban security forces, he was an easy target for those within the U.S. that wanted his head. Goodwin wrote, "The United States dispatched a special forces group to find Che and to kill him." According to Goodwin, a Bolivian operation beat them to the target and murdered him in the jungles of Bolivia.[9] Unknown to Goodwin at the time and during the period that he wrote his tome, the CIA's secret assassination program to murder Cuban leaders was still operative. Theodore C. Shackley of CIA had already sent Tony Sforza and David Sanchez Morales to Bolivia to capture and murder him.

David Sanchez Morales was a Yaqui Indian that was known for his "hard drinking" and his intimidating demeanor as one of the most loyal CIA operatives that would do anything for the Agency. Wayne Smith a 25-year veteran of the foreign service observed, "Dave Morales did dirty work for agency. If he were in the mob, he'd be called a hit man."[10]

The reason for this is that the CIA had recruited Morales and provided him with an opportunity to escape the poverty of his youth and to acquire a lifestyle he could never have imagined as a child growing up in Phoenix.

The Hidden War

Because of this, his family was the Agency. Consequently, he and the CIA's long list of bloody exploits of those who fell victim to their carnage was astounding. His fingerprints appeared to be always present when prominent leaders died. For instance, Morales admitted to a friend that he "was in the palace when Allende was killed."[11] He also, after a few drinks, exclaimed to his attorney Robert Walton that, "I (Morales) was in Dallas when I, when we got the mother fucker, and that I was in Los Angeles when we got the little Bastard."[12] In fact, Ruben Carbajal who was one of his lifelong friends not only verified that statement by Walton but also added that Sforza and Morales had divulged to him in confidence that the CIA was involved in the murder of President Kennedy.[13] According to CIA officer Ed Wilson who was Shackley's deputy, Morales "actually led the capture of and assassination of Che Guevara."[14] Talbot in his explosive book "Brothers" corroborated Trento when he wrote, Morales was "involved in the hunting and execution of Che Guevara in 1967."

Operation Mongoose was authorized by President Kennedy in November of 1961 to encourage internal dissent within Cuba with the hope that it would eventually overthrow Castro's regime.[15] This secret operation would continue through most of phase II. The augmented group that would coordinate its activities included Robert Kennedy who was the Attorney General.

The chairman of the group was Major General Edward Lansdale who was involved in the overthrow of the Philippines' government in the early 1950s and the rise to power of Ngo Dinh Diem in South Vietnam. Harvey was chosen in early February of 1961, and he brought in agent QJWIN who was implicated in the Patrice Lumumba assassination to assist in ZR/RIFLE. He also communicated with Johnny Roselli as a conduit to his Mafia contacts. This assassination program was not part of Mongoose. John Newman in his book "Into the Storm" asserted that Harvey kept this program close to his vest and never did, according to the documentary record, inform Lansdale of its existence.

The idea of "executive action" was discussed by the augmented group but was rejected by most of the members. Ironically, it was CIA Director John McCone who had been appointed by Kennedy to replace Allen Dulles who vehemently objected to the U.S. sanctioning such tactics. Lansdale I am sure was amused by his comments, recognizing the naïve ignorance of the new director. Operation Mongoose would be terminated in November of 1962 because of the accord that resolved the Cuban Missile Crisis in late October of that year.

The IG Report concluded that there were no executive authorizations issued for the assassinations. It was determined after interviewing everyone involved with exception to former director Allen Dulles and Deputy Director General Charles Cabell that Presidents Eisenhower and Kennedy were not apprised of the operations. As we shall see, the failure to interview Dulles significantly impaired the conclusions of the investigation.

The IG Report did cite an incident when Robert Kennedy was made aware of the CIA-Mafia alliance on May 22, 1961, via a memorandum from FBI Director J. Edgar Hoover. In that memo, Hoover advised the Attorney General that the CIA had solicited members of the underworld such as Giancana to assist in Cuban operations. This information was obtained through an illegal FBI wiretap. Kennedy wrote in the margins of the memo to his aide Courtney Evans, "I hope this will be followed up vigorously." RFK was assured by Edwards of the Agency that the alliance with organized crime was terminated.

Robert Kennedy would not become aware of CIA-Mafia alliance again until May 7, 1962. It was at this time that he was briefed on the Castro plots that occurred in the first phase. RFK was furious because this was hindering his investigation into these mob bosses. As a result, he met with Richard Helms who was at the time the Deputy Director of Plans (DDP). He then met later that afternoon with agent Sheffield Edwards and CIA general counsel Lawrence Houston for a briefing on pre-Bay of Pigs Castro assassination plots. Kennedy was irate and told them never to do this again without consulting with the Department of Justice (DOJ). RFK then divulged to Hoover everything that he had learned about the plots against Castro.

The CIA in an internal memo admits that RFK was never informed that the CIA-Mafia plots against Castro had entered another phase. As far as Kennedy knew, they had ceased. In an article published in 1998 titled "The Castro Plot Thickens -Again" by Evan Thomas, Kennedy told an aid after reading a newspaper account of his authorization of the Castro plots that, "I didn't start it. I stopped it...I found out that some people were going to try an attempt on Castro's life, and I turned it off." During a trip to Latin America with Dick Goodwin, RFK remarked, "I'm tired of all these Latins attacking me for going after Castro. The fact is that I'm the guy who saved his life."[16]

The Church Committee was formed in response to allegations that the CIA was assassinating foreign leaders and had attempted on many occasions to kill Castro. They were able to get the 1967 IG Report that had been requested by

The Hidden War

President Johnson. There were only two discussions that the committee was able to determine that involved President Kennedy in these matters.

The first was a meeting that special assistant Richard Goodwin arranged between foreign correspondent for the New York Times Tad Szulc with Robert Kennedy. He was one of the journalists who uncovered the Bay of Pigs story prior to Brigade 2506 hitting the beach. They discussed Cuban operations but did not broach the subject of assassinations. At the close of their discussion, RFK invited Szulc to meet with President Kennedy.

The second meeting with the President occurred on November 9, 1961. It was made clear to him before the meeting began that this private discussion was "off the record." Szulc testified before the committee that they initially had a general discussion of post Bay of Pig Cuban strategies. The President then without warning asked him what his perspective would be if he authorized the assassination of Castro. Szulc replied that he did not think that the death of Castro would significantly impact Cuban activities. He also asserted that he did not believe that the U.S. should be engaged in murders and political assassination. The President responded that, "I agree with you completely." He further elaborated that he and his brother felt that for moral reasons the U.S. should not resort to assassinations as part of our foreign policy. JFK then revealed to him that he brought up the matter because he was under tremendous pressure from advisors (Szulc thought he meant intelligence people) to order a hit on Castro. Goodwin corroborated Szulc's account of the meeting. He remembered vividly Kennedy's assertion, "We can't get into that kind of thing, or we would all be targets."[17] The second conversation was between Kennedy and his good friend Democratic Senator George Smathers of Florida.

The Church Committee concluded that "...Neither conversation aided us in our effort to determine whether President Kennedy or any other President specifically or implicitly authorized the CIA's assassination plots and plans."

It was after this conversation with Szulc that Kennedy made his final decision. He delivered a speech that had been written by Theodore Sorensen on November 16, 1961, at the University of Washington in Seattle. According to Sorensen, this was Kennedy's archetypal expression of his foreign policy that incorporated a new realism on the limits of American power that he had learned over the first year of his presidency.[18] For Sorensen, this was not only one of his favorite speeches but was one of the most important that Kennedy had orated. In this speech Kennedy had declared, "We cannot, as a free nation, compete with our adversaries in tactics of terror, assassination, false promises, counterfeit mobs and crises."[19] It is true that Kennedy had not issued an executive order condemning such activity, but, nevertheless, it had been made clear by this speech that this was not to be part of his agenda.

One of the most provocative plots on Castro's life was initiated during a period in which the Kennedy administration was fully exploring what was referred to as the "sweet approach." This was a back-channel effort initiated by ABC journalist Lisa Howard and Ambassador William Attwood with the approval of Kennedy. The CIA and Joint Chiefs of Staff were deliberately not briefed on these secret negotiations. The goal was to seek rapprochement with the Cuban government. President Kennedy opined that if this effort was successful that the U.S. could take Castro "out of the Soviet fold and perhaps wiping out the Bay of Pigs and maybe getting back to normal."[20]

DDP Richard Helms and his agents had their suspicions and were closely monitoring everyone who was involved in the negotiations. The CIA most likely leaked this information to the anti-Castro Cuban community as they began their clandestine activities to sabotage Kennedy's back-channel diplomacy. In the fall of 1963, Operation AMLASH was initiated by Helms and William Harvey. Desmond Fitzgerald in October met with a close associate of Fidel Castro named Rolando Cubela (AMLASH) to discuss killing him. Cubela wanted to know how high Fitzgerald's authority went. Fitzgerald responded that the Attorney General had personally approved of this mission. He added that he would have the full support of the U.S. government. Fitzgerald had used a pseudonym to conceal his identity to protect the Agency. As Professor Peter Dale Scott reported, CIA operative Sam Halpern had been asked by the Schweiker-Hart Subcommittee if this operation could have exposed the CIA by placing it in an embarrassing predicament. Halpern testified that the CIA was protected because agent Fitzgerald had not revealed his name to AMLASH. As Scott observed, "Only Robert Kennedy would be embarrassed."

The IG Report referenced this event in a glib fashion when it indicated that at "the very moment that President Kennedy was shot a CIA officer was meeting with a Cuban agent in Paris and giving him an assassination device for use against Castro." This operation was clearly an attempt by CIA officers to sabotage Kennedy's negotiations with Cuba, for this project was initiated when these back channel diplomatic efforts were gaining momentum. This plot may have also been part of the assassination of the president to make it look like Castro killed Kennedy to avenge the attempts on his life allegedly authorized by

The Hidden War

RFK. In fact, an emissary of Kennedy named Jean Daniels was meeting with Castro when news came over the radio that Kennedy had been assassinated in Dallas. Castro immediately understood the implications for Cuba when he blurted out, "Everything is changed. Everything is going to change!"

Helms testified before the Church Committee that he had never discussed AMLASH with Robert Kennedy or the President. This was also conceded by others that were involved in the plot. They had essentially conveniently assumed that this is what RFK would have wanted. Nevertheless, the Church Committee and the IG Report found no supporting evidence that any of these plots on Castro were authorized by President Eisenhower or the Kennedys.

Debra Conway who co-founded JFK Lancer surmised from her research that the Kennedys were not involved in the original orders, for the plots were activated during the Eisenhower administration. Thus, the Kennedys were completely unaware of the Castro assassination attempts in Phase I. She indicated that they were never told that Phase II was in effect when RFK had thought he had shut down the CIA-Mafia plots against Castro in May of 1962. She believes that the Kennedys may have speculated that the CIA attempts on Castro might have been in effect in the early part of phase III and did nothing to verify their suspicions. But as the negotiations with the Cuban government became more optimistic, and as these covert activities resulted in formal Soviet grievances that the U.S. was violating the Cuban Missile Accord, the President issued an executive order in the late Summer of 1963 to terminate all anti-Castro operations being conducted within the U.S. They were essentially attempting to eradicate these clandestine activities that they suspected may have included assassination operations as the administration was seeking an end to the Cold War through diplomacy. They, however, never authorized them or approved of them. And yet, the assassination program continued through 1965, and possibly beyond that year, in complete defiance of a presidential order.

The reason that the Church Committee and the IG Report never ascertained how far up the chain of command the assassination orders for Patrice Lumumba and Fidel Castro had gone was because Allen Dulles had never been interviewed in 1967 and was dead by the time the Church Committee was formulated in 1975. It is clear because of a sworn statement by Robert Johnson whose responsibility was to transcribe the minutes for the group that was created by NSC 5412/2 - in which Dulles was in attendance - was that Eisenhower had given the order to kill the Congolese leader Lumumba in the summer of 1960. He intuitively understood that this segment of the discussion should not be memorialized in the transcript of the meeting. He, however, was so shocked by Eisenhower's order that it was engraved into his memory.[21]

Eisenhower of course was not so rash as to use such explicit language to express his command. In a meeting held on May 13, 1960, "after a briefing from Allen (Dulles), Eisenhower told the Special Group that he wanted the Cuban leader 'sawed off'. His second target Lumumba had not yet risen to power."[22] Years later Richard Bissell who was the Deputy Director of Plans of CIA during the Eisenhower years and was the officer who "set both assassination plots in motion, testified that Allen (Dulles) ordered him to do so."[23] On both occasions, Dulles revealed to him that the orders had been approved at the "highest level."[24] Thus, we know today that the only President prior to the drone program to authorize the murder of foreign leaders was President Dwight D. Eisenhower. At least, he is the only one we have credible evidence against.

The idea of killing political enemies was clearly discussed in the Nixon administration. In fact, Kissinger and Nixon may have sanctioned Salvador Allende's murder in 1973 when the CIA and Chile's military overthrew his government and installed the brutal regime of Augusto Pinochet. Nevertheless, these attempts by CIA officers such as Richard Helms, E. Howard Hunt and Sam Halpern to tarnish the Kennedy legacy by blaming the Kennedy brothers for these despicable acts was another one of their perfidious tales.

As the Church Committee findings were made public, President Ford issued executive order 11905 in February of 1976 which included a ban on political assassination. Carter would strengthen this order in 1978 by removing the word "political."[25] All of this unfortunately would be ignored by our intelligence community during the Reagan administration. The assassination of our enemies would officially be sanctioned by Presidents George W. Bush and Barrack Obama as a legitimate tactic in our war on terror.

This absurdity known as the drone program is now being continued by the Trump administration. This idea of murdering our alleged adversaries to achieve our objective was once considered by the media and general public as something that the U.S. would never engage in - which is why these assassination plots were considered highly sensitive top-secret operations concealed by the most elaborate of security measures - are now conducted openly by each succeeding administration as justifiable tactics against our

The Hidden War

enemies. President Obama promoted it as a "cleaner" way to achieve our objectives as opposed to sending troops in harm's way.

Operation Neptune Spear which resulted in Osama bin Laden's death in 2011 was the exception. This covert operation, however, is heralded as a heroic mission that enhanced the legacy of Obama's presidency. When in fact, it could be argued that this murder was nothing more than a vigilante operation that we would have immediately objected to if Putin had done the same to one of his professed enemies. We do not approve of it on a community level so why do we condone it when our national government does it. The answer is we should not and that the enforcement of the rule of law should be our primary goal.

These programs that justify murder weaken the spiritual and moral integrity of our nation in that we have essentially become just like our professed enemies. These operations and tactics are not a representation of our ideals but of our power. And yet when our adversaries do it, we are outraged and quick to condemn their actions. We appear oblivious to the hypocrisy of our words as we continue to activate policies, and the rationalizations that justify them, that unequivocally contradict what we claim to be defending. We seek false pretexts to initiate our absurd wars that in some cases were simply false flag operations, meaning that they were built upon lies or events we created. Despite all the proclamations that this is being done on our behalf to preserve and protect our liberty and to reinforce our security, I think for those who have objectively and analytically dissected this false reality know that our liberty has been diminished and that our security has become more precarious by these insidious policies.

The worst aspect of this secret assassination program is that it was hijacked and turned against our own leaders. The overwhelming evidence that exists today implicates many of the participants in the Castro plots in the assassination of President Kennedy.

John Kiriakou a former CIA analyst who became a whistle blower when he revealed the extent of the CIA torture program stated, "One of the things that most observers don't understand is that the CIA will do anything – anything – to survive. All CIA officers are taught to lie. They lie all the time, about everything, to everybody. And they justify it by trying to convince themselves that they are doing it in the national interest, for national security. From my very first day in the CIA, it was drilled into me, as it is into every other employee, that 'the primary mission is to protect the Agency.' That was the

Murder Incorporated (The 1954 Guatemalan Training Documents)

Mantra. Couple that with the CIA's ability to intercept and to take over virtually any communication device (WikiLeaks disclosure of Vault 7), and you have a Frankenstein monster. Is it really that hard to believe that such an organization would resist a president who challenged it? Is it hard to believe that it would do so surreptitiously? I don't think so."

It was not just a president that fell victim to the secret CIA assassination apparatus. Malcolm X's murder in 1965 is lesser known than the other prominent assassinations of the 1960s and yet it has the fingerprints of an intelligence operation all over it.

Malcolm X's father was murdered by the Klan when he was a child. He ended up as a disgruntled angry young man who gravitated to a world of crime and drugs that eventually turned him into a heroin addict. During his stint in prison, he turned to God to assist his courageous journey to pull himself out of the thralls of his disease. He would initially find his purpose as a devout Muslim and member of Elijah Muhammad's pro-black Nation of Islam.[26] He became a very effective preacher and vehement supporter of black pride and self-defense in a nation that treated African Americans, as well as Muslims, as second-class citizens. He initially advocated for tactics to defend their rights that included an eye for an eye or as he famously orated "by any means necessary."

It was a trip to Mecca in Saudi Arabia that ironically transformed him and provided him with examples that multi-racial societies could exist in harmony. He brought this epiphany back with him and began to modify his message in quest of seeking an alliance with Dr. King. These two influential civil right leaders joining forces caused significant anxiety within the U.S. intelligence community. Declassified documents reveal that at the end of his life the FBI, ONI and CIA were monitoring his activities daily.[27] Television news reporter Louis Lomax in 1970 was producing a documentary on Malcolm X's death that included commentary that the CIA had played a role in the assassination. This documentary was never aired for on July 31, 1970, Lomax died in a car crash. Investigating authorities indicated to the press that the accident had been the direct result of his brakes being cut.[28]

Professor Koerner had discovered in his research two incidents leading up to his death that had the earmarks of intelligence. Malcolm X traveled to Cairo, Egypt in July of 1964 to address the Organization of African Unity Conference. He was planning to present a petition at that conference that would solicit

The Hidden War

their support to bring U.S. human right violations before the United Nations. An act that surely would incur the wrath of the CIA and its covert operators.

The night prior to delivering his highly anticipated speech, he was having dinner with his entourage which included New York City Councilman Milton Henry at the Nile Hilton Hotel. Henry and Malcolm noticed two Caucasian males sitting at a nearby table constantly glancing over at them as they ate their dinner. In fact, they had recognized them as the same men that had been following them that entire day. Suddenly, Malcolm became violently ill and was rushed to a nearby hospital where he almost died. The doctors immediately had his stomach pumped and the contents analyzed by their medical lab. The lab technician had determined that there was a "toxic substance" in his food. A substance that could not have been present as a result of natural circumstances. They further determined that it would have been lethal if the doctors had not been able to treat him as quickly as they did. Another suspicious factor is that when they searched for the waiter that served them, he had "mysteriously disappeared" and was never located.[29]

The second incident occurred just prior to his death. He flew on February 5, 1965, to Orly Airport in Paris for another speaking engagement. Upon his arrival, he was confronted by French police and informed that he would not be permitted entry into the country. As a result, he was compelled to fly back to London. Malcolm was completely baffled by the French reaction because he had visited France on other occasions without incident. The most recent had been only three months before. He could not understand why they were now inexplicably treating him as a criminal.

In April of 1965, just two months after his assassination, investigative journalist Eric Norden while researching the circumstances that surrounded his death had stumbled over the reason the French had acted the way they did on that day. He was apprised by a source who was a "powerful" African diplomat that wanted to remain anonymous that his nation's intelligence agency had been informed by the "French Department of Alien Documentation and Counter-Espionage that the CIA was (plotting) Malcolm's murder, and France feared he might be liquidated on its soil." This was only 15 months after JFK's assassination. The French leaders did not want Paris to become another Dallas. The French agency was apparently advising this African nation that they had anticipated was a destination of Malcolm X to warn them, so they might provide the requisite security to save his life.[30]

Malcolm in the last year of his life was under constant harassment and surveillance that he knew was not consistent with the capabilities of the Nation of Islam that had become his nemesis after he had been forced out by their leadership to venture out on his own. He told author Alex Haley, "The more I keep thinking about this thing...the things that have been happening lately (including the bombing of his house), I'm not at all sure it's the Muslims. I know what they can do, and they can't do some of the stuff recently going on."[31] Researcher and author James Douglass observed, "Malcolm realized (just prior to his death) that...the Nation of Islam was now serving as a proxy, much like the CIA used the Mafia...in the attempted killings of Castro." Malcolm of course was murdered by three gunmen while giving a speech in New York City. There are a multitude of books that describe the murder and how his security was removed and the culprits behind it. The evidence convincingly supports that the Nation of Islam had essentially joined forces with intelligence assets to kill a common enemy.

There is something decomposing within the foundation of our democratic institutions that is exuding a malodorous odor that is indicative that something has gone terribly wrong. The assassination and torture programs are just two examples of many that confirm that we have drifted into a dark place and that something is rotting within our national spirit. We need to wake up and pull ourselves back into the light to defend our liberty and protect our Constitution if we wish to have any chance of rebuilding our republic. To do this, we as a nation must decide if we stand for anything. Do we desire to be feared for our power or respected for our ideals and our culture? We cannot choose to ignore this for the stench of our institutional decay will become revolting and not even those that reside in their gated communities will be able to escape it.

We can change our direction by terminating the operational side of the CIA and by reverting it back to what it was intended to be an intelligence gathering and analytical agency. But we cannot stop there for the entire intelligence community must be revamped such that their loyalty is to country and that their primary mission is to preserve and defend the Constitution of the United States. There also must be an internal mechanism governed by an objective group to judge the credibility of the grievances submitted by employees regarding the programs and policies being pursued by their employer. This group similarly should have congressional and/or judicial oversight to *assure* the integrity of the process.

The Hidden War

The most important reform should restrict what is classified to narrowly defined criteria that is truly related to national security. This must be vigorously enforced by objective overseers that are not dependent upon the good faith compliance of the agencies.

In my opinion, most of the actions of our national security complex should be transparent so that their activities can be scrutinized by our elected officials, the public and most importantly the media; a media that is objective and independent. This can be achieved by reinstituting net-neutrality, the Fairness Doctrine, and the repeal of those portions of the Telecommunication Act of 1996 that permitted 6 corporate giants to gobble up 97% of our media outlets.

As referenced above, a major threat, among others, to our nation is from the secret government that operates with impunity, without oversight or accountability. Its mission is to expand its power in quest of building an empire not to defend a republic. It mandates that all its members sign secrecy oaths and pledge their loyalty to the agency they work for and not the Constitution they were sworn "to preserve and to protect." Secret oaths and secret organizations are repugnant to a democratic republic, and thus cannot be allowed to exist within our governing institutions. Most of the demons we face were created by our intelligence community to maintain a level of fear among the citizenry to manipulate them to support their large budgets and tolerate their illegal covert activities. I do not think it was a coincidence that the only president to challenge their influence and was attempting to limit their power through his policies was assassinated. British historian and writer in the 19th century, Baron John Emerich Edward Dalberg-Acton, observed, "All power tends to corrupt and absolute power corrupts absolutely."

CHAPTER 6
A Horrifying Discovery by the Green Onion

The Cuban Missile Crisis was the pinnacle of the Cold War in that those two anxious weeks in October of 1962 was the closest the two superpowers ever came to a nuclear conflict. A war that would have killed in the span of an hour hundreds of millions of innocent civilians whose impact would be felt for decades. Like all dark events created by man, the crisis had manifested because of short sighted policies that were the constructs of ideological fictions that attached themselves to a manufactured reality based on power, greed, and irrational fear. Thus, the origins of the crisis began years before in our perceived innocuous support of the brutal regime of Fulgencio Baptista who ruled Cuba during the 1950s.

Cuba at that time was an ally of the U.S. against any communist incursions into Latin and even in South America. We propped up the dictator with military aid and large sugar quotas that made him and his cohorts extraordinarily rich. Large companies like United Fruit and Freeport Sulphur (renamed Freeport Mineral Company in 1971) extracted the natural resources of Cuba at minimal cost to the detriment of the citizenry who received miniscule benefits from their operations. While all this was occurring, the mob set up large gambling casinos and multiple exclusive brothels in Havana. In addition to their drug routes that ran through Cuba and into the United States, organized crime generated $100 million of revenue in that decade.

The Cuban island became the playground of the rich who travelled long distances from within the U.S. and other western nations to participate in the debauchery of a culture while impoverishing a people. Like the U.S. today, there was a significant chasm between the affluent who benefited from Baptista's rule and the working class. It became so intolerable as the severe conditions in which the poor and working class toiled that it culminated in a Cuban uprising led by Fidel Castro, Che Guevara and others that successfully toppled the dictator's government in 1959 much to the dismay of the CIA that became known as the Cuban Revolution. The pace of events essentially caught the Eisenhower administration by surprise.

Castro understood that the U.S. was the power that propped up Batista's dictatorship but nevertheless in a trip to New York City in September of 1960 - in which he was to deliver a speech at the United Nations - was hoping to meet with representatives of President Eisenhower to negotiate recognition of his

The Hidden War

newly formed government for the establishment of diplomatic relations between the two countries. He was rebuffed to such an extent that he was denied lodging in all the major hotels in Manhattan until a hotel in Harlem, quite familiar with the policies of oppression, opened its doors to him and his entourage.

The prior year, just 4 months after his victory, he traveled to New York in which he was able to schedule a meeting with Vice President Richard Nixon in April of 1959 who reported to the President that Castro was a "communist" and could not be trusted. The Director of the CIA Allen Dulles and his brother John Foster Dulles, the pious Secretary of State who hated communism to its very core for its "heretical" views on religion, zealously advocated to Eisenhower that these developments were a threat to our national security. They argued that the mere existence of a communist regime in the region only 90 miles from our most southern shore was intolerable and ardently sought permission to remedy the problem. In a secret meeting held on May 13, 1960, after being briefed on the Cuban issue by the CIA director, President Eisenhower told the 5412/2 group that he wanted the Cuban leader "sawed off." Allen Dulles understood this command as an authorization to assassinate Fidel Castro of which he assigned that task to Richard Bissell who was the Deputy Director of Plans.[32]

These notorious assassination attempts began shortly thereafter. The CIA would solicit the assistance of organized crime who still had lethal assets in the country that could facilitate the murder of Cuban leaders. These abhorrent plots would secretly continue through the Kennedy administration and beyond.

During that same period, a plan to overthrow the Cuban regime began in earnest as the CIA commenced the training of Cuban exiles who were primarily from the upper class that had fled Cuba after Castro had taken power and confiscated much of their family's land. This plan was codenamed "Operation Zapata." Initially, this was an attempt to instigate rebellion in Cuba through propaganda and infiltration, but as power was being transitioned to Kennedy, the plan morphed into a major amphibious assault of the island by Brigade 2506 which consisted of 1400 anti-Castro mercenaries that were being trained on the Pacific coast of Guatemala by CIA officers.[33]

This is the plan that was presented to Kennedy shortly after he was inaugurated. Kennedy initially was very reluctant to authorize such a large-scale assault that would be extremely difficult for the U.S. to maintain plausible deniability. He felt the original landing site would implicate American involvement and ordered that another landing site be chosen that was more remote. The landing site that was eventually selected by the military and CIA officials was the "Bahia' de Los Cochinos" which in English translates to "Bay of Pigs." The name that would become synonymous with utter failure.

Even after this remote bay was chosen, Kennedy remained unenthusiastic about the proposal. The Joint Chiefs of Staff and CIA Director Allen Dulles, CIA's Deputy Director of Plans Richard Bissell and the CIA's Deputy Director General Charles Cabell assured Kennedy that the plan had a reasonable chance of success and that once the Brigade got control of a beachhead and infiltrated the countryside they would be joined by thousands who wanted to oust Castro's regime. These assertions were all based on dubious intelligence that included intentional omissions and deceptions by Dulles and Bissell to entice the President's authorization for their ambitious operation.[34]

Dulles was not concerned whether the plan failed or succeeded because as he wrote in coffee stained notes later discovered by researchers that it was his view that once the assault began to fail, as he knew it would, the young president would be forced to choose between a humiliating defeat or ordering the military to support the Brigade to salvage the operation. He opined that a young president given those stark choices would inevitably decide to avoid humiliation and defeat.[35] President Kennedy of course had emphatically told Dulles and his CIA colleagues that under no circumstance was he going to authorize U.S. forces to participate in a war in the jungles of Cuba.[36]

When the plan began to fail miserably as Castro's forces mopped up the invaders, the President to the dismay and shock of the Joint Chiefs and the CIA leaders refused to authorize the Naval fleet sitting off shore just over the horizon to engage in the battle in support of the Brigade. More than 1000 were taken prisoner and the rest were casualties left on another battlefield of the Cold War.

The young President by doing so had perplexingly, as viewed by his national security team, stood by his principles, and accepted defeat. Kennedy had realized after the fact that the generals and the echelon of the CIA had attempted to entrap him in a CIA scenario that would compel him to drop his advanced stated restrictions against the introduction of U.S. combat forces because of circumstances they had set him up for.[37]

He shared his frustration with Dave Powers and Ken O'Donnell when he stated, "They were sure I'd give in to them and send the go-ahead order to the Essex (Navy aircraft carrier)." He added, "They couldn't believe that a new

The Hidden War

President like me wouldn't panic and try to save his own face. Well, they had me figured all wrong."[38]

In a press conference, Kennedy personally assumed responsibility for the failure and in private ordered an investigation that was chaired by General Maxwell Taylor to determine what went wrong. He also gave a speech defending his position by pointing out that it was contrary to our traditions to invade another country that had not attacked us first.[39]

The conclusion of that study ominously had revealed what Kennedy had suspected. The military had essentially approved an operation that had minimal chance of success without U.S. military support and that the CIA had essentially lied to him regarding key points of the plan to solicit his approval. The deceit of CIA leaders led to the removal of Dulles, Bissell, and General Cabell. A bold act by a president that was unprecedented at the time and has not been done since his presidency. As Senator Chuck Schumer inadvertently revealed on the Rachel Maddow show (9/27/19) when discussing President Trump's verbal tweets against CIA and NSA officials, he chillingly blurted out, "Let me tell you: You take on the intelligence community – they have six ways from Sunday at getting back at you." He added that this was "...really dumb to do this."

The exiling by Kennedy of internal hero and leader of the CIA, Allen Dulles, who secretly continued to manage his former agency out of his plush residence in Georgetown, Maryland, had irreparably damaged Kennedy's relationships with CIA officers who were fervently involved in the planning and execution of the Bay of Pigs and extremists within the anti-Castro Cuban community that mistakenly blamed the President for the failure of the operation. Even the CIA's internal probe of the disaster written by Inspector General Lyman Kirkpatrick, Jr. had concluded that the project had progressed beyond the Agency's capabilities and responsibilities. Kirkpatrick wrote, "The Agency became so wrapped up in the military operation that it failed to appraise the chances of success realistically. Furthermore, it failed to keep the national policymakers adequately and realistically informed of the conditions considered essential for success."

The Cuban issue continued to haunt Kennedy's administration. The Generals and the CIA just could not let it go and of course the President's ire towards Castro remained in his thoughts. But mostly, he kept kicking himself for being so "stupid" to approve such a plan. Within this political environment, a top-secret false flag ruse was being devised by the Joint Chiefs of Staff known as

A Horrifying Discovery by the Green Onion

Operation Northwoods. The Chairman, General Lyman Lemnitzer, presented the plan several times to Kennedy and the Secretary of Defense, Robert S. McNamara, in 1961 and 1962. Essentially, Lemnitzer, with the unanimous backing of the other Joint Chiefs, described a covert operation that through deception would rile up the American public for the purpose of manufacturing their consent for a Cuban invasion. He reported to McNamara that this could be achieved by sinking a U.S. ship off the coast of Cuba, or by shooting down a jetliner, or by lobbing missiles into Guantanamo and blaming it on the Cubans with fictitious intelligence. Kennedy eventually dismissed the covert operation and by the end of 1962 had sent the General to NATO Command and replaced him with General Maxwell Taylor on October 1, 1962.[40]

In November of 1961, Kennedy initiated Operation Mongoose which was managed by an augmented group that included his brother. The hope of these sabotage missions was to encourage the destabilization and eventual demise of the Cuban regime. It did not, however, include assassinations of Cuban leaders. This was an ill-advised policy that Kennedy enacted that never achieved any of its purported goals. It was one of many mistakes he made attempting to appease the rabid anti-communists in his administration that kept hounding him to do something about Cuba. The operation was terminated after the Cuban Missile Crisis in November of 1962.

The repercussion of all these actions, operations and policies was to encourage Castro to reach out to the Soviet Union to assist his defense against the goliath that was situated just north of him. His security forces had gathered intelligence that the mob while working for the CIA was trying to kill him, his brother, and Che Guevara. The Bay of Pigs assault clearly revealed that his enemies within the U.S. were willing to use covert para-military operations to overthrow him. He feared at some point the military might convince Kennedy to authorize an invasion. This began a long process of Soviet military aid that included weaponry and aircraft, as well as thousands of military advisors. Eventually, the Soviets had deployed 40,000 men that included not only elite combat troops, but state of the art military technology.

According to secret Soviet documents, the leadership in Moscow in ciphered telegrams emphatically wrote to Soviet commanders in Cuba that October, "We categorically confirm that you are prohibited from using nuclear weapons from missiles, FKR (cruise missiles), 'Luna' and aircraft without orders from Moscow."[41]   However, in prior memorandums, R. Malinovsky (USSR Minister of Defense) and M. Zakharov (Chief of the General Staff), after sending IL-28s

The Hidden War

and Luna missiles in early September, instructed the Commander of Soviet forces in Cuba that "In a situation of an enemy landing on the island of Cuba and of the concentration of enemy ships with amphibious forces off the coast of Cuba in its territorial waters, when the destruction of the enemy is delaying (further actions) and there is no possibility of receiving instructions from the USSR Ministry of Defense, you are permitted to make your own decision and to use the nuclear means of the 'Luna', IL-28 or FKR-1 as instruments of local warfare for the destruction of the enemy on land and along the coast in order to achieve the complete destruction of the invaders on the Cuban territory and to defend the Republic of Cuba."[42] If U.S. forces had invaded, the first wave of targets would have included Soviet communication outposts which of course could have created the circumstances for Cuban Soviet commanders as authorized above the discretion to use tactical nuclear weapons to defend themselves and their ally.

History always records the actions of the large figures who guided, or misguided in some cases, the events that formed the reality in which we lived. But much like the Soviet Captain of a nuclear submarine that was attacked by the U.S. Navy with depth charges to compel him to surface during the Cuban crisis had maintained his composure and did not give the order to launch his nuclear arsenal, thinking that the war had already begun, there exists many other unsung heroes that rose to the challenge at that precise moment when their nation needed them.

One of those heroes was my Uncle Charles Alexander Bay who was my mother's younger brother. He stood 6' 7" tall and had a commanding personality that often intimidated me as a child. And yet with fondness, I still vividly remember when we lived in Bethesda, Maryland, having picnics at Rock Creek Park with him and my Aunt. My father and my uncle would play a game of catch with a football as my mother and aunt would set up the feast on a picnic table situated near the creek.

Decades later he would reveal to me his contribution to his country during the Cuban Missile Crisis. He at first was reluctant to discuss it. I inquired if his actions were still classified. My brother amusingly interjected "that if he told us, he would have to kill us." Our uncle snapped, "That's not the reason. What my secret unit did has all been declassified!" I then walked away and visited with other family that had gathered to celebrate my father's life not to mourn his unexpected death. Later that afternoon, he approached me and asked me "If I wanted to talk about the 1962 crisis?" We had a brief but remarkable discussion. He later sent me a package that included documents that in detail explained his participation in the formation of history.

He had been transferred from the Fleet Intelligence Center Europe (FICEUR) located in Lyautey, Morocco to a highly classified Naval department named the Atlantic Intelligence Center (AIC) that was part of the Second Fleet Command of Admiral Dennison. AIC's commanding officer was Captain H. A. Kelley who was a highly decorated pilot.

He began his classified duties at AIC in February of 1962. The name of the space they were housed was oddly named the "Green Onion" which apparently referred to the two-cypher locked green doors that were the only ways to exit or enter the department. It was a relatively small space that consisted of three rooms that were utilized at one time for patients as part of a hospital on the CINCLANT compound that had been disbanded.

He had been in the Targeting Branch which was composed of 20 officers that mostly consisted of senior enlisted men that were engaged in deadly nuclear war games on the Soviet Union by the Sixth Fleet. He at the time was a Lieutenant (junior grade) of USNR as an Air Intelligence Officer with an expertise in aerial photographic analysis. At AIC, he created a Targeting Department that worked with aircraft of the Second Fleet that focused on targets in the northern Soviet Union next to the Arctic Ocean and the Baltic States.

The situation in Cuba was "heating up" when he arrived and U2's were initially being frequently flown over the "imprisoned island", as President Kennedy would later describe it in a televised address to the nation, announcing the presence of Soviet missiles in Cuba. The Soviet build up was in its early stages. The evidence indicated that conventional arms such as tanks and artillery had been offloaded onto the island. Joe Parker, a security officer, and photo analyst, had discovered while examining U2 photographs at AIC "anti-shipping missiles" deployed on the coast of Banes which created a "huge stir in the White House." They were instructed to keep this "under wraps."

In the summer of 1962, SA-2s were deployed along with Fishbed fighters, Komar Patrol Boats, and IL-28 light bombers. This created concerns of U2 flight detection, making them vulnerable to being shot down. This resulted in fewer flights that were primarily being flown over what was referred to as the "waist of Cuba." This was done to reduce the risks of being locked onto by Soviet and Cuban detection equipment.

The Hidden War

Essentially, the U2 photos would be picked up by AIC and officers would be randomly assigned a can and would begin the arduous process of examining each aerial photograph.

Only the National Photographic Interpretation Center (NPIC) under the auspices of the CIA could report the results of photo analysis at the national level. AIC could disseminate "finished intelligence" stemming from the U2 program. If NPIC had errors in its reporting, AIC when authorized could correct the record. Over time the AIC analysists developed a sophisticated familiarity with Soviet weaponry and deployment patterns.

The situation was tense and as a result there were many false reports of offensive weaponry, including missiles, being deployed in Cuba. These mistakes were debunked quite readily by those at the Green Onion.

Then the day of reckoning that had been anticipated for months finally came. The basic dissemination protocol for U2 photographs contained in "cans" was to send them to the Technical Support Center in the form of negatives. After being developed, duplicate positives were made. NPIC got the first wave and the Navy would receive the second group.

Joe Parker would routinely fly up to get AIC's "dry copy" as soon as it was "spooled off of the production line." The photographs that would initiate the Cuban crisis were brought to AIC the morning of October 15th and were available for examination by analysts at 8:00 am that morning. As reported above, the Soviets had introduced SA-2 missile systems to Cuba. Lieutenant (junior grade) Dick Helfrich asked my uncle to analyze frames of objects that he could not identify. They looked like a "super S" site.

The initial fears were that it was a MRBM. There was something "big" occurring because SA-2s would not be deployed to protect conventional forces. My uncle and his colleagues had all surmised that the deployment of Soviet state of the art defensive weaponry would only be deployed "to be used to defend more threatening offensive systems not yet introduced – possibly MRBM and IRBMs." He added, "In my view...given the secretive nature of the Soviet system, they would not risk the capture of their newest weapon systems unless the stakes were going to be extremely high in the event of a conflict."

My uncle using a 1:500,000 scale began the task of measuring 7 long objects that were suspected to be "missiles." He referred to the Army handbook which had pictures of Soviet MRBMs that were displayed as part of their annual Moscow parade. The pictures included information regarding the length of the rockets and the separate warhead that would be attached when deployed. His preliminary measurements of the objects in the U2 photos were a few feet short. He then remembered that his calculations did not include the warhead. When he added them, he knew he had proof of offensive soviet missiles in Cuba. He immediately went across the hall to apprise Captain Kelly of his discovery. After looking at them, the Captain blurted out, "Are you sure this is right? Because if it isn't, it will be our asses!" He assured him he was correct.

As my uncle explained to me in our conversation about that moment that he was basically, "A cocky young man who was confident about what I believed I had discovered, and that it never entered my mind the potential consequences to my career if I had been wrong." It turned out he was right and as a result received a Commendation from the United States Atlantic Fleet for "outstanding performance of duty while serving the Atlantic Intelligence Center from February of 1962 to December 1962." The information was reported out and eventually the following day ended up on President Kennedy's desk.

President Kennedy and his brother would after two excruciatingly tense weeks resolve the crisis diplomatically despite serious attempts within his national security apparatus to circumvent the chain of command through unilateral actions that could have jeopardized Kennedy's delicate negotiations with Soviet leaders.

General Thomas Power ordered that all Strategic Air Command (SAC) forces be placed on DEFCON 2 without consulting with the Commander- in - Chief. Additionally, William Harvey in charge of a top-secret CIA assassination program - which was never revealed to President Kennedy - sent in a team to assassinate Cuban leaders without the President's knowledge. Robert Kennedy was livid when he discovered Harvey's unauthorized stunt and wanted him relieved of his duties. Richard Helms who at the time was the Deputy Director for Central Intelligence of Plans stepped in and transferred Harvey to a post in Italy with the idea that if he was out of sight he would be forgotten as the crisis came to an end. Helm's actions saved Harvey's career.

The accord that was reached with the Soviets had resulted in the removal of the missiles. Although the rest of the world were relieved and had appreciated Kennedy's heroic statesmanship, the generals and the covert operators of the CIA that were responsible for Cuban operations were enraged.

The generals for instance had felt that Khrushchev had provided them with the pretext that they had been waiting for to activate their secret plan held within the archives of SAC to not only invade Cuba but launch our massive nuclear arsenal against the Soviet Union and China, killing an estimated 400

The Hidden War

million people that included 15 to 30 million Americans described casually as acceptable collateral damage.[43]

The object was the destruction of the communists through military action that would end the Cold War. A war that they ardently believed was inevitable, so it was in our national interests to hit them when circumstances were in our favor. Therefore, the only real choice from their perspective was to achieve total victory through warfare over their much-maligned adversary. To negotiate with the enemy for that generation was tantamount to appeasement. All the Joint Chiefs were decorated World War II veterans who vividly remembered Prime Minister Chamberlain's ill-fated diplomacy with Adolph Hitler to avoid war with the Nazis at Munich in 1938, an act that became synonymous with "appeasement." Hence, the crisis for them was an opportunity handed them by Khrushchev that Kennedy's negotiated settlement had thwarted. As Daniel Ellsberg reported after the crisis, there was a "coup atmosphere" that permeated the halls of the Pentagon because of the President's accord.

Kennedy inadvertently captured this rage for posterity when his Secretary Evelyn Lincoln forgot to turn off his secret recording system while he was meeting with the Joint Chiefs during the crisis on October 19th. Kennedy had invited them to the Oval Office to further discuss the developments of the crisis.

As the generals entered the room, Kennedy opened the discussion by explaining the quarantine proposal and the other alternatives. During the heated discussion one of the exchanges between Airforce General Curtis Lemay and Kennedy illustrates dramatically the lack of judgment of the Joint Chiefs and their determination to recklessly attack Cuba and their Russian ally. Lemay asserted that the best course of action is to engage in a surprise attack on the Russian missiles as soon as possible. Kennedy had asserted in prior Ex Comm meetings that his concern was that if we attacked Cuba the Russians would respond by invading West Berlin. Accordingly, Kennedy skeptically inquired, "What do you think their reprisal would be?" Lemay indicated there would be none if we made it clear we were ready to fight in Berlin as well. Admiral George Anderson chimed in supporting Lemay's position. Kennedy then interjected, "They can't let us just take out, after all their statements, take out their missiles, kill a lot of Russians, and not…not do anything."[44]

This prompted Lemay to retort later in their meeting, "this (blockade and political action) is almost as bad as the appeasement (of 1938) …I just don't see any other solution except direct military action right now." Kennedy remained poised and did not respond. The rest of the Joint Chiefs added that we needed to rectify the matter and invade Cuba and bomb the missile sites. Lemay then jumped in reaffirming his original point, "I think that a blockade and political talk would be considered by a lot of our friends and neutrals as bein' a pretty weak response to this. And I'm sure a lot of our own citizens would feel the same way, too. In other words, you're in a pretty bad fix at the present time." Kennedy responded, "What'd you say?" Lemay repeated his words. Kennedy while laughing scornfully stated "You're in there with me, personally."[45]

The discussion continued with the generals arguing for a massive invasion of Cuba and the bombing of the missile sites. The President than exits the room after assuring them he would thoroughly evaluate all the alternatives.

The generals in his absence continued their discussion completely unaware that their conversation was being recorded. Marine General Shoup exclaims, "You were a …You (Lemay) pulled the rug right out from under him." Lemay responds, "Jesus Christ. What do you mean?" Shoup replies, "…He's finally getting around to the word 'escalation' …when he says 'escalation' that's it. If somebody could keep 'em from doing the goddamn thing piecemeal, that's our problem…" Lemay replied, "That's right." Shoup continued, "You're screwed, screwed, screwed. He could say, 'either do the son of a bitch' and do it right and quit friggin' around." Lemay added, "That was my contention."[46]

Kennedy after the meeting recounted the tense conversation to his aid Dave Powers. "Can you imagine Lemay saying a thing like that? These brass hats have one great advantage in their favor. If we listen to them, and do what they want us to do, none of us will be alive later to tell them that they were wrong."[47]

Defense Secretary McNamara recalled how displeased the generals were with the resolution of the crisis. After Khrushchev had agreed to remove the missiles, Kennedy out of a sense of courtesy invited the generals to the White House so that "…he could thank them for their support during the crisis." McNamara recalled that "… there was one hell of a scene." Lemay not holding back, after Kennedy had announced we should not "gloat" over our victory, snapped, "We lost! We ought to just go in there today and knock 'em off." Even Robert Kennedy was struck by their reaction. He recounted Admiral Anderson exclaiming to his brother, "We have been had." The President revealing his frustration over the matter later told Author Schlesinger, "The military are mad."[47b]

The Hidden War

The lesson learned from the crisis for Khrushchev and Kennedy was much different than the hardliners within their national security apparatus that fed off one another. For the two leaders, peace was the only rational choice. By the end of the following year, Khrushchev and Kennedy were moving rapidly towards that peace. Kennedy's efforts were even facilitating a negotiated settlement with Cuba that would end a dark chapter in American history and permit his administration to let the Bay of Pigs fade into the fog of historical memory. By 1964, coincidence or not, Kennedy was dead, and Khrushchev had been ousted from power ironically in a bloodless coup by the Politburo led by Leonid Brezhnev.

The Cold War would march on reinvigorated by a U.S. proxy war in Vietnam that Kennedy had resisted for three years. He not only refused to send combat troops but had even signed National Security Action Memorandum 263 on October 11, 1963, which directed the removal of all U.S. personnel by December of 1965.[48]

The Cuban people would be subjected to CIA clandestine operations, violent assaults perpetrated by rogue anti-Castro extremists and economic sanctions imposed on them by each administration for decades until President Obama late in his second term attempted to re-open diplomatic relations that unfortunately Trump terminated.

The consequence of the Joint Chief's recommended actions in Cuba would have been horrific. As an example, my uncle discussed the designated landing zone for the 18th Airborne. He knew the Captain who periodically that fateful spring and summer would visit AIC as required by his "commanding general" to be apprised of any new developments. He further volunteered that his commander as recounted by my uncle "required all his intelligence staff to be first on the jump manifests – in order to ensure maximum attention to the job."

The 18th Airborne's landing site was a large field southeast of Havana. After the crisis had ended, the Captain returned to receive a post action report. As they examined the U2 photographs of the area, my uncle noted under the canopy of trees adjacent to the landing zone the presence of dozens of highly advanced ASU-57 armored vehicles with self-propelled guns. My uncle wrote, "I showed the Captain and he visibly turned white. I suspect that the lightly armed paratroopers would have had a difficult time, particularly since the weapons were most likely manned by elite Soviet troops." Essentially, the 18th Airborne would have been decimated.

A Horrifying Discovery by the Green Onion

This reminded me of a World War II film entitled "A Bridge too Far" that was about Operation Market Garden which was the taking of 7 bridges on the Rhine River. Photographs taken by reconnaissance aircraft had revealed a German Panzer division and their equipment that was parked under the cover of trees just outside the town in which the 7th bridge was located. The leaders of the mission decided to ignore the evidence and gave the go ahead to take all the bridges. The British paratroopers that were assigned to take that bridge were either killed or captured. Sean Connery who played their commanding officer in the film was furious when he found out that headquarters had evidence of the German Panzer unit in the area prior to the initiation of the operation.

McNamara had initially informed Kennedy that he estimated that 15,000 U.S. troops would be killed if he authorized the invasion of Cuba. When he attended the 30th anniversary of the event in 1992 that was also joined by Soviet military personnel that had participated in the crisis, he learned for the first time of all the weapons that they had deployed on the island that were available to defend their positions, including the presence of tactical nuclear weapons. With this new information, he estimated that 100,000 American troops would have been slaughtered.[49] If President Kennedy had relented to the generals demands, the crisis would have rapidly escalated beyond the control of civilian leaders on both sides, ushering in Armageddon.

As to my uncle Alex, his unit's discovery, as horrifying as it was, prevented the Soviets from completing the installations of their MRBMs in secret that had the range of up to 1100 miles. The crisis could have unfolded differently if all the missiles were operational that may have emboldened Russian leaders to step headfirst into the secret plans of SAC. Of course for decades as reported by researchers, journalists and historians, NPIC and the CIA have always received the credit for the discovery of Soviet offensive missiles in Cuba when the real heroes were a small band of analysts working for AIC which was a classified Naval unit housed in a space named the Green Onion.

CHAPTER 7
A House of Cards

President Kennedy's assassination has inspired hundreds of books, articles, videos, regional and national conferences. Some of these books support bazaar conspiracy theories in which the author tortures the facts until they confess. Their premise is Castro, the KGB, LBJ or the mob were the impetus for this transformative dark event in our history. There are also those books whose objective is to reinforce the Warren Commission's determination that a lone nut with communist affiliations was responsible for this tragedy. For many, this is a reassuring scenario because the alternative is beyond their comfort zone to even contemplate much less believe. Some of these books were encouraged by the CIA, parts of the deep state and our corporate media to obfuscate the landscape so its typography for most was so unrecognizable it discouraged them to venture into the abyss. And for others, it was meant to distract them from the stubborn facts that remained that if fully appreciated would permit an informed researcher a glimpse of the truth.

The 888-page Warren Commission Report (WCR) was submitted to President Lyndon Johnson on September 24, 1964, and then was subsequently released to the public in October with 26 volumes of evidence that purportedly buttressed their conclusion. I must concede that I agree with Colonel Leroy Fletcher Prouty that the number of shots and where the professional mechanics were in Dealey Plaza are window dressing that conveniently distracts the public from what is truly important which is why Kennedy was murdered. Nevertheless, the examination of these details I think is the most efficient method to prove a conspiracy.

This is because of an 8mm movie camera wielded by Abraham Zapruder that filmed the assassination. The Warren Commission (WC) was placed in a vice by that film that restricted their conclusions. For the film did not just record the event, it also captured how much time had elapsed from the first shot until the last which was 5.6 seconds. The FBI had already concluded that a mechanic firing the 6.5 Mannlicher Carcano bolt action rifle would need a minimum of 2.3 seconds for each shot. This meant that Lee Harvey Oswald – if he was the assassin – would only be able to fire three shots in that time frame.[50] This innocuous finding would eventually create a nightmare for the WC investigators when trying to describe a scenario that was limited to one shooter. The Commission's eventual solution to this problem became the fulcrum of their case which was a fiction.

The FBI in its initial investigation had concluded prior to the formation of the commission a scenario that resolved this dilemma. The FBI had determined that there were 3 shots fired that day and that all of them had hit Kennedy and Connally. The first and third shots hit President Kennedy and the second shot had struck Governor Connally who was sitting in front of the President in a jump seat. This all unraveled when it was learned that a shot had completely missed the presidential limousine and had struck a curb on Main Street, causing a piece of cement to hit a bystander named James Tague in his right cheek. He apparently was standing just North of Main Street near the triple overpass. This meant that there were only two shots available that caused 9 wounds in Kennedy and Connally.[51] This quandary is what prompted Arlen Specter to invent the infamous single bullet theory (SBT).[52] Without this scheme, the WC would have to accept that there were at least two assassins firing at Kennedy which obviously would be a conspiracy which they preordained had not occurred. It was a result that was unacceptable and consequently everything hinged upon this theory being portrayed in a manner that would be a palatable solution to the media, the government, and the public.[53]

The essence of the single bullet theory is that the second shot hit Kennedy in the back of the neck and exited his throat. The bullet then proceeded to enter the right part of Connally's back, hitting a rib and destroying his right wrist. It then ended up in his left thigh. The bullet that allegedly did all this damage was fortuitously discovered on a stretcher that Connally had been previously placed on by emergency room medical staff at Parkland Hospital in Dallas. The bullet which is designated Commission Exhibit 399 (CE 399) had a small chip missing on the tip of the slug. Otherwise, this pristine bullet was undamaged.[54]

This explanation seems unusual but nevertheless possible if one does not examine the facts. First, Kennedy was hit 5.6 inches below his right shoulder just to the right of his cervical spine. Former President Gerald Ford and member of the WC admitted to the Assassination Records Review Board in 1997 that he had changed the wording in the WCR to reflect that Kennedy was

The Hidden War

hit in the "base of the neck" not the back to make the description more consistent with the SBT. This is an incredulous act, considering that this change was made without consulting medical or forensic experts. And more importantly, he was distorting the record.

In addition, crime scene reconstruction and blood spatter expert Sherry Fiester had concluded based on the evidence that the wound in Kennedy's back had entered his body at a 38.84-degree angle which is consistent with a shot fired from an elevation of 60 feet or a sixth-floor window.[55] The doctors at Bethesda Naval hospital who probed this wound with their fingers determined that there was no exit wound. Fiester had also calculated that Kennedy's throat wound was created by a bullet that had entered the body at 0 degrees.[56] This meant the bullet was travelling parallel to the ground and was fired at a much lower elevation. The third wound in Governor Connally's lower back had entered at a 22-degree angle which was consistent with a shot from a second-floor window in the Dal-Tex Building or the building adjacent to it.[57]

No matter how much you torture the angles of the shots they will not line up. In fact, the doctors at Parkland Hospital had surmised based on their observations that Kennedy's throat wound was an entry wound and that he had a large exit wound in the Occipital (back) region of his head the size of a baseball. Fiester had concluded that the entry wound that caused the damage to the back of his head had entered the upper right quadrant of Kennedy's forehead just above the hairline.[58]

There is additional evidence that supports a conspiracy and not a lone gunman. For example, the three shells found at the alleged sniper's nest on the sixth floor of the School Book Depository Building were found so close together that it was not consistent with being ejected from a bolt action rifle, but rather appeared to have been placed there. The forensic evidence further established that CE 543 had been "dry loaded" and that CE 545 had not been fired that day. The only shell casing that had been ejected from the Italian rifle was CE 544.[59]

Furthermore, the acoustic evidence that was obtained from a dicta belt recording from a motorcycle operated by a Dallas Police Officer in the motorcade was examined by an expert panel assembled by the House Select Committee on Assassinations (HSCA). This panel was able to fire multiple shots in Dealey plaza and compare them with the 5 acoustic sounds that were on that recording which were consistent with gunfire. The panel had concluded that one of the shots was fired from the grassy knoll and that the other 3 had originated from behind the President. The panel was unable to determine the location of the 5th shot. This finding was reaffirmed by Dr. Donald Thomas the author of "Hear no Evil" in 2003. He presented his findings at the National Archives and Research Center in 2014 in which he confirmed that the dicta belt recording was "contemporaneous with the Kennedy assassination" and that the 5 impulsive sounds that have the "acoustic waveform" consistent with gunfire are detected on that recording.[60]

Sherry Fiester in her book "The Enemy of the Truth" had concluded that the kill shot captured on frame 313 of the Zapruder film was discharged from the south knoll in a clump of trees just in front of a large parking lot and adjacent to the triple overpass. This location was opposite the infamous grassy knoll.[61] Tosh Plumlee and another individual who were allegedly part of an abort team that obviously failed to prevent the murder of President Kennedy claim they were at that location shortly after the assassination and that both smelled gun smoke at that site.[62]

This is a brief analysis of the evidence that we possess today. It is clear there was more than one shooter firing at Kennedy and that his movement "back and to the left" was consistent with a frontal shot. There was only one casing at the sniper's nest that had been fired that day and that the acoustic evidence established that 5 not 3 shots had been fired at the President. Furthermore, CE 399 when examined at the FBI lab did not have any blood, tissue, or particles of bone on it even though it allegedly had caused 7 wounds and broke a rib and smashed a wrist. In fact, there were more fragments in Connally's right wrist than were missing from the bullet. How could the sum of the parts be greater than the whole?

Also, the trajectory of the bullet and the corresponding entry wounds should have entered the body at roughly the same angle unless it hit something hard enough to alter its path. The trauma to back and throat was to soft tissue and thus did not hit a bone. Additionally, once it came out the throat it would immediately have to drop and then enter at a 22-degree angle. This of course is assuming that Kennedy and Connally's bodies were lined up such that Kennedy

The Hidden War

was slightly to the right of Connally. Otherwise, this bullet performed some amazing stunts to make the SBT feasible. CE 399 in my opinion was planted and was not part of the assassination. The conspirators needed to further link the Italian rifle that Oswald allegedly purchased to the crime with ammunition used by that type of weapon.

    The SBT was a resolution to a problem that permitted them to proffer a fiction that a lone nut was responsible to avoid any possibility of a conspiracy which they were determined to circumvent. Chief Justice Earl Warren had been coerced by President Johnson to head the commission with the explicit instruction to prevent a third world war. He was told that Castro and possibly the KGB were involved. Of course, Johnson and Hoover because of the impersonation of Oswald in Mexico City and the deceptions of the CIA knew differently. They were compelled to cover-up the crime to prevent the nation from looking like another "banana republic."[63] Warren, therefore, was essentially mandated not to find a conspiracy but sanction the lone gunman scenario. The evidence that has been discovered by researchers, historians, movie directors and government whistleblowers has debunked the validity of their SBT that has caused their house of cards they ineptly created to collapse.

CHAPTER 8
A Coup in Dallas
(The CIA's Consciousness of Guilt)

Mark Lane died on May 10, 2016, at the age of 89. His rendezvous with death was mourned by family and friends, and a few researchers that were inspired by his courage to seek the truth and to confront a government that was consumed with its censored history as it subtly manipulated the narrative that was emanating from Dallas. This narrative that was hijacked by the CIA and FBI only 40 minutes after the President was mortally wounded. Prior to taking control, the media interviewed witnesses and openly discussed the fact that gunshots had originated from the front, as well as behind the motorcade.

He stepped into the fray naïvely oblivious of how omnipotent and menacing the adversaries he was fomenting each step he made towards the truth. A truth that could have torn the nation asunder as each stubborn fact that remained amongst the obfuscation was revealed to an unsuspecting public that genuinely believed in their government. Consequently, the conspirators were inadvertently concealed by the immense wave of patriotism that justified the whitewash as a matter of national security.

Those that developed the plan had anticipated this predictable reaction and had even made it more likely by incorporating a virus that compelled this response. If the patsy were a communist that was supported by Havana and possibly Moscow, the public and the media would have demanded retribution that risked dragging us into a nuclear war. A war that Defense Secretary McNamara had estimated would cause 40 million Americans to die within an hour. And even if the government, as President Johnson and FBI Director J. Edgar Hoover eventually did, suspected a domestic plot that eliminated Kennedy over policy disputes, those that designed the plan were confident the authorities would cover it up to avoid the humiliation of resembling another "banana republic." It, therefore, was imperative from the civilian leadership's perspective, whether it was the former or latter scenario, to establish to the public's satisfaction that Lee Harvey Oswald was a lone wolf without any other accomplices who were still lurking about potentially seeking more targets.

When the Warren Commission (WC) had completed its farcical investigation and submitted its 888-page report to President Johnson on September 24, 1964, Lane after it was released to the public that October with its accompanying 26 volumes of evidence began to read their summary of events

The Hidden War

that the New York Times and CBS News had immediately endorsed. The report and its supplemental volumes of evidence that allegedly had convincingly proven Oswald's guilt clearly would have taken days not hours to examine meticulously. As Lane waded into the report and its supporting testimony and documentation, he recognized as an accomplished lawyer in New York that the case against Oswald and the sequence of events as proposed by the Commission were not only not compelling but were highly improbable.

He decided to go to Dallas and interview the witnesses and examine the scene of the crime. Each witness he spoke with contradicted, or at a minimum placed into question, the conclusions of the government's inquiry. He found numerous witnesses for instance that were never interviewed by the Commission who had seen smoke, heard shots, or felt bullets pass over their shoulder from that hill that became known as the grassy knoll. The importance of this is self-evident in that the fence that ran along this small hill was to the right-front of the President's limousine. Oswald had allegedly fired all three shots from the southeast corner window of the Texas School Book Depository (TSBD) located on the sixth floor which at the time of the shooting was behind the President.

Many of his interviews can be viewed on YouTube. In any event, this investigation culminated in his groundbreaking book "Rush to Judgment" which was eventually published in 1966. Initially, none of the New York publishers were interested in the publication of his book. Undaunted by their dismissal of his work, he printed and sold his tome quite successfully in Europe. The response was so positive that it became a best seller. It was only then that his book was picked up by a domestic publishing firm and sold in the United States. The sales catapulted his work onto the New York Times bestseller list as well.

His investigation was immediately followed up by Sylvia Meagher's book "Accessories after the Fact", "Whitewash" by Epstein, "Six Seconds in Dallas" by Josiah Thompson, and the prolific writings of dissident attorney Vincent Salandria who unfortunately recently died. Nevertheless, Lane's death for the most part was shamefully ignored by the corporate media, which to some degree was expected, but also was overlooked by Democracy Now which was disappointing.

The CIA immediately allocated resources to discredit Lane and this small band of WC critics that were beginning to awaken a public that for the most part was initially in shock after the assassination and then as the government asserted that it was back in control went back to sleep. This was strange, if not peculiar, for an agency that professed no interest or knowledge of the lone nut prior to Dallas. The echelon of this powerful Agency proclaimed that they only became aware of this disgruntled citizen, who allegedly had communist affiliations, after he was arrested by the Dallas Police Department (DPD).

In the defense of the WC, they, as well as other agencies, coerced and intimidated witnesses. Many of these witnesses committed suicide while others allegedly died by natural causes and accidents. Most of these deaths occurred at the most inopportune time and the circumstances of their deaths are considered suspicious, as caustically noted by James Garrison when he observed that "...witnesses in this case do have a habit of dying at the most inconvenient times."

The Agency also destroyed top secret documents, sabotaged official investigations, omitted important information in their communications with the Commission, committed obstruction of justice and perjury. And while the nation watched in horror, cohorts of organized crime silenced the patsy. This was all done to maintain the fiction that President Kennedy was felled by a loner. An event that was simply a random act of violence completely void of any relevance to anything they or some rogue elements within the Agency might have been involved in. The question that must be asked is why an Agency that was charged with obtaining and interpreting foreign intelligence was meddling, if not taking the lead, on a domestic matter that was primarily the domain of the FBI and the Justice Department. A state crime that occurred within the jurisdiction of the city of Dallas.

The CIA partially answered that question in a document it disseminated in 1967 to its media allies and assets around the country. In that document designated 1035-960, the CIA confronted the concern the Agency had regarding the mounting criticism of the Warren Report. They indicated that a poll in 1964 had revealed that 46 percent of the American public did not believe that Oswald acted alone. They wrote "This trend of opinion is a matter of concern to the U.S. government, including our organization...Innuendo of such seriousness affects not only the individual concerned, but also the whole reputation of the American government...Conspiracy theories have frequently thrown suspicion on our organization, for example by falsely alleging that Lee Harvey Oswald worked for us."

The purpose of the memorandum was "to provide material countering and discrediting the claims of the conspiracy theorists..." The Agency listed several strategies on how to achieve their stated mission. They encouraged publications by "friendly elite contacts", such as editors and politicians, buttressing the position that the Warren Commission was an exhaustive examination that investigated every aspect of the assassination. The CIA wrote further that it should be emphasized that "... parts of the conspiracy talk appear to be deliberately generated by communist propagandists."

The Agency further specified that propaganda assets should be employed to attack the critics. This could be achieved by book reviews and articles that discredit pro-conspiracy publications. The CIA asserted it will provide background information to assist in accomplishing this objective. They also pointed out that these publications should make it clear that no "new evidence has emerged which the Commission did not consider."

The memo goes on to proclaim that a conspiracy of this scale could never be done by the government, and if Oswald had accomplices that they most likely were a "...group of wealthy conspirators..." that were more capable of arranging such a secretive operation. They proffered this incredulous claim while they were secretly murdering foreign leaders and overthrowing governments that were all hidden from the American public for decades. This assertion may have also have been a subtle version of a "limited hangout" in that the operation may have partially been funded by affluent moguls that were entrenched in intelligence activities and, accordingly, had converging interests in Kennedy's removal. Additionally, it would be interesting to know what group of "wealthy conspirators" were capable of altering the President's motorcade route, turning off the internal alarms that protect our chief executive, reducing the security measures in Dallas in violation of Secret Service's protocol and procedures as outlined in their manual, and effectuating a cover-up that implicated the most powerful officers and agencies within our government. This would be some extraordinary group to achieve all that and remain a ghost that even several decades later cannot be clearly identified or proven to even exist except within the imagination of the CIA.

They concluded by pointing out that Oswald "would not have been any sensible choice for a co-conspirator. He was a 'loner', mixed up, of questionable reliability and an unknown quantity to any professional service." The death of multiple witnesses can also be explained as the result of "natural causes" and other reasonable grounds.

This is an extraordinary document that bootstraps the CIA with specific positions that we know are untrue or are very controversial based on all the evidence we possess today. First of all, the CIA held thousands of pages of documents on Oswald prior to the assassination. Pursuant to a program administered by the Counterintelligence Department whose chief was the CIA's liaison to the WC, they were closely monitoring his mail and maintaining close tabs on his location. Some of the files on him were designated top secret. Furthermore, we know that Oswald was not a social isolate and was quite competent and intelligent. We even have discovered evidence that he admired the President.

We also know that the Commission failed to interview witnesses or follow any evidentiary trail they surmised would undermine their thesis that Oswald was a lone nut with communist sympathies. Even Robert F. Kennedy, Jr. conceded in an interview with Charlie Rose that his father thought the report was a "shoddy piece of craftsmanship." He added that "the evidence at this point is very, very convincing that it was not a lone gunman." When asked by Rose who he thought was involved, he replied that in his opinion members of organized crime, anti-Castro militants and "rogue" CIA agents conspired to murder his uncle.

Doug Horne of the Assassination Records Review Board (ARRB) has asserted that in his opinion there are several documents that he classifies as "smoking guns" that were discovered in the declassified medical evidence. He determined that these documents when combined with all the testimony that the ARRB recorded establishes that Kennedy's wounds were altered and that the official autopsy, which by the way is the third draft, cannot be trusted. The first and second drafts of the autopsy conducted at Bethesda Naval Hospital have disappeared. In fact, Dr. James J. Humes reluctantly admitted to the ARRB that he burned all his notes after the autopsy. Therefore, their conclusion that it was a comprehensive investigation and that there was not any new evidence being discovered by these audacious researchers we know is false. In fact, the Agency deliberately failed to apprise the Commission of numerous facts and relevant documents that they possessed in their archives. And finally, this document is unequivocal proof that the Agency was actively engaged with their media assets in discrediting the publications of the critics while attempting to impugn their integrity and their credibility.

Consequently, the CIA since Dallas has not been a disinterested passive observer to each government investigation that was formed to examine what happened in Dealey Plaza, or any film or book that has galvanized public interest and support for the proposition that Kennedy's assassination was the

The Hidden War

result of a domestic conspiracy. In each case, whether it be James Garrison's investigation of Claw Shaw or the House Select Committee on Assassinations, they were actively involved in obstruction of justice and perjury, among other nefarious activities. They even joined a crusade led by the mainstream media to discredit Oliver Stone's film "JFK". If Kennedy was felled by some alienated lone wolf who got extremely lucky when he fired three shots from an antiquated Italian rifle with a defective scope, a random act of violence just like the act that resulted in his death by Jack Ruby in the basement of the DPD, why devote so much time and resources discrediting theories that have no basis in reality? Maybe the answer is in an analysis of the scene of the crime and the chain of events as we know them today.

Kennedy was visiting several cities in Texas to mend fences within the state's Democratic Party and to begin to generate support for his bid to be re-elected in 1964. He knew that Texas was an important state to hold since he anticipated the defection of many southern states to the Republicans because of his submission of a controversial civil rights bill that was being scrutinized by Congress.

On November 22, 1963, he was visiting the city of Dallas which was the last leg of his whirlwind Texas trip. He was scheduled to give a brief speech at a luncheon at the Trade Mart. His plane arrived at Love Field 30 minutes late. Other than that, everything appeared to be going well. He and his wife got off the plane and walked over to greet a large crowd that had gathered behind a small fence. The couple appeared in good spirits as they got into the blue convertible Lincoln and started their tour of Dallas. All the way to Dealey Plaza that was named after George B. Dealey, a local businessman and publisher for many years of the Dallas Morning News, enormous crowds, sometimes five or more rows deep, waved flags and cheered as the presidential vehicle passed them. The reports that this could be a turbulent visit seemed inane as the motorcade travelled further into the city.

Just outside of Dealey Plaza, a bizarre event occurred 20 minutes prior to the motorcade's arrival. An ambulance was dispatched to attend to a man who was allegedly having seizures at the corner of Main Street and Houston. He was placed into the only ambulance assigned to that area of the city and taken to Parkland Hospital. Upon their arrival, the man got out of the vehicle and disappeared before staff could admit him to the ER. This Caucasian male has never been identified. This in my opinion, in addition to the patsy, was another diversion set up by the conspirators. Unfortunately for the plotters, the motorcade was behind schedule. If it had been on time or slightly off schedule, the timing of this disturbance would have been more effective and ominous.

The lead car that held the Chief of the DPD Jesses Curry, and the President's 1961 Lincoln that followed directly behind, entered Dealey Plaza on Main Street at approximately 12:29pm. The crowds began to position themselves to get the best view of the young couple. They pulled out their cameras and double-checked their settings as the motorcade took a right turn onto Houston. Governor John Connally's wife Nellie, while observing the enthusiasm of the large crowds along the motorcade route, remarked "You can't deny Dallas loves you Mr. President."

The large Lincoln then approached the TSBD which allegedly had the lone gunman waiting for an opportunity to make his mark on history. As the presidential vehicle began to navigate the 120 degree turn onto Elm just in front of that infamous building, Abraham Zapruder was filming what ex-CIA agent E. Howard Hunt had confessed to his son, Saint John, many years later was called "the big event" by the plotters.

The large vehicle slowed to approximately 18 mph while passing the TSBD as it approached what was called the triple underpass by the natives. Dealey plaza had three major roads that travelled through the large park as tall buildings outlined three sides of the green. If facing the railroad bridge, Commerce Street was to your left while Main Street went through the center of the plaza. Elm was located to the far right which ran next to the grassy knoll. All three roads converged at the base of the plaza as they went under the bridge.

The sequence of the shooting continues to be debated. This is my interpretation of what transpired that day. The shots began at 12:30pm.

The first shot emanated from the sniper's nest on the sixth floor of the TSBD that missed its target to the left by approximately 200 feet, hitting a curb on Main Street which caused a small piece of cement to hit a bystander named James Tague in his right cheek. This was all documented by a Dallas patrolman. Many of the witnesses, including those in the motorcade, mistook this shot for a firecracker. This is the only shot fired by the 6.5 Mannlicher Carcano that the Commission alleged Oswald used to kill Kennedy. As we know from the forensic experts, CE-544 is the only shell casing located at the purported sniper's nest that was ejected from a bolt action rifle on that day. The primary purpose of this shot was to grab the attention of the crowd below to the window of the designated patsy.

The Hidden War

The second shot also emanated from the sixth floor, but at a different window, hitting the President in the back at a 38.84-degree angle. The third shot originated from the far end of the grassy knoll at a lower elevation that hit Kennedy in the throat at 0 degrees. This meant that the bullet had to be at the same elevation as Kennedy's throat while travelling parallel to the ground. An employee of the Ford Motor Company in Detroit who examined the Lincoln shortly after the assassination noted what he surmised was a bullet hole in the front windshield.

The next shot fired almost simultaneously originated from the Dal-Tex Building from a second-floor window that just missed Kennedy as he leaned to his left after being hit in the back and the throat, hitting Governor Connally in the lower right back at 22 degrees, causing all his injuries. Connally had always asserted that he was not hit by the same bullet as the President.

The fifth shot fired from the grassy knoll hit the Stemmons freeway sign, diverting the bullet into the pavement and onto the grass between Elm and Main Street. This sign was inexplicably removed shortly after the assassination.

As Kennedy pulled up his arms and leaned forward and to his left as a result of the bullet that hit him in his back and throat, the Secret Service agent, William Robert Greer, slowed the Lincoln to approximately 9 mph as he glanced over his right shoulder to ascertain what was happening. It was at this moment that a mechanic fired the fatal shot from a location next to the triple overpass in a clump of trees just in front of a parking lot that was situated across the plaza from the infamous grassy knoll. This bullet that had originated from what was designated the south knoll hit the President in the upper right section of his forehead just above his hairline, according to forensic crime scene reconstructionist Sherry Fiester.

The kinetic energy that was released out of the entrance wound caused his head to slightly move forward. As the bullet traversed through his cranium generating concentric and radial fractures that emanated from the origin of penetration, it then exited the lower occipital area of his skull, causing bone fragments, brain tissue and blood to jet out all over the trunk of the vehicle, creating a wound the size of a fist which propelled Kennedy "back and to the left."

This wound is what all the doctors from Parkland Hospital in Dallas recounted to the ARRB in the 1990s. In fact, Dr. Charles Crenshaw asserted in a 20/20 interview on ABC conducted in 1992 that before he left Trauma Room #1, he went over to Kennedy's body to observe his head wound one last time. As he gingerly lifted his head, the image of the mortal wound to the lower-right portion of the back of his head was forever embedded into his memory. A wound that the official autopsy at Bethesda Naval Hospital concluded did not exist.

The motorcade after that fatal shot then sped off to Parkland Hospital where doctors quite familiar with gunshot wounds attended to his injuries, attempting to save his life. With exception to one individual, the medical personnel had concluded that Kennedy and Connally had been hit from two directions.

They surmised after examining the President's bullet inflicted wounds that the small hole in his throat was an entrance wound. They were unaware of his back wound. However, Dr. David Mantik who had reviewed the declassified medical record at the National Archives indicated that contrary to popular belief several doctors at Parkland did observe an entry wound in his upper right forehead just above his hairline.

As reported above, the doctors also noted an exit wound the size of a baseball in the occipital region of his skull in proximity to his lower right ear. Additionally, Dr. Robert McClelland observed cerebellum exuding out of this exit wound. This part of the brain is located at the lower back of the skull and the bottom of the brain. The tissue from this section of the brain which has very distinctive structural features could not have been observed if the wound was located at the front top of the head as delineated in the autopsy report from Bethesda Naval Hospital.

It is my contention a minimum of 6 shots were fired at Kennedy not 5 or what the WC calculated to be 3. It is my belief that the poor recording captured by a microphone on a Dallas Patrolman's motorcycle that was traveling several cars back to the left rear of the President's limousine was not designed to pick up background noise but only direct communication between the officer and dispatch. It, therefore, was not capable of recording the gunshot that emanated from the South Knoll. This shot originated from the left front of the motorcycle. The Dallas patrolman and the bike, in addition to the sound of the engine, blocked the soundwaves from reaching the microphone. Any noise in my opinion that may have been recorded from that location was so degraded that it was not decipherable. All the other shots emanated from the right front and rear of the Limousine with exception of the bullet that hit him in the throat which must have come from a shooter directly in front of the motorcade near the triple underpass.

The Hidden War

Jack Ruby, the owner of a local strip joint called the Carousel Club in Dallas who was a known mob asset, had two primary duties for the plotters. His first task as speculated by researchers was to plant what became known as the magic bullet on a stretcher that had been used by Governor Connally. He was seen by two local reporters at the hospital just prior to authorities discovering the bullet. One of the reporters even conversed with him briefly. As amazing as it may sound, the WC believed Ruby's denial that he had been there over the testimony of the two journalists. His second task was to silence the patsy.

Once Kennedy had hit the kill zone, professional mechanics fired at the President from what was a triangular formation, a standard practice by experts. Some of the assassins were provided with official Secret Service identification with fictitious names that had been prepared by the Technical Service Division of the CIA. This enabled them to confiscate evidence and exit the scene of the heinous crime without interference by other law enforcement agencies. The second part of the plan was to get control over Kennedy's body and begin the cover up. They also had to get the cover story out before the public had formed an opinion regarding the event.

There were two cover stories that were available to the planners, depending on the reaction of other key elements within the government. The first one was to link Oswald's actions with Castro and the KGB in the hope that this might prompt an invasion of Cuba and the perpetuation of the Cold War. When the civilian leadership balked at the prospect of a nuclear war that could result from any aggressive action against Cuba, the CIA conspirators changed their cover story to the lone nut scenario that was eventually adopted by the WC. Oswald's alleged communist affiliations were no longer used to implicate Cuba or the Soviets, but rather to suggest a plausible motive for his killing of the President.

Once they had chosen their cover story, they had to revise history and promote the fiction that Kennedy was a traditional cold warrior whose policies were similar to his predecessor if not more belligerent. Accordingly, the narrative, as it related to Cuba for example, was that the Kennedy brothers were obsessed with revenge against Cuban leaders for the Bay of Pigs' humiliation and that the Castro assassination plots had originated with them. By establishing this mythology, it made his death appear less necessary, as well as obscured the primary motive that compelled the conspirators to act. It also made it easier for President Johnson to pursue a more aggressive policy in Vietnam, and other hot spots, while claiming he was fulfilling the objectives of the martyred President. They very cleverly used the President's own words to reinforce this image.

Without rehashing the details presented in the "The Patsy" in my first volume published in May of 2017, this is the conspiracy in a nutshell. The events in Dallas as described above and as supported by the forensic evidence were unequivocally not the actions of a lone nut and accordingly was not a random act of violence as outlined in their memorandum.

The death of Kennedy was clearly the result of a sophisticated plot that was consistent with the modus operandi of an intelligence operation. Because this operation was compartmentalized, and information was only shared on a need to know basis, the conspirators were able to get many to assist in the execution of the plan, and its cover up. Government employees or assets were assigned tasks that were so vague they had no clue what they were contributing to. Those who figured it out after the fact or were privy to matters that clearly contradicted the official version were intimidated, coerced, blackmailed, or murdered. Most of the murders were made to look like a suicide or death by natural causes. Those that were clearly executed by traditional methods were done primarily by organized crime gangsters, such as the deaths of Johnny Roselli and Sam Giancana.

The motive attributed to Oswald by the WC was pathetic. If he had killed the President to make his mark on history, why claim he was a "patsy" that was not involved in the crime? Furthermore, his word choice to describe his predicament has always bothered me. Most people in his position would have claimed that they were "framed" or that they were left "holding the bag." I heard these phrases quite frequently when I was a defense attorney. The use of the word "patsy" was primarily a term of art for intelligence. This was another piece of evidence that hints that he was not the person he was portrayed as by the government.

In retrospect, as pointed out by Garrison, it is not a mystery why rogue agents of the CIA, including Allen Dulles who at the time of the assassination had been forced into retirement by Kennedy, had joined organized crime bosses and vitriolic anti-Castro Cubans to perpetrate the crime of the century. Their motives are blatantly obvious once you become familiar with Kennedy's actual policies that threatened the Cold War orthodoxy that the covert sector of the CIA and the Pentagon zealously believed in. Essentially, there actions amounted to a coup as it was called by Colonel Fletcher Prouty.

The Hidden War

There were also those that had been tactfully approached by Allen Dulles, as surmised by the circumstantial evidence exposed in Talbot's "The Devil's Chessboard", that did not object to the proposal and as a consequence had foreknowledge of the operation. In my opinion, powerful members of the military brass and Wall Street were among those who knew a plan was being developed. They intentionally were not provided any specific details on how and when it was to occur to maintain plausible deniability. They were confident that the "old man" would take care of it.

Since Kennedy's death, the word "conspiracy" has been transformed into some mysterious and remote occurrence that is an aberration in civilian and government social structures. And those who invoke it as an explanation for an event or a policy are quickly dismissed as paranoid or attributed with some sinister motivation for making their allegations. This has become so pervasive in our society that even obvious conspiracies are dismissed by our corporate media and cynical public. Whereas in Europe, they do not discard conspiracy theories so easily.

For instance, the situation in Brazil was initially reported by the Brazilian and American corporate press as a corruption scandal that involved the President, Dilma Rousseff. The alternative media outlets more disposed at seeking the truth immediately recognized that the opposing party's leadership, many of which were under investigation for corruption, were taking advantage of an opportunity fomented by the weakened Brazilian economy to achieve what they could not in prior elections. They basically initiated a bogus impeachment process to disguise what was essentially a coup. Once they took power, they introduced severe austerity measures that had been opposed by Rousseff and began dismantling the agencies that were primarily responsible for the corruption probe. After the President was forced to step down until the trial in the Senate could determine if her accounting maneuvers amounted to "high crimes and misdemeanors", a transcript of a discussion between Senator Romero Juca and oil executive Sergio Machado just prior to the impeachment vote acknowledged that the best way to terminate the corruption probe was to oust President Rousseff. A clear indication that Rousseff was the victim of a conspiracy to usurp her authority. Brazil is currently ruled by a fascist, Jair Bolsonaro, who incongruously – considering our professed love of democracy - is backed by the U.S.

Even highly educated individuals cringe whenever they hear the word used in a sentence. Some of my close friends declared to me "that everything is not a conspiracy." They in one sense are right. Everything is not the result of two or more persons conspiring to achieve a common sinister or selfish objective. However, their broader implication which is that conspiracies are rare is clearly false. Most policies and programs developed in our government or in Wall Street are the result of conspiracies. Many of these conspirators are not necessarily seeking nefarious objectives but some clearly are.

In my opinion, there are soft and hard conspiracies. A soft conspiracy is when two or more individuals or organizations are aware of their common interests and the methodology being utilized to achieve their objective. They, however, are not coordinating their efforts through direct communication. A hard conspiracy is two or more persons or organizations that directly communicate to develop their plan of attack and the methods to be employed for its success. We see this type in the criminal courts all the time.

The other absurd assertion is that our government is not capable of such a heinous act. We are more committed to the principles of democracy than other nations who remove leaders because of a coup quite regularly. Of course, most of those coups were directly and indirectly instigated by the CIA, but I digress. If you review our turbulent history dispassionately, the above thesis begins to unravel quite precipitously.

The original sin of slavery was a brutal institution that justified its offense against humanity by relegating the oppressed as nothing more than assets of an estate or as written in our Constitution as three fifths of a human being for census purposes. Even then it was not an attempt to acknowledge their humanity but to enhance the South's power in Congress. This view of slaves as nothing more than property was affirmed by Chief Justice Roger B. Taney in his infamous majority opinion in the Scott v. Sanford case of 1857. This decision is generally referred to as the Dred Scott case.

Dred Scott was a slave that had been acquired by U.S. Army surgeon John Emerson from the Blow family in 1831 who were residents of St. Louis. Emerson travelled with Scott into slave and free states for 12 years. When he died, Scott attempted to purchase his freedom from Emerson's widow. When she refused to accept his offer, he filed his first case in state court in 1846. Scott's lawyer argued that Dr. Emerson had in prior years brought him to the state of Illinois that prohibited slavery and to the territory of Wisconsin where federal law banned its establishment as part of the Missouri Compromise of 1820. His attorney argued that his physical presence in jurisdictions that did not recognize slavery as a legitimate and legal institution should be reason

The Hidden War

enough for the court to grant his just request to be designated a free man. He lost his first trial and amazingly won his second only to have it overturned by the Missouri State Supreme Court.

He then filed suit with the assistance of abolitionists that supported his bid for freedom against Fred Sanford who was the brother of Emerson's wife in federal court. When the court ruled in favor of the defendant, Scott appealed to the U.S. Supreme Court.

President-elect Buchanan was hoping the case would be resolved by the date of his inauguration which was set for March 1857. He sided with the justices from the South that he anticipated were going to vote against the emancipation of Scott. He knew if the decision was purely made along sectional lines that this could cause a great deal of difficulty for his new administration as abolitionist groups ratcheted up anti-slavery sentiments that had significant support throughout the North. With this concern, he intruded inappropriately on the independence of the court when he pressured Justice Robert Cooper Grier, a northerner, to vote alongside the southern majority.

Chief Justice Taney wrote the majority opinion for the court that denied Scott's claim by a seven to two decision. He pontificated that a negro whose ancestors were brought into the United States and sold as slaves, whether they be enslaved or free, were not citizens and therefore had no standing to file a lawsuit in federal court. He added that the federal government had no authority to regulate, never mind prohibit, slavery in federal territories that were acquired after the founding of the nation. He concluded "…They (negroes) had for more than a century before been regarded as beings of an inferior order, and altogether unfit to associate with the white race, either in social or political relations; and so far inferior, that they had no rights which the white man was bound to respect; and that the negro might justly and lawfully be reduced to slavery for his benefit."

Abraham Lincoln as a candidate for the senate in 1858 denounced the decision and used it as the inspiration for his "House Divided" speech in which he declared "A house divided against itself cannot stand." He argued that by necessity we will all be free, or we will all be slave states. At some point, these two opposing forces would clash to resolve this crisis. Although he had accurately forecast the catastrophe that lurked just beyond the horizon, he could not have anticipated the extent of that calamity that would befall an unsuspecting nation. And much more than this, he could not have known the pivotal role he would play in that resolution.

When that crisis arose, 600,000 died in a bloody war to finally end the division so that this nation could stand and begin to purge the stain of injustice that soiled our national spirit from the beginning. Prior to his assassination in Ford's Theater, the 13th Amendment was ratified that banned Slavery. This soon would be followed by the passage of the 14th Amendment that provided equal protection under the law and the 15th Amendment which gave the "negro" the right to vote. These positive legal reforms permitted progress to spread throughout the nation.

The southern states in response to these legal rights given to their former slaves, and while antipathy towards the North lingered over the brutality of the war manifested by Sherman's march and Grant's tenacious sieges, that empowered delusions that stubbornly refused to accept that the Confederacy had lost, began to shift their tactics. The failure of reconstruction to prevent this reprehensible push back against the above amendments to the U.S. Constitution led to the black codes, Jim Crow laws and lynching of hundreds of black men for minor crimes or perceived violations of the acceptable social mores of the time. For instance, black men were hung from trees by hateful mobs for being accused of romantic relations with a white woman. These lynching laws still have not been outlawed by the Congress to this day.

In 1896, the U.S. Supreme Court in Plessy v. Ferguson sanctioned the "equal but separate doctrine" that affirmed that separate public facilities and schools based on race was constitutional. As hate groups, such as the Ku Klux Klan, enhanced their membership and began their terror campaign throughout the south that continued well into the 20th century, the court's incredulous ruling that had confirmed the legality of segregation became the spark that had ignited widespread discontent that was the catalyst for the Civil Rights movement seeking freedom and justice, and more importantly the nation's acknowledgement of their humanity. These protests led by King's Southern Christian Leadership Conference, the Student Nonviolent Coordinating Committee and Malcom X with the help of the Kennedy brothers, Hubert Humphrey, and to some degree President Johnson, led to the enactment of the Civil Rights Act (1964) and the Voting Rights Act (1965).

These monumental reforms have obviously not abolished institutional racism, as the protestors currently marching in the streets in numerous cities throughout the nation, justifiably outraged by George Floyd's recent death in Minneapolis caused by senseless police brutality, unequivocally demonstrates. The multiracial composition of the protests, sometimes marred by looting and

The Hidden War

rioting, clearly manifests that we have not confronted the injustices and disparities in our society nor the blatant failure to heal the deep wounds inflicted upon our fellow citizens of color by this abhorrent racist legacy. As Malcolm X asserted, "If you stick a knife nine inches into my back and pull it out three inches, that is not progress. Even if you pull it out all the way, that is not progress. Progress is healing the wound, and America hasn't even begun to pull out the knife."

The repetition of history is inevitable if the people remain ignorant of the past. This is the primary reason that the words of the leaders from that era still resonate for those willing to listen today. For example, while speaking about the riots of 1965 through 1968, Dr. King orated, "And I must say tonight that a riot is the language of the unheard. And what is it America has failed to hear? It has failed to hear that the plight of the negro poor has worsened over the last twelve or fifteen years. It has failed to hear that the promises of freedom and justice have not been met. And it has failed to hear that large segments of white society are more concerned about tranquility and the status quo than about justice and humanity." He further denounced the looting and the violence that occurred during the protests but added that the best "guarantors" against future riots are "social justice and progress."

Another prominent example was our despicable treatment of Native Americans that culminated in the Indian wars from 1860 through to 1890. We deluded ourselves with this concept of Manifest Destiny that we were ordained by God to possess all the land from sea to shining sea. In fulfillment of that quest, we attempted to eradicate the indigenous peoples who had lived on this continent long before we ever discovered it. We senselessly killed millions of buffalo which we had discerned were a major source of food and clothes for the tribes that lived on the Great Plains.

As the war lingered, the military became embittered. They were informed by the newspapers that Civil War hero General Sheridan had exclaimed, "The only good Indians are dead Indians." In this ominous environment, we committed many atrocities, but none more depraved than the naked savagery of Sand Creek and Wounded Knee. We essentially mutilated and massacred unarmed elderly men, women, and children.

Black Elk described what Wounded Knee had meant to his people when he said, "I did not know then how much was ended. When I look back now from this high hill of old age, I can see the butchered women and children lying heaped and scattered all along the crooked gulch as plain as when I saw them with eyes still young. And I can see that something else died there in the bloody mud and was buried in the blizzard. A people's dream died there. It was a beautiful dream...the nation's hoop is broken and scattered. There is no center any longer, and the sacred tree is dead."[64]

In their yearning for wealth, the white settlers and prospectors combed the hills and valleys, hoping to discover valuable minerals that included gold. Infected by this fever, we promised everything to cheat the Indians out of their land. And when it was over, their culture and heritage were buried beneath the onslaught of white settlers that considered their way of life as savage and uncivilized. Over time, it became apparent to even the most obstinate resistors that they were outnumbered and outgunned. And as the wilderness dwindled, leaving them with no space to hide, their people were relegated to desolate parcels of land that were called reservations. As Chief Red Cloud recounted in old age, "They made us many promises, more than I can remember, but they never kept but one; they promised to take our land, and they took it."[65]

There lies in the dark recesses of our history another ingrained cultural dimension that was intertwined with our racist social constructs that taints our innocent image. The Eugenics movement of the late nineteenth and early twentieth centuries have long been forgotten by our historically illiterate generation. It nevertheless was a significant part of our history and culture prior to World War II. The primary purpose of the movement was to purify and improve the genetic development of human beings. It was believed that those who lived in poverty, especially young women of ill repute, were considered inferior and were prime candidates for sterilization which was an offshoot of the movement. This also applied to those who were mentally retarded and as such were placed in large psychiatric institutions hidden from society. At the time, family members were embarrassed by this perceived genetic abnormality that compelled their removal from public scrutiny.

This ideology intensified during the massive emigration of Eastern Europeans to the United States in the 1920s. The mixing of inferior races as opined by many stimulated the growth of racist organizations such as the Ku Klux Klan. It also enhanced the practice of sterilization programs being implemented around the country. In 1927, the U.S. Supreme Court in Buck v. Bell constitutionally upheld the Virginia Sterilization Act of 1924.[66]

Carrie Buck was a psychiatric patient that was contesting the validity of this act. Justice Oliver Wendell Holmes, Jr., a celebrated jurist from Harvard, composed the majority opinion. He wrote "It is better for all the world, if

The Hidden War

instead of waiting to execute degenerate offspring for crime or let them starve for their imbecility, society can prevent those who are manifestly unfit from continuing their kind...Three generations of imbeciles are enough." It was considered in the interest of society to permit her sterilization. Although this practice of forced sterilization is now considered a violation of an individual's human rights, this abhorrent case has never been overturned. In fact, 70,000 U.S. citizens suffered this indignity up through the 1970s.[67]

The program did not escape the awareness of German scientists in the 1930s. Their knowledge was significantly enhanced by California eugenicists that produced literature that promoted this philosophy, as well as sterilization, and sent it overseas to German scientists and medical professionals. The forced sterilization program by the Nazis was instituted shortly thereafter. Their program was initially supported and applauded by their American counterparts until it morphed into an extermination project that eventually murdered millions that were considered inferior to the Aryan specimen that represented the future of the Third Reich. Prior to this development, institutions such as the Rockefeller Foundation funded Nazi eugenic programs, including the barbaric research of Dr. Josef Mengele before he arrived at Auschwitz.

It is also important to recognize the amoral principles internalized by those that founded the CIA and the despicable policies they promoted to achieve their dubious objectives in the name of national security. The MKULTRA program experimented with the use of powerful drugs, hypnosis and other reprehensible tests on unsuspecting patients that received care in psychiatric wards and hospitals around the country and in Canada in the 1950s and 1960s. The primary goal of the project was to create a Manchurian candidate that they could control and manipulate into position to assassinate selected targets.

Although this program was dismissed as unsuccessful by Helms and others within the CIA who were compelled to answer questions before Church's committee, its methods may have been used to place Sirhan Bishara Sirhan into a hypnotic trance when he fired at Senator Robert Kennedy in the pantry of the Ambassador Hotel. This was the conclusion by experts who examined him on several occasions prior to and after his trial. Essentially, Sirhan was another patsy that diverted the attention of most of the witnesses while a second gunman fired the shot that mortally wounded the senator.

This scenario was corroborated by the conclusion of the Chief Medical Examiner of Los Angeles, Dr. Thomas Noguchi, who conducted the autopsy of Senator Kennedy. He determined that the bullet that ended Bobby's quixotic campaign had emanated from a gun that was 1.5 inches from his lower right ear. The second gunman must have been standing just behind and to the right of Kennedy. Sirhan, according to the witnesses, was standing two to four feet in front of the senator.

There is a memorial in Montreal that attests to this abhorrent program while remembering the suffering of those who were subjected without their consent to these horrific experiments that permanently diminished the quality of their lives.

It is also imperative to examine the capacity of those within the hierarchy of the Agency to appreciate what they were capable of as individual human beings. There is one example, among many, for instance that I believe captures the essence of the evil that Allen Dulles was quite capable of when he deemed it in his interests or that of his offspring, the CIA.

He was a spy for the United States in World War I and was stationed in the beautiful city of Bern. On many occasions, his contacts caused him to wander into the remote villages surrounded by the majestic mountains of Switzerland when he became involved with a beautiful young woman of Czech descent. They had become acquainted while working together at the American legation offices. Their relationship quickly became very intimate. When it was brought to his attention by British intelligence that she was a German spy, he casually, as they had done many times before, took her to dinner. After they had finished their meal, he walked with her on the streets of cobblestone that had become quite familiar to both of them to a designated location that had been prearranged by his British counterparts and immediately transferred her to their custody.[68]

Her life was taken, as had 20 million in that war, and was quickly forgotten as collateral damage. Dulles resumed his duties the following day with little regret of what had been done that prior evening to another human being that he had shared dinner and a bed with on many occasions.

Based on the above, I submit that powerful elements within our government unfortunately are quite capable of assassinating a president over significant policy disputes that implicate the division of power in our society. This capacity is tremendously enhanced when rogue agents within our government cloaked by national security can act with impunity protected by a wall of secrecy that rarely is breached.

Those that were complicit with the murder of our President walked amongst us, talked like us, and spoke the same language. They, however, were not

The Hidden War

democrats or true proponents of the republic founded by revolutionaries, seeking independence and liberty. Their philosophy was quite opposed to government that represents and responds to the needs of the people as eloquently affirmed in Lincoln's iconic speech at Gettysburg. Many of the cabal that directed our secret government were neo-fascists, elitists and corporatists that vehemently believed that the interest of the nation was too important to be left to the ignorant masses that they so easily manipulated. Thus, the citizenry needed their sagacious guidance to protect them from their naïve understanding of global intrigue and the intricate machinations of power. Their primary objective of advancing our ordained prosperity and the sustained growth of our empire could only be achieved by supplementing the interests of the ruling class and their corporate manifestations.

Their insidious philosophy infected the secret government and spread throughout our institutions like an epidemic. The successful murder of our chief executive emboldened them to assassinate Malcom X, Dr. Martin Luther King, Jr., and Senator Robert F. Kennedy. They were traitors who hid amongst us quietly subverting every principle that made us proud to be Americans. As Cicero so pungently pointed out, we have less to fear from a murderer than a traitor that infects the instruments of power like the plague. A contagion that is unseen but nevertheless continues to contaminate the spirit of our nation to this very day.

CHAPTER 9
The Devil Collects his Price for Dealey Plaza (Remembering 1968)

The year of 1968 was a tale of two drastically different stories that persist as though neither were connected or even existed at the same time. There is the nostalgia of the adventure and innocence of my childhood that was tethered to a darker reality of national crisis that threatened to break our spirit and our solidarity. The link that held both narratives together was that my father's debt to the Navy was due that year.

The Navy had paid for my father's post-graduate education at Jefferson Medical School located in the city of Philadelphia, and in return he was a naval officer for 6 years while serving his country. He left for Vietnam in late 1968 and was stationed on the Repose which was a floating naval hospital until his return in December 1969. It cruised in the Pacific just over the horizon, waiting for casualties that resulted from the nightmare that was being ruthlessly waged on land.

As he described to me only a couple years before his death, his experience was comparable to the television series MASH which was a sardonic comedy whose context was about a medical mobile unit during the Korean War. My father added that the series accurately portrayed the long hours of boredom that were assailed by intense periods of stress and horror. He revealed that once the casualties began to arrive by helicopter it felt as though there was an endless supply of victims as a consequence of a policy that had terribly gone wrong. The helicopters would come one after the other, leaving behind soldiers from both sides, as well as civilians that had been caught in the crossfire.

He told me that Vietnam is where he learned how to drink. It was during that conversation that he admitted to me that he had post-traumatic stress disorder. He divulged that he would have flash backs every time he heard a helicopter. Although this emotional scar of the war diminished as he got older, it nevertheless was a constant reminder of the brutality of war, and the cruelty we can inflict upon each other for a perceived righteous cause. The fact that the whole war was based on a theoretical doctrine and justified by a false pretense would not be fully understood for decades.

Our family resided in a raised ranch on a street that epitomized the development of suburban life that had spread across some of the most fertile

The Hidden War

farms and mature forests as the growing middle class left our metropolitan centers for a more tranquil existence. We had moved to Framingham, Massachusetts from Bethesda, Maryland. My father commuted to Chelsea Naval Hospital in Boston that closed decades ago.

We lived there for 4 years from 1967 until the summer of 1971. Our street was full of children that became my brother's and my friends. We built tree forts, played hockey in the street and football on our lawns. My brother and I collected stamps and played with our Corgi and matchbox collections, as well as our toy soldiers. My mother brought us to one of the first malls in the country where we went shopping and ate pizza at Papa Gino's. We spent long hot summer days at the National Seashore on the Cape and visited for two weeks each summer at my grandparents' farms in beautiful Bucks County, Pennsylvania. The carnage of the war had no relevance to our daily existence. The only reminder that something was wrong was my father's absence that took a toll on my mother. She, however, made sure we were not aware of the hazards that my father was confronted with as we went to see the latest Disney movie or got ice-cream at our local fast-food dairy.

The other tale of 1968 was a country being torn apart by racism, social unrest, poverty, and violence. The year before we had been swayed by the government that we were winning the war and that our mission of protecting an ally had been fulfilled. This fictional narrative General Westmoreland and President Johnson repeatedly told us to placate the growing discontent among many as a result of the violence our government was thrusting upon the citizenry of a poor nation situated thousands of miles from our most western shore. This falsehood was being voiced despite the savageness of the war being portrayed in our newspapers and periodicals, as well as the photographs and news footage being shown to us in our living rooms. This fairy tale persisted even though the bodies of our young men were being brought back in caskets by the thousands. This false depiction continued to defend our national honor as our soldiers committed many atrocities, including the My Lai Massacre in which 500 civilians had been raped and murdered in March of that year.

Dr. Martin Luther King, Jr. was so appalled by the pictures of children being bombed by napalm and the images of their burned naked bodies running in agony that he could no longer remain silent to this immoral policy. He orated one of the finest speeches on April 4, 1967, at the Riverside Church in New York that revealed to the public the insanity of this depraved policy and how it was undermining our national objectives and our national integrity. Senator

The Devil Collects his Price for Dealey Plaza (Remembering 1968)

Robert Kennedy was also becoming more outspoken that same year against Johnson's policy to Americanize the war. This was all playing out as the Viet Cong and North Vietnam were planning a major offensive that was to commence during the Tet Nguyen Dan holiday. This was a celebration of Vietnam's lunar new year and the arrival of spring. It is more commonly referred to as "Tet."

The Tet offensive that began the nightmare that 1968 would become caught the South Vietnamese and our military completely by surprise. Their initial success in taking over the cities and government buildings removed the curtain of deceit that our government had been reporting to us. Even Walter Cronkite questioned on the air if we could win this war. This prompted President Johnson to blurt out in frustration that, "If I've lost Cronkite, I've lost middle America." Although the South Vietnamese Army and U.S. forces eventually regained all the territory that was lost and could legitimately assert that they had won the battle, it, nonetheless, was clear that this offensive was a major blow to Johnson's policy and to his public support. This of course only verified what Ho Chi Minh had observed as the United States entered the void created by France's abrupt exit. He prophetically remarked, "We can lose longer than you (United States) can win."

Senator Eugene McCarthy waited on the sidelines to ascertain what Robert Kennedy's decision would be regarding his entrance into the presidential primaries scheduled for the winter and spring of 1968. Bobby waivered back and forth for several weeks in the late fall of 1967 until he finally said he was not throwing his hat into the ring. For Senator Kennedy, this was a terrible time because he vehemently opposed Johnson's war and the consequences it imposed on our domestic policies. He felt despondent and disconnected while watching the struggle being waged by many seeking racial and economic justice, and of course the movement to end the war being promoted by groups such as the Students for a Democratic Society (SDS) headed by Tom Hayden, from the sidelines. He was determined to be part of the fight to change our policies and fulfill his brother's mission. However, he had to contend with a multitude of factors that some were familiar with and other matters that only a few in his inner circle understood.

Many in the press knew that he and President Johnson had a turbulent and difficult relationship. Bobby did not want the race to digress into a discussion about their antipathy which he feared would overshadow the issues that he opined should define the election. He also knew because of his secret

The Hidden War

investigation into the death of his brother that the same forces that were behind his brother's murder would coalesce to prevent his ascension to the presidency. By entering the race, he had to be willing to risk his life.[69]

As Senator Kennedy assured the press that he was not going to challenge the incumbent president of his party, McCarthy saw his opportunity to enter the race as the anti-war candidate. His promising performance against President Johnson in the New Hampshire Primary clearly had established that Johnson was very vulnerable. As Johnson's political future became more precarious each day the Tet offensive continued, Johnson not only began to reconsider his candidacy for reelection, but also began an initiative to end the war at the diplomatic tables in Paris. These negotiations began in earnest in May of 1968.

As the president contemplated his political future, Bobby could not stand to be on the outside looking in any longer. He decided to announce his candidacy on March 16th of 1968. He made his declaration in the U.S. Senate Caucus Room which was the same room that his brother had announced his candidacy for president on January 2, 1960. In a clear reference to his adversarial relationship with Johnson he stated, "I do not run for the presidency merely to oppose any man, but to propose new policies. I run because I am convinced that this country is on a perilous course and because I have such strong feelings about what must be done, and I feel obliged to do all I can."

President Johnson in an evening telecast on March 31rst would announce to the nation that he would not seek another term. He informed the country that he felt it was necessary to focus on the nation's problems of which included the war and that he could not be distracted by the campaign. He did not concede in his speech that there was a significant chance that he was on the verge of being humiliated in primaries scheduled in the coming weeks as his approval ratings plummeted. This was probably the primary reason that prompted his announcement not to seek reelection.

The Republican primaries were also underway. Richard Nixon was hoping to redeem his 1960 loss to President Kennedy and ascend to the presidency. He watched with significant interest the events as they unraveled on the Democratic side. He was not over-joyed with Senator Kennedy's entrance into the race. When Johnson pulled out, this political battle with another Kennedy seemed eminent. However, 1968 was not your normal year and was anything but predictable. It was a year that rivaled 1860 and 1932. The fabric of our national cohesion seemed to play out before our eyes as we watched one tragedy fade into another. Dr. King was felled in Memphis on April 4, 1968, and

The Devil Collects his Price for Dealey Plaza (Remembering 1968)

Senator Kennedy would succumb to another conspiracy on June 6th of that same year. The world watched and was horrified as we killed our progressive leadership and burnt our cities to the ground. They watched as Mayor Richard Daley's police force brutalized protesters from SDS and other groups opposing the war in the streets just outside the doors of the Democratic National Convention. Hubert Humphrey who had never supported Johnson's policy nevertheless was imprisoned by it. Nixon and his inner circle must have relished how the Democrats had imploded which of course enhanced his chances for victory in November.

Nixon, however, was concerned that if Johnson were successful at consummating an accord with North Vietnam in Paris that this could catapult Humphrey into the White House. He decided through third parties to contact the North Vietnamese delegation to implore them to hold out until after the election. His contacts enticed them with assertions that Nixon would tender them better terms. Despite his treasonous actions, Johnson was able to negotiate a ceasefire and stopped all bombing missions that fall. Johnson would discover Nixon's subterfuge and confronted him in two conversations that were recorded.[70] These brief telephone conferences are held at his library as part of the Johnson tapes. Johnson curiously never did make this public which would have destroyed Nixon's candidacy for president.

It was a tight race but when the political dust had settled Nixon and his cronies were in the White House. He ran on a platform that he would end the war with honor. He not only did not end the war, but he expanded it secretly into Cambodia and Laos. He also dropped more bombs on Vietnam than his predecessor did. In addition, we had the shootings of students peacefully protesting the war by the National Guard at Kent State and lesser known Jackson State. His administration would unceremoniously end when he resigned over the revelations of Watergate and other illegal chicanery his administration was involved in.

The year of 1968 was the year that shaped a generation. It was a year that caused our nation to continue our drift into an Oligarchy with unlimited political bribery as former President Jimmy Carter has recently described it. It was the year that ended the hope of a better world and an opportunity for our nation to live up to its ideals. It was a year in which Nixon finally fulfilled his dream to occupy the White House. His administration would become one of the most corrupt in our history.

The Hidden War

This nightmare that 1968 personified to so many that lived through it owed so much of its chaos, violence, and insanity to what transpired in Dealey Plaza. If President Kennedy had lived, there would have been no war, and Dr. King and his brother Bobby would have continued their battle for racial and social justice well into a future that is now our past.

The following are samples of my father's letters he sent home from Vietnam:

December 29, 1968

Dear Mom and Dad;

We are at present in Subic Bay, Philippines. The Repose (floating hospital) crossed the South China Sea yesterday and Friday. She arrived Tuesday morning at about 11:30am.

My trip to Vietnam has been uneventful except for minor complications. It took about 15 hours ...to reach Danang.

On Tuesday, I will have been on board (the Repose) 14 days. I am not very busy which makes the time more difficult, but I am not complaining – would rather it stay quiet. Danang is a huge military facility that you would not believe how large it is. You only can realize how tremendous the commitment there is by seeing it. It was quite depressing to reach the conclusion that it seemed almost impossible that the USA could be thinking about leaving all (military equipment) that is in Danang behind. The people are living for the most part in abject poverty while all of us thrive on this monstrous billion-dollar complex. They seem totally oblivious to it all. It was the most freakish set up I had ever seen. A mingling of primitive people and a highly advanced military technology. It was not a very pleasant sight to see and rather frightening because you had this feeling it was autonomous and out of control. The terminal was filled with filthy dirty, exhausted glassy eyed boys dressed in fatigues. Some sleeping while others staring blankly into space. Weapons were everywhere and it was unnerving to realize what the purpose was. Surprisingly, there were young Vietnamese women all over the place sweeping up and so forth. Children running around and civilian Vietnamese men as well. They also seemed unconcerned, undisturbed and not unfamiliar with their (incongruous) surroundings. We drove from main terminal about four miles through Danang the city and the base. There were literally thousands of jeeps, trucks, armored personnel carriers and planes; acres of stockpiled war material. It was fantastic and depressing to take in all at once.

As I mentioned before, casualties received on Repose have been light since I arrived. But 10 – 20 are enough. 18-21-year-old guys blown in three or four different directions missing legs, arms, eyes, untreatable because of severe brain damage, hemorrhaging from everywhere or nearly dead from shock. Some we do nothing for and just let them die because there is nothing we can do for them. Lord knows the people here treat many that are doomed before they arrive. My involvement in all this is only through the blood bank.

There are about 60 Vietnamese aboard. They are about in the same shape as our wounded, children, women and men – Lord only knows what percentage these small groups of fortunate people represent of the entire number mutilated and dead on the beach.

Well enough said about that...The ship is fine; my quarters are comfortable. The food is good to excellent (served by Philippine waiters). All the comforts of home. The people on board are an exceedingly fine group. My crew in the lab is excellent. Everything is just dandy except for just one overwhelming important aspect. Everything that matters to me is 13,000 miles away. I will not quibble. The last two weeks have been as close to emotional – well as I want to get. A whole year seems intolerable to me and to my wife I am sure also. But I am afraid that's just what it's going to be unless something miraculous happens. I must provide something for my wife and myself to look forward to that is within a reasonable distance to travel for R & R. But it can be terribly expensive.

I pray to God Cecilia can manage this terrible year. I also pray to God I will come home. We are so God damn close and involved with one another for this kind of thing. It makes it very difficult.

Love to all, Newt.

10/16/69

The Hidden War

Dear family;

Well it's been quite a while since I wrote to you. Your letters indicate that there has already been a trip intervening to the southern part of the USA... I am just returning from Subic Bay in the Philippine Islands – my last trip there. There are less than two months to go and I suppose I should be jubilant about that, but you can't imagine how long 55 days looks from here.

I had to laugh at one of Dad's notes to me with The New York Times stating, "Thank you for the letter it was much appreciated." As I recall that particular letter was anything but appreciable. The tone of the war has tapered off considerably since late September and all I can do is pray it stays that way. The word from the Sanctuary is that they have had very little to do and only had a bed census of 300 patients while we (USS Repose) were gone. This is a little unusual from my experience since the hospital ships are generally bulging with patients when one (ship) is gone to Subic Bay.

It was interesting to hear that my sister is becoming involved with orphaned children. I had considerable aspirations in that direction several months ago but the mechanics of putting anything constructive together has somewhat discouraged me. I am not entirely out yet though. The family I was interested in I have not been able to see for over two months and at that not the important member, the father. I have not seen him since July. It's too dangerous. He lives off limits in Danang and if I were caught it would cost me 800 – 1000 dollars for the visit. I have seen him before but then not totally aware of the penalties or actually not officially informed in person. I shall see what I can accomplish in the next 8 weeks – all on the up and up of course.

Mother mentioned the people lost in the plane (reported by Dad in a prior letter) ...no Mom they are not counted in the battle casualties. I don't hesitate to inform you, however, that they are just as dead and dead for what?????? The more that has seeped out about this war in the last six months the more bewildered and disillusioned I have become. It must be strange to you that I should feel that way but I must confess an almost total lack of understanding about what we are attempting to do over here – everything seems to be contradictory – each political force playing against the other, playing some weird game while men die, children starve and women suffer.

The Devil Collects his Price for Dealey Plaza (Remembering 1968)

I received Dad's paper today. For a moment after reading the attached note I confess some anger but after a little reflection realized that I had no such right, considering that I don't even really know what is happening. The war Dad goes on with to me is inhuman. After 50,000 American lives, 600,000 NVA and VC lives, possibly over 1,000,000 civilian dead and 200 billion dollars spent and countless injured permanently. We have also created 4 million refugees or living in absolute destitution.... those are the statistics. I am ashamed to admit that I still see little to be optimistic about, little changed in the blight of the peasant (95% of the population) and the same old slogans being blasted about excusing this war as necessary and just. There still exists a blindness to the stupidity of it all, an almost willing sabotage of one's own sense to cover up for the terrible, horrible, immoral war that we have taken part in the last 8 years. I refer you to the picture story in Life Magazine several weeks ago in which I read carefully. There is much truth in it as far as I am concerned. These people are disheartened. Most of the population are anguishingly caught in the middle between the political aspirations of General Thieu, the USA and Hanoi. They are poor uneducated and yet industrious and capable but as the article points out their lives revolve within a rather narrow sphere of existence. They live from day to day in fear of VC reprisals and American bombs and guns. They have little if any security for without notice they can be rudely uprooted from their homes and transported miles and relocated while their homes are burned. The Saigon Government has done hardly anything to encourage loyalty from these people of South Vietnam and if one talks to the right people (like the director of the pacification program in Danang) the outlook for any meaningful effort on Saigon's part is indeed bleak. What I am saying Dad is that the little people – the ones this war is supposedly being fought for – are the ones being hurt most by it and helped least by it.

Peace will come I am sure. I just hope we do not feel we have accomplished something noble and consistent with the teachings of a supposedly Christian nation.

Love to all, Newt

CHAPTER 10
The Urgency of Now
(The Words of Jesus Inspire a Non-Violent Crusade for Justice)

The solutions we seek are not hidden in the stars, awaiting some philosopher king to discover them. They are not some impractical ideal practiced by saints that long for utopian society's that flourish beyond a golden horizon. They exist just below the surface to be raised above all the deception, ignorance and fear that buried them.

These natural laws made known by a vision, an attitude or even a perspective that was reborn in the minds of honorable sages that overcame their human frailties that enabled them to appreciate their meaning despite the prejudices that threatened to banish them.

In every generation, there are those that benefit from the status quo and those who suffer from it. This political and social construct that the elite perpetuate to sustain their supremacy and power. If these orthodoxies are threatened by social movements, no matter how reasonable and righteous their demands, the inclination by those with power is to maintain it. Consequently, history has shown time after time that the aristocracy will use whatever is at their disposal to squash dissent even if that means assassinating the leadership of the opposition. Therefore, the messenger must remain true to their cause and be willing to risk everything to achieve it, including their life.

We are fast approaching the 50th (4/4/18) anniversary of the death of Dr. Martin Luther King, Jr. (King) who like the Kennedys and Malcolm X was not a saint that implored us to worship him, but rather was an honorable man who rose above his personal flaws whose dream of justice and peace became, if only for a brief moment, our dream. He refused to be defined by his adversaries or intimidated by their threats to publicize his personal indiscretions that they had so insidiously recorded. He rejected the paradigm of hate which many had implored him to accept as retribution for past injustices that his country refused to confront. He was counseled that only through violence could his demand for racial equality be achieved. He rejected all that not because he wished to be a martyr, but rather he had accepted the command of Jesus "to love your enemy."

He orated in his 1957 speech at the Dexter Avenue Baptist Church in Montgomery, Alabama that "…these are great words, words lifted to cosmic proportions. And over the centuries, many…have argued that this is an extremely difficult command. Many would go so far as to say that it just isn't possible to...practice this glorious command. They would go on to say that this is just additional proof that Jesus was an impractical idealist who never quite came down to earth. So, the arguments abound. But far from being an impractical idealist, Jesus has become a practical realist. The words of this text glitter in our eyes with a new urgency. Far from being the pious injunction of a utopian dreamer, this command is an absolute necessity for the survival of our civilization."

And so, with all the hate and violence that many invoked to derail his movement for racial and social justice that had been thrust upon him and his followers, he continued to preach non-violence, so he could remain true to his higher calling to despise the system but to love his enemy. He opined that to succumb to hate would undermine the integrity and moral authority of his message. In political terms, violence would alienate most of white America that had some empathy for his cause. He espoused that, "For the person that hates, the true becomes false and the false becomes true...You can't see right. The symbol of objectivity is lost. Hate destroys the very structure of the personality of the hater." As to his aversion to violence, he observed "Returning violence for violence multiplies violence, adding deeper darkness to a night already devoid of stars."

He reminded us in his eloquent speeches to honor those promises that were made at our founding. He summoned us to live up to our national ideals and protect the fundamental rights memorialized in our Constitution. Those rights that should be applied to all our citizens and not just become the privileges of white America.

As authorities such as Commissioner Bull Connor unleashed the dogs and the fire hoses upon the protesters in the spring of 1963, he stated, "...But somewhere I read of freedom of assembly. Somewhere I read of the freedom of speech. Somewhere I read of the freedom of the press. Somewhere I read that the greatness of America is the right to protest for right." This observation seems so simple and self-evident that to continue to debate its merits seems like an absurdity maintained by a social pathology we cannot eradicate from our national psyche. Hence, we are still arguing over the same issues that King's movement attempted to ameliorate by his non-violent resistance.

As the movement progressed and social legislation was passed, King began to realize that a man may not be interested in his right to vote if he did not know where his next meal would come from. He also understood as the Johnson

The Hidden War

administration diverted more resources into Vietnam that the programs that were sponsored to create jobs and reduce poverty were consistently being underfunded to support the war. A war that in his mind became more immoral each year. Consequently, his social movement began to transform and broaden its mandate to confront the major evils in the world which consisted of militarism, extreme materialism, and racism. This led to his condemnation of the war in Vietnam in a speech he delivered on April 4, 1967, at the Riverside Church located in New York City. He stated, "I knew I could never again raise my voice against the violence of the oppressed in the ghettos without having first spoken clearly to the greatest purveyor of violence in the world today…my own government."

He also returned in April of 1968 to Memphis to support a strike by sanitation workers, seeking better wages. His intent after Memphis was to continue his work on a massive protest in Washington D.C. to confront the issue of poverty. An idea that Robert F. Kennedy had suggested earlier that spring to civil right leader Marion Wright Edelman as an effective way to bring the issue of poverty to the forefront of our national discourse just like the march on Washington in August of 1963 had done for civil rights. Edelman told King of Bobby's idea which led to a partnership between Kennedy's staff and King to help organize the "Poor People's Campaign of 1968."[71]

Dr. King was hoping that the crowds might be large enough to shut down the federal government. I can just imagine the fury within J. Edgar Hoover of the FBI the more he contemplated the potential consequences of this subversive act being organized in his backyard that he clearly had surmised, or had deluded himself, was influenced by communists. After all, King was directly assaulting two sacrosanct tenets of American power – militarism and capitalism.

He would never live long enough to make that protest on poverty in our national capital a reality. He was assassinated on April 4, 1968, at the Lorraine Motel in Memphis while standing with a few of his close advisors on a second-floor balcony. It was exactly one year after he had denounced the war which had infuriated President Johnson who had felt the speech constituted an unforgiveable betrayal. In fact, he never spoke to King again. We were told that another lone nut named James Earl Ray had killed him. And just like Oswald before him and Sirhan just two months after him, there was no real trial in which the accused had a zealous advocate to challenge the evidence presented by the prosecution.

Ray spent the rest of his life seeking an appeal that was always denied regardless of the evidence that was presented. This fictitious narrative that supports his guilt continues even though the House Select Committee on Assassinations had concluded that King's murder was "probably" the result of a conspiracy. This narrative persists even though the King family won a wrongful death lawsuit in 1999 against one of the conspirators in which a jury had found that King's death had been the result of a conspiracy that included elements of organized crime, the Memphis Police Department, and federal agencies. 70 witnesses testified at that trial.

The most important legacy King left behind for future generations was his fidelity to the concept of non-violent protest. He staunchly believed that this method of resistance was the most potent form of protest in that it disarmed your opponent and exposed their absurd moral defenses to justify their prejudices. He opined further that the means by which you achieve your objective was just as important as the objective itself. He stated, "immoral means cannot bring moral ends." In fact, it contaminates and undermines your message and eventually corrupts the integrity of your mission. He asserted that "Darkness cannot drive out darkness; only light can do that. Hate cannot drive out hate; only love can do that." As his mentor Gandhi observed, "I object to violence because when it appears to do good, the good is only temporary. The evil it does is permanent."

His dream remains unfulfilled five decades after his assassination. Even though Obama's presidency revealed that progress had been made, it also unveiled that we were still a racist country. And although the 1964 Civil Rights Act and the 1965 Voting Rights Act have obviously not resolved our racial divide, these historic achievements nevertheless have permitted significant progress. These landmark pieces of legislation that are periodically threatened by conservatives in congress and on the Supreme Court who have spent their entire careers salivating for an opportunity to undermine their effectiveness. These political edicts that espouse that federal legislation as it related to civil rights had extended federal authority beyond its constitutional limits and, therefore, had unlawfully interfered with state rights. In addition, they proffered that these laws in any event did not ameliorate this national stain but inflamed local passions amongst those that were impacted by these laws.

King addressed the critics such as Senator Goldwater that made the same arguments in the early 1960s when he replied, "The law can't change the heart,

The Hidden War

but it can restrain the heartless." He further asserted, "It can't make the heart accept integration, but the law can stop segregation."

The day before he died Dr. King delivered this prophetic and heartfelt oratory to keep the movement hopeful while acknowledging the dark days ahead. His goal was to inspire them to march on with or without him, whatever fate may lay in his path as a man, and to stay focused on their quest for righteous change and justice. He reflected, "Well, I don't know what will happen now. We've got some difficult days ahead, but it really doesn't matter with me now, because I've been to the mountain top and I don't mind. Like anybody, I would like to live a long life; longevity has its place. But I'm not concerned about that now. I just want to do God's will, and he has allowed me to go up to the mountain, and I've looked over, and I've seen the Promised Land. I may not get there with you, but I want you to know tonight, that we, as a people, will get to the Promised Land, so I'm happy, tonight. I'm not worried about anything. I'm not fearing any man. My eyes have seen the glory of the coming of the Lord."

CHAPTER 11
The Case for Conspiracy (The RFK Assassination)

The reluctance to be a witness for the reality we live in was disappointingly revealed again in what initially began as an inquisitive examination of Robert Kennedy's assassination to commemorate the fiftieth year since his death by Zac Stuart-Pontier (Zac), an editor and producer. He had persuaded Bill Klaber a radio commentator, journalist and author of "Shadow Play" which is a provocative study of RFK's murder in 1968 to participate in this investigative odyssey. Klaber had researched this dark event for years and had concluded that Sirhan Bishara Sirhan (Sirhan) was another patsy that diverted the attention of the witnesses and the media from the real assassins. If true, this is a conspiracy.

The definition of this dreaded word "conspiracy" that so many roll their eyes and begin to tune out the instant it is mentioned is basically a secret plan to do something unlawful or harmful. All you need in the simplest of cases is two people to constitute a conspiracy. This is hardly the sinister-paranoid term it has evolved into in modern times. In any event, the task Zac and Klaber were to explore in their documentary was whether Robert Kennedy was murdered by Sirhan - as concluded by a court that initially sentenced him to death that was eventually reduced to life imprisonment after the California Supreme Court repealed their capital punishment statute in 1972 - or were hidden conspirators responsible for his death.

This series was aptly entitled "The RFK Tapes" which were presented in 10 podcasts. Klaber only agreed to participate because of the assurances by Zac that this would not digress into another mainstream media whitewash to obscure the truth. Zac gave that pledge not realizing what he was assenting to. Nevertheless, the first 6 episodes were highly informative especially those segments that dealt with former Congressman Allard Lowenstein who was a friend of RFK.

The audio tapes of Lowenstein discussing his investigation of his friend's murder had never been publicly aired prior to this episode. Initially, it was too painful for him to objectively assess Kennedy's assassination and because of this he never seriously contemplated that conspirators had ended his friend's campaign for the presidency. It was not until Watergate and the revelation of

The Hidden War

President Nixon's enemy list of which he was listed as number 7 that he began to ponder that if someone as innocuous as himself was designated that high on a president's enumerated list of enemies where would someone as influential as Bobby Kennedy be. And more importantly, who else in Washington had similar lists. He then teamed up with Paul Schrade who was not only part of RFK's campaign staff but had been struck in the head allegedly by one of Sirhan's bullets in the pantry of the Ambassador Hotel that night. Their quest to ascertain the truth became a crusade to reopen the case and objectively reexamine all the evidence that the Los Angeles Police Department (LAPD) had ignored or had destroyed.

By the seventh episode, it became obvious to me that Zac was getting cold feet as he entered the sinister world of the CIA and its black operations. MKULTRA for instance was a program that researched the possibility of creating a Manchurian candidate that could be hypno-programmed to murder assigned targets designated by CIA officials. The experts that performed this research in many cases used unwitting subjects from psychiatric institutions within Canada and the United States that were exposed to experiments that included hypnosis, sleep deprivation, electroshock and drugs such as LSD to develop dependable methods to control their minds with the ultimate objective of behavioral modification. In limited cases, date-rape drugs were administered to kidnap potential subjects.[72] Their conclusions were that with a susceptible candidate they could overcome their internal moral values through deception and program them while under hypnosis to perform acts that in a conscious state would be morally repugnant to them such as deviant sexual acts and of course murder.

Because this program was way out of Zac's comfort zone, he latched onto anomalies such as a vicious letter Sirhan had written to author Dan Moldea. His colleague - as this became apparent to him - became more frustrated as his co-host drifted further into the establishment's fictitious world.

They reviewed the autopsy report by Dr. Thomas T. Noguchi who had determined that all the shots that hit Kennedy had been fired by a gunman that was positioned just behind and to the right of the Senator not in front of him as all the witnesses had placed Sirhan. In addition, the mortal shot had been fired by a 22-caliber pistol that was positioned close to RFK's lower right ear. He had further concluded that the gun was 1.5 inches, but no more than 3 inches away

The Case for Conspiracy (The RFK Assassination)

from Kennedy's head. Sirhan's gun by all accounts was never closer than 2 feet in front of Kennedy.[73]

They also met with Philip Van Praag a forensic audio expert who had performed tests utilizing twenty-first century technology to decipher the sounds that could be detected on Pruszynski's Tape. This was a recording inadvertently made by a freelance Polish journalist named Stanislaw Pruszynski that by providence had memorialized the auditory sounds of the assassination. Its existence had been virtually unknown by researchers until modern technology was able to reveal the hidden evidence that was captured by this extremely poor audio of that tragic night. Praag had essentially concluded that he could identify 13 gunshots on that recording. He added that some of the shots were so close together that they had to have been made by different weapons. Since Sirhan's gun only held 8 bullets, this was definitive proof that there had to have been at least two guns in the pantry that night.

There also was a study by the Stanford Research Institute completed in 1982 that conducted an acoustic analysis of an ABC broadcast tape that was recorded contemporaneously with the assassination. Their conclusion was that there were at least 10 gunshots identified on that tape.[74]

In addition, in another episode, they interviewed Sirhan and discussed with psychologists how easy it was to hypnotize him. They likewise surmised from their interactions with Sirhan that his claim that he could not remember most of the event was sincere.

Zac by this point was way out of his realm and began to reach out for anything that would return him to a reality that was more palatable to him. He sought out a friend who was an electronic and computer technology expert to examine the Pruszinski Tape. He confidently asserted after conducting his own testing that there were only 8 shots that could be detected on that recording. Zac then referred to a tome published in 2014 written by psychologist Jesse Walker entitled "The United States of Paranoia: A Conspiracy Theory." For him, this was his piece de resistance. He no longer had to contort his brain to make sense of the palpable evidence that cried out "Manchurian assassin." Not to mention that other contemptible word "conspiracy."

Walker in his volume wrote about our mystical past and the Salem Witch Trials. He proffered that human beings were "hardwired" to find conspiracies or see patterns that were essentially created by irrelevant facts to make sense of the signals they had detected. Much of these matrixes are a manifestation of our fears and thus reflect the anxieties and experiences of those who believe in them, even if the theory says nothing "true" about the objects of the "theories themselves." The fact that on rare occasion there are real conspiracies reinforces this national paranoia.

This is what Zac in podcast 10 avidly referred to as the apprehensions that exasperated him were vanquished as each of Walker's theories written in his book came out of his mouth. Klaber by this point was obviously aghast by these concepts that had contaminated what was initially to him an objective search for the truth. For him, this whole show had digressed into the same old rationalizations for suppressing a new trial for Sirhan or any real inquiry that included all this new evidence. He in fact in their last meeting refused to talk about their collaboration, ending his participation in what he surmised had become a farce.

Zac in the end felt that Praag and Klaber were engaged in confirmation bias to make sense of all the anomalies in the evidence and the multiple incidences that exposed the incompetence of LAPD's investigation. He asserted that these factors were simply coincidences and that no intelligence agency would have devised such a complex scenario when there were obviously much "easier methods" available to them. A common cop-out for many.

When I interned in the Summer of 1987 for the San Francisco District Attorney's Office, I was supervised by Assistant District Attorney Chuck Haynes who was part of their Vertical Prosecution Unit. This unit prosecuted all felonies with exception to homicides. He told me while he was picking a jury for an attempted murder case that whenever the fact pattern was unusual that he always wanted jurors who lived in the communities in which the crime occurred. The reason for this is that potential jurors from middle or upper-class neighborhoods would be disinclined to believe that these fact patterns were possible in our society. However, those that resided in these districts because of their life experiences were very much aware of what human beings were capable of.

Robert Kennedy's assassination was one of those unusual fact patterns that for those that are unfamiliar with the underworld of intelligence and their "wilderness of mirrors" would appear more suitable for a Hollywood science fiction movie than an actual murder investigation. The documents that the

Church Committee examined and the corroboration of many experts in this field have verified that the capabilities to create a "Manchurian candidate" can be achieved by utilizing specific methods on a susceptible individual.

I can certainly understand Zac's reluctance to accept the fact that trained psychologists in hypno-programming techniques had developed the capacity with Sirhan to place him in a trance by using a signal that would trigger him to automatically start shooting as though he was at a firing range. They were also able to create barriers within his mind to prevent him from remembering who programed him, as well as the event itself.

As Sirhan was firing his pistol at the Senator, all of those around RFK grabbed him and wrestled him onto a table. While most of the attention was on the young Palestinian, the professional assassins fired the shots that killed Kennedy. A simple diversionary trick commonly used by intelligence. Unfortunately for Zac, the plethora of evidence that supports this scenario is astounding.

Sirhan's activities according to family members were unknown to them for the 3 months that preceded the assassination. During this period, he was accompanied by others at a gun shop and at a firing range on numerous occasions as reported by witnesses. In fact, he arrived at the Ambassador Hotel that night with an unidentified male and a woman wearing a polka-dotted dress.[75] In addition, it was emphasized by experts in hypnosis that to accomplish what apparently had been done to Sirhan would have taken at least 90 days. Furthermore, the diary in which Sirhan had repeatedly written "RFK must die" is called automatic writing which occurs when someone is in a trance or under hypnosis.

Dr. William J. Bryan, Jr. was proficient in hypnotic techniques that he used on many subjects while employed by the CIA. He was one of the nation's leading experts and as such was ironically the consultant for the iconic film "The Manchurian Candidate."

His relationship with the Agency began in the early 1950s when he worked with Korean War veterans who had been exposed to brutal interrogation techniques by the North Koreans. His main practice where he treated patients with various complaints by applying his hypnotic methods was situated in Los Angeles.

The Hidden War

He was an obese man who weighed almost 400 pounds. He was known for his sexual exploits and had even been reprimanded by the California licensing board for sexually assaulting some of his female patients while they were under hypnosis. Because of this, he was not permitted to treat the opposite sex without a female professional present during these treatment sessions.

Professor Philip Melanson of the University of Massachusetts, who was the chancellor of their Policy Studies at the Dartmouth campus, interviewed several CIA consultants and colleagues of Dr. Bryan. One of those interviewed only provided his CIA pseudonym which was Gilbert Marston. He indicated that Bryan admitted to him that he had been solicited to hypnotize Sirhan.[76] Although Bryan would deny this in an interview with Betsy Langman in 1974, there were many former sexual partners and close professional colleagues that disclosed that he boasted on many occasions that he did it. In fact, two investigators, William Turner (former FBI agent) and John Christian, in the early 1970s tracked down two young call girls who primarily worked in Beverly Hills who had several sexual encounters with Dr. Bryan. Both asserted that during their sessions with him he would brag that he was hired by the CIA and LAPD to work on top-secret projects. Sirhan's name came up often during these discussions. Bryan was essentially an "egomaniac" that could not help himself. While consuming alcohol and drugs, he would often ramble that he was the one who had hypnotized Sirhan.[77]

Dr. Bryan by all accounts was an expert in tricking clients while under hypnosis to perform acts they would not ordinarily be inclined to do. As forensic historian Patrick Nolan wrote, "He had mastered the art of concealing his work by establishing amnesia – or a mental block – in subjects to prevent them from remembering him or what had happened, or what they had done while they were hypnotized."[78] This certainly is consistent to what happened to Sirhan.

There are many more CIA connections to this assassination. The two primary LAPD detectives that would manage Special Unit Senator (SUS) were assigned by Chief of Homicide Detectives Hugh Brown. This unit was set up separately from LAPD's central structure. The two officers that were entrusted with this historical task were Lt. Manuel Pena and Sgt. Hank Hernandez. Pena was brought out of retirement to manage the investigation while Hernandez was to focus on aspects of the case that suggested a conspiracy. Both were known CIA operatives within the intelligence community and LAPD's leadership. They had participated in several operations in South America. In addition, according to declassified CIA documents, both were involved in a program to train other major law enforcement departments on how to infiltrate and confront leftist subversive groups in their cities. As reported by FBI agent Robert J. LaJeunesse, Pena had been assigned projects by the CIA for almost a decade. This was also corroborated by Pena's brother.[79] Consequently, it is not surprising that these officers kept the focus of the investigation on Sirhan and ignored all the witnesses and forensic evidence that was indicative of a conspiracy.

Witnesses in the pantry reported that they saw two other guns that night. One of the handguns brandished at the scene was by an Ace security guard named Thane Eugene Cesar. Although he denied that the pistol that he had in the pantry was the same caliber used by Sirhan, he conceded that he had owned a 22 pistol but had sold it prior to the assassination. This turned out to be a lie when researchers tracked the gun to the person that he had sold it to. The receipt indicated that the transaction occurred two months after RFK's murder. Even more curious, Cesar had been standing just behind and to the right of Kennedy. The perfect position to inflict the gunshot wounds suffered by the Senator. More importantly, he had been hired by Ace only several days prior to the assassination. Another curious fact is that he was employed by Lockheed where he was assigned to a restrictive area of the facility related to the CIA's U2 spy plane. He, however, may not have been the gunman but rather was placed there to dispose of the patsy but because of the chaos and the confusion was unable to get Sirhan in his line of fire. For another gunman was observed by witnesses approaching Kennedy from behind. This man was never identified by LAPD.

There also was the unidentified male and woman in the polka-dotted dress that had been observed entering the kitchen area with Sirhan. Sirhan was seen by witnesses speaking briefly with this woman who had her hand on his arm just prior to the shooting. They were also seen hastily exiting the back door of the pantry just after the assassination and racing down a stairway to the street passing by Sandra Serrano who happened to be sitting on the steps, sipping from a glass of Vodka with orange juice. As they brushed by her on the stairs, the woman exclaimed, "We shot him!" Serrano impulsively asked, "Who?" The woman shockingly replied, "We've shot Senator Kennedy." This was verified by another witness named Albert Ellis who had overheard the interaction they had with Serrano.[80]

She initially recounted this event to Sander Vanocur of NBC that was part of a nationally televised broadcast late that night. As a result, she was requested by LAPD to provide a statement at the offices being occupied by SUS investigators. Hernandez handled the interview that was more consistent with an interrogation of a potential suspect than a vital witness. He bombarded her with accusations that she was lying and could not have witnessed what she had claimed. He shamed her by indicating that she was further traumatizing the Kennedy family by unnecessarily confusing matters that essentially was an open and shut case. This audio is available on You Tube if you want to judge for yourself. In my opinion, his aggressive method was not consistent with someone who was in search of the truth but rather was attempting to bully a witness to revise her statement to cover it up. This is eventually what happened. Serrano finally relented after several hours and provided a revised statement that Hernandez had demanded from her. She was one of several witnesses that reported similar treatment by LAPD personnel.

LAPD's lead criminologist and ballistic expert was Dewayne Wolfer. His report to Pena concluded that his team had determined that 8 bullets were fired and that one of them was lost in the pantry's ceiling. He also later claimed that he had matched the bullets obtained from Kennedy's body with Sirhan's gun. Both findings by Wolfer are contradicted by other experts, FBI agents, witnesses, and discrepancies in his own ballistic analysis.

In FBI documents that were released pursuant to a Freedom of Information Act lawsuit, their findings revealed that in addition to the eight bullets discharged from Sirhan's gun there were 5 additional unaccounted for bullet holes located in the pantry area. Two bullet holes were found in a doorjamb from the pantry's swinging doors, two in the center divider post and one in the stage doorjamb.[81] This of course would be a total of 13 bullets which corroborated Praag's acoustic analysis of the Pruszinski recording. Additionally, FBI agent William Bailey personally inspected the scene just after the tragedy and discovered evidence of two bullet holes unaccounted for lodged in the center divider between the swinging doors in the kitchen pantry, verifying what was reported by an LAPD patrolman who Zac capriciously dismissed because that officer had no prior forensic training. Agent Bailey's observations were subsequently included in the FBI documents discussed above.

Wolfer's other conclusion in his LAPD Ballistic Report is that the bullets fired by Sirhan's gun had consistent markings as those retrieved from Kennedy's wounds. There have been studies completed more recently and those done in the 1970s that contradict Wolfer or at a minimum had determined that the findings were inconclusive. Even more disconcerting, the serial number of the gun used for LAPD's ballistic examination included in Wolfer's report does not match the numbers on Sirhan's pistol. LAPD has over the years casually dismissed this as a clerical error.

Dr. Henry C. Lee, an internationally known forensic scientist, whose previous employment included such distinguished positions as the director of the Connecticut State Police Laboratory from 1978 until 2000, a professor of forensic science at the University of New Haven and the founder of the Henry C. Lee Institute of Forensic Sciences, as well as the author of multiple books, has asserted in his forward of Nolan's volume that, "From Judge Robert Joling's documents and photographs, it is clear that the ballistics and autopsy evidence in the case conflict with the official version of events." These documents of the RFK assassination that were assembled by Judge Joling, a foremost expert on the assassination, were donated in 2002 to the University of New Haven's Henry C. Lee's Institute for Forensic Sciences. It was because of this generous gift that Dr. Lee was able to thoroughly examine the forensic evidence on this transformative tragedy.

In all homicides, the investigators must establish from the totality of the evidence a credible motive to commit the crime. The one assigned to Sirhan by LAPD was that he was extremely angry because of Senator Kennedy's support to send fighter jets to Israel that he knew would be used to kill his decedents that resided in his former homeland. As a young child, he had been traumatized by some of the violence that was pervasive in that area of Palestine. They conveniently found a cutout copy of an article discussing this issue at his home where they also located his diary. Many of his family and friends reported that he had lived in the U.S. since he was 12 years old and considered America his home. They argued that he had no affinity for guns and was a quiet peaceful young man. They asserted further that in fact he admired Robert Kennedy and supported his bid for the presidency.

The Hidden War

Another factor many overlook or ignore is that the path through the kitchen pantry was chosen at the last second as Kennedy was stepping off the podium. His arm was grabbed and was slightly pulled to go in that direction by an aid that was instructed to guide RFK through the pantry. Kennedy's original instinct was to turn to his left not his right. If Sirhan was acting alone, the question that should be asked is how he would have known to wait for RFK in the pantry of the Ambassador Hotel. The more logical answer is he was brought there by others who were subtly controlling the events that led Kennedy to him and their treacherous trap.

The motive that can be attributed to the CIA is linked to what happened in Dealey Plaza on November 22, 1963. In my opinion, you cannot accurately examine this murder if the relevant factors of his brother's assassination are not applied to what happened in Los Angeles. The reason for this is that if President Kennedy had not been assassinated there would have been no motive to kill Bobby that night. For instance, RFK had told his family at the dinner table shortly after his brother's death that he believed there were powerful right-wing forces behind Oswald's gun. He indicated that he was not able to confront these influential men until he could recapture the presidency and get control of the FBI and the Justice Department. Because of this, he and a handful of trusted colleagues were secretly investigating his brother's assassination right up to his victory speech at the Ambassador Hotel. He in fact was planning to announce at the press conference that he was walking towards that if elected he planned to reopen the investigation of his brother's murder.

The motive was to prevent him from telling the world what he really thought of the Warren Commission. And most assuredly, they could never let him be president for none of them would have been able to escape his vengeance for his beloved brother's murder if he obtained the power of that office. They would all be expeditiously taken into custody and rightfully prosecuted. In addition, many have confessed and admitted to their involvement in President Kennedy's assassination. This list includes, but is not limited to, Johnny Roselli, Chauncey Holt, Sam Giancana, E. Howard Hunt, John Martino, and David Sanchez Morales. Morales even admitted to his attorney that he was involved in Bobby Kennedy's death as well. I believe this motive is more compatible with all the evidence.

And finally, another incredulity manifested in this case is that the District Attorney's Office of Los Angeles and LAPD assented to the destruction of thousands of photographs and pieces of physical evidence, including the doorjambs that the FBI concluded had contained unaccounted for bullet holes. This was all done prior to all the appeal strategies available to the alleged assailant were exhausted. This is not just incompetent indifference to the integrity of the justice system but is more indicative of an utter contempt for the truth and for history.

The more we uncover the more untenable the government's tortured narrative becomes. Distinguished researcher Lisa Pease recently published her volume entitled "A Lie too Big to Fail" that was the culmination of 25 years of research into the assassination of Robert Kennedy. I read this enthralling and compelling account of what happened to Kennedy in the pantry of the Ambassador Hotel that tragic night and who was behind it. I encourage anyone who is interested in our real history to read it.

One of the chilling chronicles she recounts at the end of her book has left an indelible impression on my thoughts that I felt compelled to recite. Pease fortuitously was able to procure the diary of John Meier who was a top aide for the reclusive billionaire Howard Hughes from 1966 until 1970. In that Diary, Meier recorded for posterity occurrences that certainly would not have been memorialized by anyone else who were implicated in these events.

Don Nixon – the brother of Richard Nixon – was curiously apprised of the events that pertained to the assassination of RFK by a notorious CIA operative and former FBI agent named Robert Maheu. He was involved in CIA operations in South East Asia and had been a conduit between William Harvey and Johnny Roselli in their quest to assassinate Cuban leaders. He was a well-connected and highly proficient clandestine operator. This meeting took place prior to the Senator's death being widely known to the public on the morning of June 6, 1968.[82]

Meier wrote, "Bob Maheu called to ask about the Don Nixon meeting and suggested 8:30 breakfast at the Desert Inn Country Club (in Las Vegas)." Meier continued, "I went to the club. Maheu was all smiles, and Don Nixon walks in all smiles. What followed next had to be seen to be believed. They embraced each other and Don Nixon said, 'Well that prick is dead,' and Maheu said, 'Well it looks like your brother is in now.' At the time, I did not know what they were talking about."[83]

The Hidden War

"Mahue joked that he should now be called 'Mr. Vice President.' I still did not realize that Robert Kennedy had died and when they saw I was unaware Maheu told me, 'John you are out of it. Why don't you go home and Don and I will carry on without you.'"[84]

Meier indicated that when he learned that "Thane Cesar" had been in the pantry that night as an Ace security guard he began to get suspicious. Because of a conversation he had with Jack Hooper, an associate of Maheu who knew Cesar, he began to make inquires of his own. When Maheu got word that he was asking questions regarding Cesar, he angrily told him to stop, or he would suffer severe consequences.[85]

Meier told Pease that J. Edgar Hoover later had revealed that he knew that Robert Maheu was behind the assassination of RFK.[86] This would be substantiated by other intelligence officers.

As to Walker and his paranoia theory, there are many fallacies with his arguments. For instance, nature is full of patterns that human beings became aware of initially as a matter of survival. To state that human beings are "hardwired" to find conspiracies as though he was asserting something profound is somewhat disconcerting. This to me is obvious but is not something that prevents us from understanding our environment but is a tool used to fully appreciate the hazards that exist in our natural surroundings. For example, primitive societies in Africa recognized that Lion prides mostly hunted at night. This meant that they had to seek shelter after sunset to avoid becoming a meal for these apex predators. There are many examples of humankind learning from these discernable behaviors of the animals that shared their environment and the recurring patterns of their physical world. For instance, the three laws of motion as observed by Isaac Newton are patterns that he was able to explain by mathematical formulas. Every time a medical professional or a psychologist makes a diagnosis of a patient's ailment, they are observing a pattern that are categorized as symptoms.

Another example of professionals using predetermined patterns can be found in objective risk assessment tools that encompass a range of pretrial release practices that are consistent with what has been established as legal and evidence-based practices. In the study guide for Pretrial Release Practitioners it clearly states, "With objective assessments, we look at data that form patterns from the past to try to measure the likelihood of what will happen in the future."

The Case for Conspiracy (The RFK Assassination)

Those that deny conspiracies or obvious historical patterns are engaging in pre-conditioned biases to affirm the paradigms that comprise their accepted reality. Of course, there are times when researchers fall victim to confirmation bias or view matrixes in clouds that clearly are not the actual representations of the objects they see. But this does not mean that conspiracies can be dismissed as nothing more than the paranoid delusions of their professed observer no more than those that capriciously dismiss these patterns are the arbiters of truth. Conspiracies are rampant in human history because we are essentially social beings that recognize that there is more power in organized groups than by standing alone. Thus, in the power struggles of the past, we rarely see these battles being waged by individuals. In most cases, it is between groups whether they are members of political parties, religions, races, tribes, nation states or even secret societies or militias.

Of course, there are some who see conspirators behind every tree and offer conspiratorial explanations for every dark event. These examples, however, are not evidence that conspiracies are aberrations that rarely assist our understanding of these transformative tragic events. In fact, they are indicative of how human societies behave and expose our innate proclivity to seek power over others. There are numerous examples of conspiracies that even the corporate media, mainstream historians or the intelligence agencies that were implicated in them can frankly deny. For instance, the CIA has been involved in at least 81 regime changes around the world since its inception in 1947. Every one of them was a conspiracy that they fervently attempted to conceal their involvement in.

There are of course many examples of conspiracies in history that are undisputed facts. The murders of Emperor Julius Cesar and President Abraham Lincoln, the succession of southern states from the Union, the quest for independence from the authority of King George III, the attempted assassinations of Adolph Hitler and Fidel Castro, Watergate, Iran-Contra, the Gulf of Tonkin, the claims that Iraq had weapons of mass destruction, the subterfuge of Bernie Sander's primary campaign by Clinton and the DNC, the murder of CIA agent Frank Olson, the case against Alger Hiss, the assassinations of Secretary General Dag Hammarskjold, Patrice Lumumba, Rafael Trujillo, Salvador Allende, Ngo Diem, Berta Caceres, Dr. Martin Luther King and

The Hidden War

Malcolm X are all proven conspiracies. I of course would add President John F. Kennedy and Senator Robert F. Kennedy to this endless list.

The reason we have these debates can be directly linked to a document that was surreptitiously disseminated in 1967 by the CIA to its media and political allies to discredit the Warren Commission critics that effectively associated this pejorative connotation with this word ever since. In that document, the CIA wrote that a persuasive technique to discredit their message is to label them "conspiracy theorists." The word "conspiracy" prior to 1967 was used quite frequently by those who wanted to distort the truth, as well as those who were righteously seeking it. In short, we need to stop this nonsense and view each event objectively by tracking the evidence to its source, even if that trail leads to a conspiracy. As Sir Author Canon Doyle's fictional incisive sleuth Sherlock Holmes asserted, "Once you eliminate the impossible, whatever remains, no matter how improbable, must be the truth."

CHAPTER 12
The Looking Glass (Rethinking America)

Don Miguel Ruiz is a spiritual teacher that is also an internationally known author. He has attempted through his teachings and writings to help his students find individual freedom by understanding the true nature of our reality. In that vein, he astutely observed, "People like to say that the conflict is between good and evil. The real conflict is between truth and lies." Although in many cases, those seeking nefarious objectives prefer lies and deceptions while those who want to promote the common good are well versed in universal truths.

The reflections of my country I so admired in my youth has gone through many evolutionary transformations in search of the truth. In many ways, it is like that television game show of the 1960s "To Tell the Truth" where four panelists would ask questions of three guests to determine the two imposters. In the end, the host would ask the real celebrity to stand up. The three guests would all attempt to stand until one stood alone.

This in many ways resembles my quest to ascertain the real America. My research has enabled me to identify the imposters that in youth I would never have chosen. Of course, along the way, I had glimpses of this America and yet it never became the looking glass from which I inevitably would draw my conclusion. To be fair, my view was never one dimensional or guided by patriotic nationalism that in many cases is nothing more than a cultural delusion created by the aristocracy to solicit our devoted allegiance to fight their wars. Wars that are always portrayed as a humanitarian mission. Hence, John Lennon and Tom Hayden are identified as the enemies of democracy not the imperialistic wars brutally waged against poor nations that never threatened us, so we can assert our power in regions rich with natural resources and are considered strategically important.

To comprehend the real America, you must maintain an open mind devoid of any preconditioned paradigms taught in our schools which are subtly reinforced by advertisers, the media and our entertainment that perpetuate this national narrative. A story that does not necessarily omit the dark side of our country's growth, but rather it is the emphasis enmeshed in what is described as the courage of rugged pioneers that forged a nation out of an untamed wilderness that creates this distortion. This is not because this

The Hidden War

narrative is patently false, but rather its focus exposes the partiality of this history.

For instance, the concept of "Manifest Destiny" was justified as a fulfillment of God's will that our land was preordained to reach from "sea to shining sea." The Indian Removal Act signed by President Andrew Jackson that resulted in the "trail of tears" and the savage Indian Wars that consumed most of the second half of the 19th century was tragic but necessary to achieve our national objective which was to democratize and civilize a continent. It was not described as an attempted genocide to augment our national wealth by exploiting all the natural resources found under the tribal lands that Native Americans considered sacred. And yes, it is true that our history books mention the massacre at Wounded Knee that signaled the end of the wars, but it was presented as an anomaly not a pattern of behavior that was implicitly encouraged by our national leaders just as the My Lai Massacre was insidiously framed by our military a century later in Vietnam. To not appreciate the significance of omission verses emphasis is to be oblivious to the perspective in which the objective arbiters of history will use to judge it.

Most of us believe that patriotism is saluting the flag, standing at attention during the national anthem and supporting the troops. These gestures of respect, however, are not the patriotism that our founders contemplated or what astute observers of a true republic would label genuine patriotism. You can love your country while criticizing the policies of our federal government and the sacrosanct orthodoxies that are reinforced in our schools. As historian Howard Zinn espoused, "Dissent is the highest form of patriotism."

This perspective is more aligned with the founders' vision because they knew from their extensive reading of history that all governments – even benevolent governments – over time incrementally digress into tyranny if their power is not challenged by their people. Because of this, the founders placed safeguards in our Constitution to ensure that one branch of government did not become too powerful and that the people had a voice in their hallowed chambers. The watchdog was to be an objective and independent media that was not only responsible for informing the citizenry of their government's actions but also to hold power accountable by exposing deceit and corruption. This is the reason the media was included in the first amendment.

Even a conservative military commander such as former President Eisenhower understood this concept when he asserted that, "May we never confuse honest dissent with disloyal subversion." And as we have witnessed through the decades, the conservative agenda was to limit government, to protect our traditions and to preserve individual liberty. It is the neo-conservative perspective that equates blind loyalty to country with being a true patriot. This is the premise that caused President George W. Bush to declare at the beginning of the Iraq invasion that you are either "with us or against us." Another example of how the Republican Party has drifted far from their roots.

There are many examples of the political elite imposing policies that echoed the intentions of a powerful cabal to limit if not undermine President Franklin Roosevelt's New Deal that for the most part empowered the "common man." The attempts to thwart Roosevelt's post-war vision were not blatant frontal assaults that the working class could easily identify but rather were cloaked in Orwellian language to obscure their real objectives, as well as employing diversionary tactics by creating false enemies that threatened our survival. The goal was to recoup all that power that the New Dealers had transferred to the people in order to build a more humane and equitable society; a society that was not beholden to the whims of the callous markets that had collapsed in 1929 that precipitated the economic desolation of the Great Depression. This historical movement, however, on occasion would reveal itself and to the educated observer there was indicia that if fully appreciated could expose the reality the power elite were so diligently attempting to conceal.

The Kennedy assassination unwittingly changed the dynamics of the problem that confronted the deep state by exposing the hidden battles for power that were waged within the bowels of our government. This is the reason this seminal event and the hidden knowledge tucked away in the crevices of this case is so important even for us living in the present. The truth of what we had become in 1963, and what is so patently obvious to the dissenters of today, can be found in the motivations of those that killed him and by those who chose to cover up this heinous crime to prevent the truth from leaking into the mainstream of our society.

President Kennedy was not a traditional cold warrior or a reactionary politician that desired to maintain the status quo that was so ardently promulgated by revisionist historians and the spineless journalists that had been coopted by secret elements within our intelligence community. The real Kennedy challenged our foreign policy paradigms in his quest for peace while domestically he was determined to augment Roosevelt's New Deal by extending it to millions while simultaneously creating new incentives for business to invest in technological development while upgrading their plants.

The Hidden War

His most prescient domestic policy was to develop a safety net to ameliorate the ravages of poverty and to create jobs that provided a livable wage.

One of the primary tasks that confronted the nation, as he envisioned it as we entered the New Frontier of the 1960s, was to provide our citizens with public schools that bestowed upon our children with the finest education to prepare them for the future. He also advocated for those that desired to attend institutions of higher learning to make those degrees affordable to the average family. He astutely opined that the education of our citizenry was one of the utmost functions of government. As Jefferson and Adams knew, the survival of the republic required an educated and participatory citizenry to sustain not only our form of government but also to defend our liberty from government encroachment.

By strengthening and updating the New Deal, he was essentially reversing everything the deep state, the national security complex and its Wall Street supporters were building to further entrench and expand their power. The primary reason the Kennedy assassination is so difficult to understand for many is because to truly comprehend what happened in Dealey Plaza on November 22, 1963, you must be willing to confront the lie that your whole reality was dependent upon in order to appreciate the context in which this event was permitted to occur.

Dr. E. Martin Sholtz was a well-known psychiatrist whose practice was in Boston. After reading the Warren Commission Report (WCR), he wrote to his good friend dissident attorney Vincent Salandria to express what he had discovered while examining the documents. His long letter became a book entitled "History will not Absolve Us" which was first published in 1996. Sholtz wrote, "To know the truth—as opposed to only believe the truth—is to face an awful terror and to no longer be able to evade responsibility." This according to reviewer John Kelin is the "heart" of the volume. The central premise asserted by Dr. Sholtz according to Kelin is that the government is "holding American citizens in a state of confusion in which anything can be believed, but nothing can be known for sure, is one of the 'primary means of keeping us politically impotent'." This method is not only used to obscure the hidden truths of dark transformative events but also is a tool utilized by the power elite to create doubt and confusion regarding other important issues that confront our nation and humanity such as climate change.

Sholtz asserted further, "In confronting the murder of JFK, we are not confronted with the task of repairing something that has been injured. We are confronted with the task of addressing a society that in 1963 was already profoundly ill, and if anything has become sicker in the intervening years. At the core of this illness is that mentality which pursues anti-communism and the Cold War above all else, a mentality which will subordinate any crime, including the threat to annihilate mankind, in pursuit of defeating this supposed enemy." He emphasized that what made Kennedy's murder necessary "was his effort to depart from this insanity."

Sholtz deemed from an analysis of Leon Trotsky's murder made by Isaac Don Levine who was an associate of Allen Dulles was that "The classic manner by which an intelligence agency attempts to cover itself is by the use of confusion and mystery. The public is allowed to think anything it wants, but is not allowed to know, because the case is shrouded in supposed uncertainty and confusion." Under such circumstances, it was not necessary for the Warren Commission (WC) to convince everyone that there was no conspiracy, they just had to present the lone nut explanation in such a fashion as to make it a credible debate. Their fallback position if evidence of a conspiracy was proven was that the Mafia or Castro did it.

John J. McCloy who was one of its prominent members inadvertently revealed the paramount importance of the formation of the Warren Commission when he asserted it was to "show the world that America is not a banana republic where a government can be changed by conspiracy." Thus, it was not as important to ascertain what happened to Kennedy and why, but rather to prove we were not another "banana republic." The cause of the assassination had to be hidden to maintain the integrity of the government and to prevent a massive rebellion from disrupting our society if the truth was known.

This view is consistent with President Charles de Gaulle's assessment who had also been targeted by intelligence forces for assassination that he surmised included elements of the CIA. He understood the tactics deployed by this intelligence underworld and was conversant with their extremist agenda because of his inquiry into this milieu of secrecy and deceit in which his enemies resided. With this insight, the French leader told his information minister, Alain Peyrefitte, on November 24, 1963, that, "What happened to Kennedy is what nearly happened to me. His story is the same as mine…It looks like a cowboy story, but it's only an OAS (secret army organization) story. The security forces were in cahoots with the extremists."[87]

The Hidden War

The minister asked, "Do you think Oswald was a front?" De Gaulle replied, "They got their hands on this communist who wasn't one, while still being one. He had a sub-par intellect and was an exalted fanatic - just the man they needed, the perfect one to be accused...The guy ran away because he probably became suspicious. They wanted to kill him on the spot before he could be grabbed by the judicial system... a trial would unearth the whole conspiracy. Then the security forces went looking for a cleanup man they totally controlled, and who couldn't refuse their offer, and that guy sacrificed himself to kill a fake assassin (the patsy) – supposedly in defense of Kennedy's memory."[88]

The French leader then began to explain the political context in which the murder had taken place. "The Security forces all over the world are the same when they do this dirty work. As soon as they succeed in wiping out this false assassin, they declare that the justice system no longer need be concerned, that no further public action was needed...Better to assassinate an innocent man than to let civil war break out. Better an injustice than disorder." He concluded, "...They (other U.S. leaders who suspected a conspiracy) will close ranks. They'll do everything to stifle any scandal...They don't want to know. They don't want to find out. They won't allow themselves to find out."[89]

The Cuban leader Fidel Castro tried to quell what he suspected would be a wave of accusations levied at his regime by the CIA and their anti-Castro allies by delivering his prescient speech only 24 hours after Kennedy's death. His views were remarkably similar to French President de Gaulle. Furthermore, his understanding of the internal intrigue within the hidden corridors of power in Washington was incredibly accurate, considering he had none of the benefits of declassified documents, witness testimonials and countless books meticulously researched by concerned citizens in search of the truth.

He astutely observed, "And thus, on a whole series of issues of international policy, there are in the United States elements that support a preventive nuclear war, who are in favor of launching a surprise nuclear attack, because they stubbornly think that this should be the policy of the United States. Reactionary and neo-fascist elements without any consideration whatsoever for the most elementary rights of nations or the interests of mankind." He continued, "Even up to this moment, the events that led to the murder of the President of the United States continue to be confused, obscure and unclear." He warned that "the most reactionary forces of the United States are at large...For instance, the worst symptom is the advantage they are taking of the event to unleash within the United States a state of anti-Soviet...and of anti-Cuban hysteria."

The question that any reasonable person should be asking is why the press and the liberal establishment became complicit by endorsing this perfidious tale of a lone gunman as the solution to the assassination of their friend and the champion of their causes.

Mort Sahl a highly revered nightclub comedian and political satirist of the time who had become a friend of President Kennedy observed, "He decided to save America – a dangerous occupation in this country." He elaborated that the optimism that anything was possible "...is all gone now." He lamented, "The social Democrats in this country have a lot of guilt. They did not stand up to Vietnam. They did not stand up to the encroachment of the intelligence community. And they walked away from Jack Kennedy. The best they could come up with after he was shot in the street like a dog was to say he wasn't that good of a president anyway." He rhetorically deplored their treachery by asserting, "Let me tell you, you have a strange group of friends."[90]

Sahl after reading the Warren Commission Report and meeting with James Garrison in 1967 decided to join his investigation to ascertain why Kennedy was murdered and who really was culpable for this seminal event. He assisted Garrison's probe by examining documents, interviewing witnesses and by introducing the District Attorney to powerful people he knew. He summed up his view of Garrison in an interview in the late 1960s by stating, "He is a very important American."[91] Because of that support and his personal views on who killed his friend, no one would be his agent. He lost money and jobs. He essentially became a heretic within the same community who only years before had showered him with praise as his gigs made them lots of money. He caustically warned in that interview, "There should be a sign within the CIA. Be careful of the governments you overthrow, it may be your own."[92]

Dr. Sholtz opined that The Nation, I.F. Stone and Noam Chomsky remained silent for a multitude of cowardly reasons. Their silence essentially "revealed that when push came to shove, when they had to make a choice, this liberal establishment was more addicted to the military and the CIA than the Constitution." The Massachusetts Institute of Technology for instance where Chomsky has been a professor for decades receives millions of dollars from defense contractors and the government to research new weapon technology among other related projects annually; To think that this did not influence his public views as it related to Kennedy's assassination as a young professor just starting his career would be absurdly naïve. We know from researchers such as David Lifton that he personally was intrigued by the evidence he provided Chomsky to solicit his support.[93] It is also important to note that the CIA's top-secret program Operation Mockingbird was surreptitiously coopting most of the media to support their schemes and disseminate their propaganda during that period.

We likewise see this same phenomenon today as it relates to the treatment of Julian Assange and WikiLeaks, as well as the Russiagate narrative that has created a second Cold War in order to divert the masses from examining the true causes of Trump's rise to power. Sholtz added that "by and large the American people are part and parcel of this addiction." The need to believe in institutions and agencies even though these same organizations have lied to them on numerous occasions and have promoted policies that undermined our democratic institutions and diminished our liberty outweigh the natural inclination to defend these important aspects of our republic. For instance, it is more comforting to acquiesce to the fiction that Kennedy was murdered by a disgruntled communist with an antiquated Italian rifle with a defective scope than to confront the reality that our society was dominated by "Orwellian forces" that controlled the media and our government.

These same forces that Robert Mueller, James Comey, James Clapper and John Brennan so ascetically represent in modern times as they promulgate their lies to achieve the objectives of the power brokers that proclaim their mandates from within their institutional perches in the FBI, NIA, NSA and the CIA. These same agencies that in prior administrations most liberals scorned as a threat to our democratic institutions and our national integrity, as well as the propaganda they disseminated to whip the masses into a patriotic frenzy to support their wars while silently eviscerating our fundamental rights. They now are lionized as a savior for democracy by these same political elements in their myopic pursuit to get Trump. By doing this as Jimmy Dore has declared, they have essentially "entered a Faustian bargain" with those deep state actors and the agencies that are the source of their insidious power. For their opposition to Trump is not founded on the same tenets, and if they are successful in his removal, we will be burdened with Vice President Mike Pence who in many ways is more dangerous and as a result will be the repentance of our sins.

Pence is naturally perceived as more palatable to the secret government and the deep state because he knows the codes and consequently is a polished politician. Thus, this will enable him to present their positions in a more

The Looking Glass (Rethinking America)

appealing framework while concealing their true objectives to maintain and expand their power. At that moment, these so-called champions of democracy will be seen for who they truly are which are wolves cloaked in sheep's clothing.

Just a generation ago these same men were lying to the American people to solicit their approbation for the war against Iraq by fictitiously claiming Saddam Hussein was aligned with Al Qaeda and had weapons of mass destruction (WMD). These same weapons that UN inspectors had incessantly reported did not exist got no traction within the mainstream media. In fact, these same media outlets overwhelmingly supported the invasion of Iraq by parroting what government officials had leaked or had espoused in press releases.

At the time, Robert Mueller was the director of the FBI when he testified before congressional committees in support of military action against Iraq. He also was instrumental in the attempt to falsely charge William Binney and other whistleblowers from the NSA with crimes they had not committed. Binney for instance was targeted because he was attempting to bring these massive surveillance programs that were in violation of the Constitution to the attention of the public. Mueller not only supported this secret program, but his FBI benefited immensely as they used this information collected by the NSA to harass and discredit Americans it deemed were a threat to our national security.

In addition, Mueller conceded to Ray McGovern, a retired CIA officer, that he supported this clandestine procedure called "Parallel Construction." This was basically a program that permitted the government to obtain evidence against U.S. citizens in violation of the 4th Amendment. The FBI would access this mass of information deposited in NSA computer banks and would disseminate this data to local law enforcement who would use it to get search warrants authorized by a local judge. They then would gather evidence to prosecute citizens without the judicial authorities knowing the original source of this information.

Many might say that they do not understand the threat espoused by civil liberty advocates for many of these citizens were committing crimes. Unfortunately, many innocent people – some intentionally and others unintentionally - were caught in these nets and harassed or totally smeared by federal and local law enforcement agencies. But more importantly, this Parallel Construction practice and the surveillance program that it remains dependent upon essentially eviscerates the 4th, 5th, 6th and 14th Amendments.

The Hidden War

In addition, these same political insiders and their agencies were part of an administration that committed war crimes and openly supported enhanced interrogation techniques that were defined by the international community and the Geneva Convention as torture. They supported the drone project which was essentially a U.S. government sanctioned assassination program. The agencies they so loyally protected were responsible for all the atrocities and violations of law that were committed in Iraq, Afghanistan, Guantanamo, as so profoundly exemplified by the horrific scandal of Abu Ghraib. They carried over many of these nefarious programs into the Obama administration that except for torture expanded their mandates to prolong this perpetual war on terror that appears to only benefit the oligarchs and the national security complex.

This epiphany that will eventually awaken the cerebral cortex of the liberals and their media mouthpieces is that their saviors' guiding authority is not the Constitution, nor do they firmly believe in the foundational principle of all republics that power is derived from the people. Their model of government is rather deeply rooted in the orthodoxies of empire in their quest for absolute supremacy for the plutocrats they have always worked for.

I am not advocating to abandon the investigation that could unveil impeachable offenses that the president may have committed, but rather I am attempting to reframe the focus of this coalition to the hazards of aligning with those who represent the worst of our society to seek revenge on a perceived usurper in order to rehabilitate the lesser evil; an obsession that diverts our attention from the systemic problems that Trump exemplifies, but did not create, and all those pressing difficulties that confront our nation that are festering by our continual neglect.

Their political ancestors were likewise responsible for the violence that ended the New Frontier. This treasonous crime did not just result in the death of a man that Nobel prize winning historian Arthur Schlesinger, Jr. asserted personified "the best of my generation", but a vision of America deeply engrained in the ideals we all proclaim exult our nation. This vision that was destroyed that day by a battle over the allocation of power that had been waged ever since he was sworn in as our President.

For like Trump, he was not expected to defeat Vice President Richard Nixon who was supported by the power elite. They were anticipating a president that would be amendable to their policies and their hawkish recommendations to resolve those issues left undone by Eisenhower. The result of this power struggle that most citizens were not even aware of had sealed our fate to become a neo-colonial empire that was not to be the beacon of liberty but rather its enemy. In poll after poll, the international community has determined that the United States is the biggest threat to peace not the Chinese, the Iranians, the North Koreans or even the Russians. From Vietnam to Afghanistan and Iraq, we have been a nation at war imposing our will upon the globe to maintain our hegemonic power that we consummated after the collapse of the Soviet Union.

In an article written for Truthdig.com by Major Danny Sjursen, a U.S. Army officer and former history instructor at West Point that served several tours of duty with reconnaissance units in Iraq and Afghanistan, he solemnly described what his beloved country had become. He referenced the absurd and coldhearted justifications our leaders have made in support of our draconian policies.

For instance, the first Gulf War had been insidiously provoked by a 15-year-old Kuwaiti girl named Nayirah. She was summoned by the Congressional Human Rights Caucus where she deliberately provided false testimony that Iraqi military forces were taking babies out of their incubators and depositing them on the cold floor to die. This testimony was cited on numerous occasions by U.S. Senators and President George H.W. Bush to justify military action against Iraq. It was later discovered that this girl's full name was Nayirah al-Sabah the daughter of Saud Al-Sabah the Kuwaiti Ambassador to the U.S. She had been recruited by the Citizens for a Free Kuwait that was part of a campaign managed by a U.S. public relations firm. President Bush, Sr. had essentially replicated the same deceitful tactics implemented by President Johnson to justify the invasion of the Dominican Republic (1965) and President Reagan's military incursion into Grenada (1983). Another example of modern atrocity propaganda often employed to manipulate the U.S. public to support their wars.

After the war ended, the United States imposed a blockade and severe sanctions on Iraq to prevent the regime from reasserting its power and becoming a threat to its neighbors. The United Nation's Humanitarian Coordinator in Iraq, Denis Halliday, resigned in protest in 1998 because he was so appalled by the extent of the human tragedy that was a direct result of our harsh policy. When Secretary Madeleine Albright was asked in a "60 minute" interview to justify the deaths of 500,000 Iraqi children and whether it was worth it, she callously replied, "I think this is a very hard choice, but...we think the price was worth it." Would she and her cohorts think the same if it were their children and grandchildren that died?

Major Sjursen penned that since the 2003 invasion of Iraq 200,000 Iraqi citizens have been killed. This does not include all those cancer deaths attributable to the depleted uranium ammunition we used in Gulf War I that impacted tens of thousands of families. The collateral consequence of this is still haunting the Iraqi people as significant numbers of children are born today with birth defects.

He added in another U.S. supported blockade with its ally Saudi Arabia that recent reports coming out of that war traumatized nation of Yemen that 85,000 Yemeni children have starved to death or died of curable diseases since the war started three years ago. This nation that supposedly has some strategic interests as asserted by our military is the poorest country in the region.

In 18 years of U.S. wars, we have lost 7,000 soldiers, have caused the deaths of over 500,000 innocent civilians, and have created 21 million refugees (now the estimates are as high as 30 million). The cost to the taxpayers of the U.S. has been a whopping $6.4 trillion (recent numbers indicate almost $7 trillion).

We have over 800 military bases around the globe and are presently dropping bombs in seven countries. We are terrorizing citizens in many nations as our drones survey the landscape seeking new victims. We have created failed states in Libya and Iraq while attempting to sentence other nations to similar fates in Syria and Afghanistan. We have sponsored regime changes in Ukraine (2014), Bolivia (2019) and Honduras (2009) and are attempting to overthrow the governments in Venezuela and Iran.

The consequence for the residents in these countries has been catastrophic. In Libya for example, terrorists' organizations and human traffickers' control much of the territory outside the cities. This nation that under its former leader Muammar Gaddafi had a large middle class that had a standard of living unsurpassed by most of the continent with the possible exception of South Africa.

Furthermore, the intelligence community with the cooperation of the Pentagon and our British ally has successfully demonized Vladimir Putin and the Russian Federation by accusing Russia of using weaponized chemicals known as Novichok nerve agents in the attempted assassination in London of former double agent Sergie Skripal and his daughter Yulia. They likewise have accused Russia's ally Bashar Al-Assad of dropping chemical weapons on his people in 2013, 2017 and 2018 and that Russian intelligence agents interfered in the 2016 election by stealing the DNC emails and delivering them to WikiLeaks. The evidence in all three cases is either non-existent or completely contradicts the official western version promoted by the corporate media.

This is the America that the rest of the world must tolerate and hopefully survive. It was not necessary that all of this come to pass as it is currently that so disturbs and saddens those that fervently believe we are a better nation than this. The nation that we could have become was eloquently described in a speech commemorating the works and life of poet Robert Frost by President Kennedy at Amherst College on October 26, 1963.

He poignantly orated, "I look forward to a great America, a future in which our country will match its military strength with our moral restraint, its wealth with our wisdom, its power with our purpose. I look forward to an America which will not be afraid of grace and beauty, which will protect the beauty of our natural environment, which will preserve the great old American houses and squares and parks of our national past, and which will build handsome and balanced cities for our future.

I look forward to an America which will reward achievement in the arts as we reward achievement in business and statecraft. I look forward to an America which will steadily raise the standards of artistic accomplishment and which will steadily enlarge cultural opportunities for all our citizens. And I look forward to an America which commands respect throughout the world not only for its strength but its civilization as well. And I look forward to a world in which we will be safe not only for democracy and diversity but also for personal distinction."

Kennedy's assassination brought this power struggle within our government out onto the streets of one of our most populous American municipalities. As a result of Dallas, his vision was quickly shoved aside into oblivion while their vision became our future. Although his death was planned and executed by rogue elements within our intelligence community and the Pentagon who had formed alliances with the Mafia and extremists within the anti-Castro community, the rest of the establishment felt compelled to save the Union by covering the trail that led to the conspirators.

The Trump presidency, the decline of the middle class as a result of neo-liberal free trade agreements and unencumbered markets, and the disparity that exists between the one percenters and the rest of us that have been exacerbated by neo-conservative tax cuts and by enormous defense budgets to continue all the wars we are involved in all have their origins in the shots that

The Hidden War

rang out in Dealey Plaza that day. The death of Kennedy was a victory for those who opposed the New Deal and for those who wanted to create a "Pax Americana" imposed on the rest of the world by our weapons of war. Consequently, this is the reality we presently live in.

We as a nation now suffer the fate of Robert Frost's "Hired Man". The prospect of having "nothing to look backward to with pride, and nothing to look forward to with hope." Hence, we have mass shootings perpetrated by misguided desperate men, rising suicide rates, broken families and an opiate epidemic that kills more of our sons and daughters than those that die annually on our nation's highways.

We are a nation who has lost its capacity to dream of things bigger than ourselves and who can take pride in the things that we create. Almost every tangible material item we have has a made in China label attached to it. And although the deep state and its minions won the battles for our national soul in Dallas (1963), Memphis (1968) and Los Angeles (1968), there is still time to win the war if we can summon the trumpets of revolution once again to reclaim those national ideals nourished by liberty to rebuild our republic.

But first, we must set aside this perfidious myth that we are exceptional and that the natural laws extant since the dawn of civilization that govern humankind and their societies do not apply to us. This insidious doctrine promoted by the entrenched elitist establishment whose primary purpose is to solicit our consent for policies that do not benefit the U.S. nor humanity. The righteous path to social, economic, and political justice can only be realized by accepting the truth.

Just like Dr. King, I can still dream of the nation I thought existed when I was a child that President Kennedy so vividly personified to the world. Otherwise, I fear as Thomas Jefferson did when he contemplated how the stain of Slavery would be judged by our creator. He lamented, "I tremble for my country when I reflect that God is just; that his justice cannot sleep forever."

CHAPTER 13
A Bitter Harvest (The Perfidious Manipulation of History)

James Garrison the former besieged District Attorney for New Orleans in the 1960s and early 1970s ardently asserted in 1967 that, "The United States Constitution, assuming that it has not accidentally been burned to a crisp, does not give anyone (or agency) the power to re-write history." His comment was made in the context of the Kennedy assassination and how the Warren Commission and its apologists were attempting to obfuscate and manipulate the facts to cover up a conspiracy that involved rogue government officials – primarily associated or employed by the CIA – while implanting in the history books the fictitious narrative of Lee Harvey Oswald's culpability for this transformative tragedy. Implicit in his observation is that the integrity of our history is essential to accurately preserve our cultural identity as individuals and a people so that we can learn from our prior mistakes and celebrate our national triumphs.

The veracity of our historical narrative may seem like some academic endeavor relegated to discussions in our institutions of higher learning but that view only culminates in the ignorant conclusion that history is not relevant to our present reality. This is a dangerous perspective that many within the power elite have encouraged as they remake our past so that it comports with their world view. And it is for this reason, we must defend the integrity of our history so that it reflects the truth and not the insidious views of those who want to maintain their power. As author George Orwell wrote in his dystopian novel "1984", those who control the past will control our future and those elements of our society that dominate our present will control our past. Orwell also avowed, "The most effective way to destroy a people is to deny and obliterate their own understanding of their history."

The Kennedy family has contributed significantly to our national heritage over the last 100 years since Mayor "Honey Fitz" dominated the politics of Boston in the early twentieth century. He was President Kennedy's maternal grandfather. Even though their family and most particularly JFK and RFK have been admired by millions around the globe, they have been the victims of many pejorative myths most often promoted by their most fervent enemies and by scandalous writers attempting to get wealthy by smearing their family. Many historians and journalists by accepting these narratives have unwittingly kept these malicious lies alive, ignoring the facts that eradicate their validity. Some of

The Hidden War

these attacks on the family are enmeshed in half-truths that are exaggerated to such an extent that these perfidious stories also distort history. The objectives by some is to disparage their character to such an extent so that their deaths, although tragic, would be perceived as inconsequential because these men were ruthless narcissists that used people for their own quest for sex and power.

This is evident in the claims that Joseph P. Kennedy, Sr. (JPK) made some of his wealth as a bootlegger during prohibition and as a result of his contacts during this period would later make a secret accord with Chicago mob boss Sam Giancana to steal the state of Illinois from Nixon which aided his son's ascension to the White House. Although there are some disturbing witness accounts and assertions that need to be further examined to determine their validity, there presently exists significant research that disprove the above referenced assertions. As pointed out by Nobel prize winning historian, Arthur Schlesinger, Jr., in his article in 1998 entitled the "The Truth as I see It", he wrote that the allegations that JPK was involved in bringing liquor into the country during Prohibition and as a result became associated with organized crime is not consistent with the facts. Schlesinger penned that Richard Whalen in his book "Founding Father" published in 1964 made no mention of bootlegging in that biography. In addition, he cited Professor of Temple University Mark Haller's comprehensive review of all bootleggers listed within the intelligence files of the U.S. Coast Guard found "no mention or reference" to JPK anywhere in the documents. He further pointed out that when Kennedy, Sr. was appointed by President Franklin Roosevelt to head the Security and Exchange Commission, the Maritime Commission or when he was appointed as Ambassador to the Court of St. James he would have been thoroughly vetted prior to his confirmation by the Senate. If the FBI or the Senate had found evidence that he was bootlegging in the 1920s in violation of the 18th Amendment of the Constitution, he would have been denied these very important posts or would have had to withdraw his name.

Prohibition was subsequently repealed in 1933 by the 21^{rst} Amendment. Schlesinger concedes that JPK was involved in shipping whiskey to the U.S. in the 1930s, but this was a time when it was legal to do so.

Robert F. Kennedy, Jr. in his book entitled "American Values" also confronts the claims that his grandfather was a "bootlegging confederate of Al Capone and Frank Costello during Prohibition." He corroborates Schlesinger's assertion that Kennedy, Sr. had purchased with the assistance of FDR's son Jimmy

A Bitter Harvest (The Perfidious Manipulation of History)

Roosevelt the British company White Horse Scotch and Dimple Pinch just as Prohibition was ending. He indicated further that historian David Nasaw who had written a comprehensive biography on his grandfather entitled "The Patriarch" published in 2012 emphatically wrote, "Kennedy neither imported nor sold any liquor during his years in Brookline (Mass.) or at any time during Prohibition." In addition, Nora Ephron in preparation for her book on the history of the liquor industry in which her research spanned several years before publishing her extensive volume stated, "It's not true (bootlegging allegation). And I happen to be an expert on this subject. No one seems to care about (the truth) but me..."

It has been established by researchers that former CIA officer Sam Halpern was the primary source of the allegations of bootlegging, Nazi appeaser claims, illegally fixing the 1960 election with the mob's assistance and the Kennedys involvement in the Castro assassination plots. Halpern was the executive assistant to Desmond FitzGerald and had been employed by the CIA since the early 1950s. In 1961, he worked with FitzGerald and Deputy Director of Operations Richard Bissell on various plots to overthrow the Castro regime in Cuba. As was the case for other CIA operatives such as David Sanchez Morales, E. Howard Hunt, William Harvey and David Atlee Phillips, his intense hatred of the Kennedys began in the aftermath of the disastrous Bay of Pigs operation. In an interview in 1997, Halpern did concede that there existed widespread hostility (within the Agency) in 1963 towards JFK. What struck the interviewer, however, was his "insistence on voicing a certain contempt for JFK and his brother. His tone and body language said it all. JFK had it coming."

He was not the only CIA officer involved in spreading these malicious lies to smear the Kennedys. John Dean, who broke ranks with the Nixon administration and testified before Congress on Watergate, recounted that when he opened E. Howard Hunt's office safe that he found forged documents falsely implicating President Kennedy for the Diem assassination. The former Counterintelligence Chief James Jesus Angleton of the CIA was also implicated in spreading falsehoods to undermine the Kennedy legacy and to divert investigators from discovering the CIA's capacious associations to Kennedy's alleged killer Lee Harvey Oswald. RFK, Jr., however, asserted that Halpern encouraged the most vicious claims hurled at his family and that most of the assaults on their reputation "were all the pap of Halpern's fabrications."[94]

The primary focus of the myths against his grandfather appear to have been aimed at his uncle, Jack Kennedy. It was an attempt to smear him after his death to taint his legacy and delegitimize his presidency, as well as the origin of their family's wealth.[95]

The other prominent lie was the claim that Kennedy, Sr. had made a secret alliance with Chicago mob boss Sam Giancana to steal the state of Illinois to help his son win the election. As Schlesinger indicates in his article, the state of Illinois was not that crucial to Kennedy's 1960 victory. Even if Nixon had taken that state, Kennedy still would have won by 276 to 246 in the electoral college. It may be true that Mayor Richard Daley stole votes in Chicago, but it was also a fact that the Republicans had stolen votes in the southern counties. Schlesinger also asserted that the state electoral board that was 4 to 1 Republican had unanimously certified the Kennedy electors.

This fictitious argument in favor of the secret alliance disintegrates once you examine the vote tallies and the history that proceeded this alleged agreement and the events that followed it. If you scrutinize the number of votes for Kennedy in counties that Giancana supposedly had influence, they are consistent with those that voted for Adlai Stevenson in 1952 and 1956. If there was an alliance, Giancana did not hold up his side of the bargain. As Schlesinger observed, why go to Giancana as opposed to Mayor Daley who was the "last of the great political bosses." In addition, Richard Nixon had far more connections with organized crime than the Kennedys. The Teamsters under Jimmy Hoffa were a great supporter of his which lasted well into his years in the White House when he commuted Hoffa's sentence in return for a $500,000 donation to his reelection campaign.

The actual history of the Kennedys and the mob was a combative and antagonistic one ever since Robert Kennedy was named the chief counsel for the Senate's Rackets Committee in 1957. His brother Jack was a prominent member on that committee which has also been referred to as the McClellan Committee. The purpose of this subcommittee was to investigate improper activities in organized labor and their management. It quickly became self-evident that organized crime had infiltrated the management of some of the labor unions most predominantly the Teamsters headed by Jimmy Hoffa. Hoffa was apparently using the Teamster's pension fund as a cash cow for other mob bosses to avail them of 0% and low interest loans for their business operations or even for their own personal use. The Hoffa cabal was also engaged in intimidation and other tactics which included murder to discourage and eliminate threats to his leadership.

A Bitter Harvest (The Perfidious Manipulation of History)

Robert Kennedy was appalled by this discovery and went after these mob bosses with a zealousness that impressed the members of the committee, the press, and the public. He appeared fearless as he cross examined these dangerous thugs that were subpoenaed to appear before the committee. He relentlessly combated with Jimmy Hoffa and others with such zeal that it made them squirm in their seats as their eyes fixated with hatred on their tormentor, the young attorney.

In one encounter, Bobby asked Giancana a question that clearly would have incriminated him if he had truthfully answered it. The mob boss after the query was posed leaned over to speak with his attorney and then laughed as he replied that he was pleading the 5th Amendment. Robert Kennedy acerbically observed, "I thought only little girls giggled, Mr. Giancana." On many occasions, Jack would join his brother in asking tough questions and making poignant observations.

After the committee had finished its work, Robert Kennedy helped write its final report that was not flattering to those who had testified before the committee. In addition, he wrote a book called "The Enemy Within" during the 1960 campaign that portrayed his father's so-called ally in the most "scorching and contemptuous way" according to Schlesinger.

As attorney general and with his brother's assent, he went after organized gangsters with such tenacity in ways that none of his predecessors and successors have ever done. The initiation of prosecutions filed against members of organized crime went up 400% to 800%, depending on the study, during his tenure as Attorney General. Sam Giancana for instance was under 24-hour surveillance by the FBI and was indicted multiple times and served 1 year in prison. The head of the New Orleans syndicate Carlos Marcello pursuant to an order made by Kennedy's Justice Department was abducted by U.S. immigration officials and deposited in a remote jungle in Guatemala. He eventually made his way back and reassumed his position in his criminal organization that encompassed the southern part of the country. Jimmy Hoffa would eventually be convicted of attempted bribery of a grand juror and sentenced to 15 years to a federal penitentiary in 1967. It is incredulous to believe that these mobsters would not have disclosed this secret alliance with the Kennedy Patriarch to discredit their nemesis, the Kennedy brothers, while they pursued their political careers.

President Kennedy was also the victim of many malicious accusations, lies, myths and exaggerations to smear his character, to undermine his legacy and

The Hidden War

obfuscate the motives for his assassination. These distortions of history include allegations that he was a fervent cold warrior, was obsessed with Cuba and ordered the assassination of Fidel Castro, was not a true liberal whose administration had diminutive legislative achievements and that he was essentially a narcissist playboy whose reckless personal life jeopardized our national interests and future. One critic wrote that Kennedy was "the biggest serial, mass fornicator and adulterer in the history of the White House." This of course is an outrageous embellishment of Kennedy's relationships with women. His claim that other Presidents did not engage in this behavior to the same extent as Kennedy is also false.

President Lyndon Johnson once bragged that he "had more women by accident than Kennedy had on purpose." There was an incident in which Lady Bird Johnson walked into the oval office only to find her husband on top of one of his secretaries on the couch. Johnson was furious that no one had warned him that she was nearby. After that occurrence, he had the Secret Service install a buzzer that they were to push to notify the President when she was heading his way. He told off colored jokes in mixed company and was known to slap women on their derriere in the White House. I would also be remiss if I did not mention President Clinton's salacious affairs or Trump's misogynistic behavior.

President Kennedy's failure to honor his wedding vows with his wife Jacqueline Kennedy is clearly disappointing and is a negative aspect of his character that should be examined. However, his relationship with women was far more complex and redeeming than many who have accepted these unfounded distortions have understood or have been willing to admit. For example, the sibling he was closest to was his sister Kathleen who was nick named "Kick." He confided with her on matters that he never shared with his parents and his other siblings. He was devastated when his sister died in a plane crash in 1948. Although he was a shy young man, he felt comfortable in the company of women and had many close relationships with the fairer sex of which some were sexual, and others were platonic.

Many who were employed in the White House during the Kennedy years were unaware of this component of his personal life. Schlesinger wrote that the voluminous claims of all the women Kennedy was to have bedded is an exaggeration. He observed that if all these allegations were true Kennedy would not have been able to lead his administration. Schlesinger wrote, "Kennedy was a hard-working fellow, concentrating intently on the problems at hand. At no point in my experience did his (alleged) preoccupation with women (apart from Caroline crawling around the oval office) interfere with his conduct of the public business." In fact, he was completely ignorant of the President's womanizing when Kennedy was alive. He added that this was true for many of his close friends as well. "Vague rumors" would float around from time to time according to Ben Bradlee, who was Kennedy's closest friend, but he was not privy to this aspect of his friend's personal life. Hugh Sidey of Time Magazine was shocked when he became aware of Kennedy's reported affairs.

Schlesinger further pointed out that history has shown little connection between personal morality and public conduct. He argued that Dr. King was not faithful to his wife and yet his moral leadership and courage inspired a movement for social, economic, and civil justice that was never as potent and as unified after his assassination. He asserted that Pol Pot of Cambodia was reportedly a faithful family man who murdered one million of his "fellow countrymen."

I would add that President Abraham Lincoln as a young man was introduced to brothels by his close friend Joshua Speed that he frequented to satisfy what was described by friends as his large libido.[96] I cannot imagine our nation surviving the great calamity of the Civil War and the eventual passage of the 13th Amendment that ended slavery without the moral leadership of President Lincoln.

Sigmund Freud taught us during the Victorian era when sexuality was not to be discussed in public, and women were completely clothed to prevent even the exposure of an ankle which was considered scandalous, is that human sexuality has a significant influence on our motivations and our behavior. The biological desire to procreate ingrained in our nature is only second to our will to live. It is an important part of what it is to be a human being. This is not to excuse President Kennedy's sexual endeavors but to place them in a proper context. Individuals with strong libidos or those that may have sexual addictions are not inherently evil or amoral, but in fact can be compassionate moral beings. We should all be thankful for instance that President Kennedy was in charge during the Cuban Missile Crisis and not John Foster Dulles the former Secretary of State in the Eisenhower administration who was a pious family man. He clearly because of his intense antipathy for the Soviets and Castro's Cuba would have bombed the missile sites that inevitably would have ushered in Armageddon.

The Hidden War

The women that worked in the White House during his administration had a much different view of him than the tabloid mentality of our media today. In Deborah Becker's article "The Women in Kennedy's White House" written in 2013, she reported that all of the women described Kennedy as a president "who deeply relied on them" and was a politician who acutely recognized the importance of women in the workplace. 75% of those employed in the White House during the Kennedy administration were women. These women wrote letters, coordinated media coverage, campaign logistics and some were involved in creating and organizing new government agencies. For instance, Marlo Orlando helped establish the Peace Corps.

All the women that were interviewed had fond memories of that time. Sue Mortensen Vogelsinger stated, "I was so happy being where I was, it was the most exciting job in the world." Barbara Gamarekian who worked in the White House Press Office and would later become a journalist for the New York Times reflected, "It brought back vivid memories (their reunion) of that happy, congested workplace where we all operated in arm's length of each other." They all agreed that working with Kennedy was "the best experience of their careers, and they thought they were helping usher in a new era of social enlightenment."

The women described Kennedy as "fiercely intelligent, charming and interested in their lives." Jill Cowan remarked that he "worked terribly hard..." Priscilla Wear stated in her oral history that the President's definition of happiness was consistent with the Greek philosophy as he referenced in a statement to the press. She remembered President Kennedy's response to a question posed at one of his heralded press conferences on whether the presidency provided him happiness. Kennedy replied that his definition of happiness was "The full use of your powers along lines of excellence" and to that extent Kennedy added that the presidency does provide a sense of fulfillment and happiness. Wear stated, "I think this really was his definition; he always tried to live up to it. In everything he did, there was always that 5% of extra effort." The interviewer than inquired, "That made the difference?" Wear replied, "Made the difference. Everything down to his personal friendships...another thing, he was always aware of the necessity of friends – really good loyal friends. He believed you could go through anything in life if you had your friends and your family behind you, and he'd do anything for his friends and family."

A Bitter Harvest (The Perfidious Manipulation of History)

Jill Cowan and Priscilla Wear were nicknamed "Fiddle" and "Faddle." Dallek in his biography of JFK entitled "An Unfinished Life" implied that these were Secret Service code names for sex kittens that fulfilled the sexual desires of the men of the New Frontier, including the President. Greg Parker in his research found these women to be extremely intelligent and knowledgeable about Kennedy's policies. He reported that the women were close confidant's to Jackie Kennedy and inferred that they would have to have been "sociopaths" to befriend her while bedding her husband. He asserted that Wear and Cowan were not the "bimbos" they have been portrayed as and that Dallek should be ashamed of himself for perpetuating this tawdry rumor. Cowan in a separate interview many years later confronted the rumor when she made it clear that Priscilla had already been nicknamed "Fiddle" prior to Cowan joining the Kennedy campaign. She was latter called "Faddle" because of their close relationship. They went everywhere together. This was another tabloid tale that became part of the Kennedy narrative that was accepted as fact even by respected mainstream historians who should have independently verified the matter.

Dallek was also the source that claimed that 19-year-old Mimi Alford was a White House intern when she had an affair with Kennedy. Parker pointed out that Gamarekian had asserted that there was no intern program during the Kennedy administration. She stated that Dallek was attempting to analogize this relationship with the Monica Lewinski scandal to sell books. She declared that the only intern at the time worked for Press Secretary Pierre Salinger, Nora Ephron, who would later become a script writer in Hollywood and a respected author. Mimi had written that she enjoyed her affair with Kennedy and that she would do it all over again if she could. The relationship was clearly consensual.

Ms. Ephron lamented after reading about all of Kennedy's illicit affairs that she must have been the only one that he did not make a pass at. In fact, all the women with exception to Alford were never privy to Kennedy's sexual liaisons and were treated with respect. He was described by many as a charming gentleman in their presence who genuinely appreciated their contributions to the New Frontier.

Becker in her article wrote that Kennedy's commission on women in the workplace was "extremely progressive" and way ahead of its time. The recommendations included in its final report was that there should be

The Hidden War

guaranteed maternity leave and subsidized daycare which still have not been enacted today.

Kennedy in an interview with commission chair Eleanor Roosevelt in 1962 commented on their work. He stated, "This is a great matter of great national concern, and in this society of ours we want to be sure that women are used as effectively as they can to provide a better life for our people…"

The President's Commission on the Status of Women was an advisory committee that was established in December of 1961. This commission was unique in that none of his successors or the administrations that proceeded him have ever formed anything like it to advance the rights of women. It was chaired by Mrs. Roosevelt until her death in 1962. It was composed of 26 members which included legislators and philanthropists who were women right activists. The primary purpose of the commission was to examine and document employment policies that were operating within the workplace and to make recommendations on how to form new policies that were more equitable. Their final report that was named after Esther Peterson who succeeded Roosevelt as chairperson was published in October of 1963.

They had determined that there was "widespread" discrimination against women in the workplace. For instance, women were paid 59% of the earnings that a male was paid doing the same job. The initial finding released earlier that year that highlighted wage discrimination was the impetus for The Equal Pay Act signed by President Kennedy on June 10, 1963. During the laws first decade, it has been determined that 171,000 female employees received back pay totaling an estimated $84 million. Both the commission and The Equal Pay Act were the foundation of much of the changes that occurred in the following decades that benefited and improved the conditions in which women worked.

I would be remiss if I did not confront one of the tawdrier myths that entailed the Kennedy brothers' alleged relationship with Hollywood starlet and sex symbol Marilyn Monroe. And more importantly, Bobby Kennedy's suspected culpability for her death in 1962. This mendacity asserts that President Kennedy had a brief fling that was followed up by his younger brother who fell in love with her. RFK was so enamored with the glamorous Monroe that he told her he was planning to divorce his wife so that they could pursue their intimate relationship. When RFK failed to honor that promise, Monroe allegedly threatened to announce their secret romance to the press. As this story has been repeated and embellished by Kennedy's detractors over the years, it has been suggested that he had her murdered to prevent her from revealing their secret.

This perfidious tale was only believed by those who were unaware of the strength of Bobby and Ethel's close relationship and his devout Catholic faith. He had a special bond with children that obviously was more profound with his own kids. In my opinion, he would not have left them for anyone. I am certain that those that were part of his inner circle would be unanimous in their agreement.

Marilyn at the end of her life was suffering from numerous health problems that included anxiety and insomnia. Dr. Ralph Greenson, her personal psychiatrist, had stated that his famous client had admitted to him that she was prescribed several medications from different doctors.

On August 5, 1962, she was found lifeless in her bed by Dr. Greenson who immediately called 911. The honorable Dr. Thomas Noguchi of the Los Angeles Coroner's Office, who would six years later administer the scrupulous autopsy of Robert Kennedy, performed her post-mortem examination. He determined that the cause of death was "acute barbiturate poisoning" as a result of a "probable suicide." After her death, there have been many conspiracy theories that have been promulgated by various dubious sources. Some of them have advanced the proposition that she was murdered by the Mafia and the CIA, as well as Robert Kennedy.

Gerald Blaine in his book co-authored by Lisa McCubbin entitled "The Kennedy Detail" rebuked this narrative as another myth that became part of President Kennedy's mystique and legend. Blaine pointed out that the Secret Service have a code that is vigorously enforced to protect the office of the president and the private lives of those that occupy it. He elaborated that because of this code those that become members of the presidential detail must remain silent "…in the face of rumor's even though the rumors are false."

One of those rumors as revealed above was Kennedy's alleged affair with Marilyn Monroe. Blaine adamantly avowed, after consulting with many other agents that were part of Kennedy's detail, including Clint Hill, that Kennedy had only met the highly lauded movie actress on two occasions during his presidency.

The first time was at a party held in Santa Monica at Peter and Pat Lawford's home who were his brother-in-law and sister. Peter Lawford was part of the Rat Pack which included Joey Bishop, Dean Martin, Sammy Davis, Jr. and of course the chairman of the board Frank Sinatra. He, therefore, knew Marilyn

The Hidden War

and many others in Hollywood, as well as Las Vegas, and on many occasions had parties at his home that included prominent members of the entertainment industry. Her presence at that gathering was on behest of Lawford not Kennedy. This brief encounter occurred in the summer of 1961 during one of Kennedy's visits to Los Angeles. It was at this event while reading a book on a chaise lounge chair that Kennedy spontaneously and without notice to his security swam out into the Pacific Ocean and when he returned to the beach was greeted by admirers that casually conversed with the President that was memorialized by a famous photograph.

The second meeting took place on May 19, 1962, at Madison Square Garden in New York City. This was a Democratic fund-raiser, celebrating the President's 45th birthday. Blaine was on duty that night and witnessed the "highlight of the evening" which was Monroe's sensual singing of "happy birthday" to the President in her provocative – if not "transparent body tight evening gown." Marilyn was also present at the reception at Kennedy's suite at the Carlyle Hotel that was attended by many of the Kennedy clan, including his brother Bobby.

Blaine concluded that he could not rule out the possibility that Kennedy had other telephonic contact with the actress, but he could confidently assert that these were the only two events in which they physically met.

The mainstream media, nevertheless, continue to portray this allegation as a fact. When pushed to justify their reports, they refer to tapes of Marilyn talking to her psychiatrist in which she briefly unveils her sexual relations with Jack and Bobby. What they never reveal is that these tapes have never been produced and that the only evidence that exists are notes written down by John Miner decades after he allegedly listened to them. As James DiEugenio has penned, many of his assertions in those notes pertaining to the iconic actress have been disputed by those who knew her. DiEugenio further elaborates that Miner was an Assistant District Attorney in Lose Angeles that participated in the Sirhan trial and was the executor of the estate of William Joseph Bryan who many have claimed programmed Sirhan to fire shots at Robert Kennedy in the pantry of the Ambassador Hotel that tragic night, as part of a larger conspiracy.

DiEugenio further writes in his essay, "Part II: Sy Hersh and the Monroe/JFK Papers: The History of a Thirty Year Hoax," that the origins of RFK's involvement with Monroe and her death first appeared in a pamphlet entitled "The Strange Death of Marilyn Monroe" that was written by Frank Capell who was described as an extreme right-winger that was associated with the John Birch Society. This absurd tale claimed that Bobby had her murdered by communist agents under his command because she had threatened to expose their policy of appeasement towards Castro's regime. This pamphlet was disseminated during RFK's New York senatorial campaign in 1964.

One of the prominent promoters of this narrative was journalist Walter Winchell who was a close friend of FBI Director J. Edgar Hoover and was also a known FBI asset. It is well documented that Hoover reviled the Kennedys and certainly did not grieve over their deaths.

William Sullivan was the former director of the FBI's security division that eventually became the third-ranking member in the Bureau behind Director Hoover and Associate Director Clyde Tolson. He was notoriously involved in the scurrilous letter and tape sent to Dr. King and his wife in 1964 that apprised him that his sexual dalliances captured in hotel rooms were on that tape. He contemptibly goaded him in that correspondence to commit suicide or his "degeneracies" would be circulated to the media. Sullivan obviously was no civil libertarian and was clearly not a King or a Kennedy admirer.

Sullivan noted that the dissemination of "Capell's invention was encouraged by Hoover." In fact, as written by DiEugenio, the FBI had RFK under surveillance for months, seeking any information they could use to blackmail him for political leverage or disparage his reputation. This was a common method employed by Hoover that had files on almost everyone who held a prominent position in government. Many in the congress feared him and complied with his legislative recommendations to avoid any retribution from his office. Thus, because of their shadowing of his activities, Sullivan was very familiar with Robert Kennedy's personal habits. Because none of their efforts caught him in any compromising perversions, he often in frustration referred to Kennedy in private as a "saint" or a "near-puritan." He divulged years after Bobby's death, "The stories about Bobby Kennedy and Marilyn Monroe were just stories. The original story was invented by a so-called journalist (Winchell), a right-wing zealot who had a history of spinning wild yarns. It spread like wildfire, of course, and J. Edgar Hoover was right there, gleefully fanning the flames."

As an aside, Sullivan was killed under suspicious circumstances, as well as 5 other FBI agents in a 6-month span before their scheduled testimony to the House Select Committee on Assassinations that was investigating the deaths of Dr. King and President Kennedy.

The Hidden War

It appears from all these insidious efforts to disparage President Kennedy and his brother's character by propagating these sexual depravities allegedly committed by them were primarily motivated to undermine their true legacy to eviscerate any notion that they were basically honorable men on an island in a sea of depraved warmongers and liars, vying for power. The objective was to encourage this fictitious narrative that Just like their adversaries they were willing to murder to maintain their secrets. This is essentially a common tactic to project onto your professed rival those same negative traits of the accuser.

The 1970s would not be kind to those that had opposed their policies and had even participated in the assassination of the Kennedy brothers. The revelations of Watergate, the Vietnam debacle and all the chicanery and crimes committed by the intelligence community as unveiled by the Church and Pike Committees was a reality that had to be rewritten. For the inevitable comparison of these clandestine operatives, and the political power they worked for, to the liberal icons that the Kennedys had become, clearly would not be arbitrated favorably for them by the judgment of history; but more importantly, by the House Select Committee on Assassinations that was formed later that decade as a consequence of all these dark revelations. Accordingly, the Kennedy brothers' memory and legacy had to be drastically humbled such that their murders were irrelevant and meaningless, and that they were just as culpable for the sleaze that the investigators of the 1970s were dredging up from the swamp of surreptitious power wielded within the high political enclaves of Washington that had appallingly gone awry.

All the above demonstrates that President Kennedy's verified relationships with women were far more complex than reported and that his legacy is incredibly positive from the perspective of women's rights in the workplace and their changing roles in our society. Every woman that had an affair with Kennedy truly admired the man and were saddened by his death. Mary Pinchot Meyer for instance was devastated and had always suspected he was murdered by a conspiracy the Warren Commission covered up. She maintained this belief until her suspicious death in 1964.

DiEugenio in his research uncovered many of the women that were a part of Kennedy's social circles. Charlotte McDonnell, for instance, who was a friend of JFK for many years revealed that their relationship was purely platonic. Another one of Kennedy's dalliances, Angela Greene, reported that he was never physically aggressive or offensive, just "sweet and adorable." There was also an incident with an intimate partner that reported an evening with "Jack" when in frustration she threw him out of her apartment for jumping out of her bed to listen to a news bulletin on the radio. In addition, His wife Jackie Kennedy adored him and missed his wit, charm, and affection for the rest of her life.

The interview she gave to LOOK magazine in 1964 on the anniversary of her husband's murder indisputably displays her devotion and affection for President Kennedy. She graciously described, "It is nearly a year since he has gone. On so many days – his birthday, anniversary, watching his children running to the sea – I have thought, 'but this day last year was his last to see that.' He was so full of love and life on all those days. He seems so vulnerable now when you think that each one was a last time. Soon the final day will come around again – as inexorably as it did last year. But expected this time.

It will find some of us different people than we were a year ago. Learning to accept what was unthinkable when he was alive, changes you. I don't think there is any consolation. What was lost cannot be replaced.

Someone who loved President Kennedy, but who had never known him, wrote to me this winter: 'The hero comes when he is needed. When our belief gets pale and weak, there comes a man out of that light – and stores some up against the time when he is gone.'

Now I think that I should have known that he was magic all along. I did know it – but I should have guessed it could not last. I should have known that it was asking too much to dream that I might have grown old with him and see our children grow up together.

So now he is a legend when he would have preferred to be a man, I must believe that he does not share our suffering now. I think for him – at least he will never know whatever sadness might have lain ahead. He knew such a share of it in his life that it always made you so happy whenever you saw him enjoying himself. But now he will never know more – not age, not stagnation, nor despair, nor crippling illness, nor loss of any more people he loved. His high noon kept all freshness of the morning – and he died then, never knowing disillusionment."

She then quoted poetry "…he has gone…among the radiant, ever venturing on, somewhere, with morning, as such spirits will." She lamented that "He is free, and we must live. Those who love him most know that 'death you have dealt is more than the death which has swallowed you.'"

The Hidden War

This certainly is not the ruminations of a wife, nor other women who knew him, that describe a narcissistic serial fornicator that used women purely to satisfy his insatiable lust.

Kennedy's domestic policies and legislative achievements have also been misrepresented over the decades to such an extent that most progressives would not list his presidency as a liberal administration. The Democratic platform of 1960, his administration's initiatives and Kennedy's personal views on the issues that confronted his presidency on the home-front contradict this fallacious narrative.

Irving Bernstein published a comprehensive analysis of Kennedy's domestic policies and his legislative record in his volume "Promises Kept" which was published in 1992. He was at the time an Emeritus Professor of Political Science at the University of California in Los Angeles. He proffered that "the most significant yardstick for measuring the President's effectiveness is qualitative, examining carefully his performance on important issues." It is also paramount to understand Kennedy's personal views on these matters and to what extent did he pursue them as he issued executive orders; the actions his cabinet enacted to advance his agenda; and the type of legislation that he introduced and supported that was being considered on Capitol Hill.

Bernstein submitted that there were three categories in which you could classify the importance of specific pieces of legislation. In tier one of Kennedy's legislative agenda, this encompassed his push for civil rights, his tax cut, aid for education and Medicare. Kennedy in order to get passage of this agenda had several hurdles to overcome. All these areas were controversial at the time and required large Democratic majorities in favor of the administration's agenda to get the votes necessary for such an innovative progressive program to get enacted.

Kennedy had defeated Richard Nixon in the 1960 election by the slimmest of margins. He faced a Congress that was significantly influenced by conservative segregationist Democrats from the south that when joined by the Republicans were able to block aggressive civil right legislation among other bills that enhanced and amended FDR's New Deal or challenged the status quo. Kennedy observed as he quoted Jefferson that, "Great innovations should not be forced on slender majorities."

This was one of many reasons why Kennedy and his brother Bobby decided to delay submitting civil right legislation until they could build a stronger majority in Congress. In lieu of legislation, Robert Kennedy filed more lawsuits supporting civil and voting rights utilizing laws already on the books in less than 3 years than the Eisenhower administration did in two full terms. Kennedy also issued executive orders that directed federal agencies to hire blacks and desegregate their facilities. He approved for instance executive order 10925 that created The Committee on Equal Employment Opportunity to promote fair employment practices in the federal agencies and among government contractors which was headed by Vice President Johnson. By doing so, as DiEugenio has pointed out, became the origin of "affirmative action" programs.

In addition, the Interstate Commerce Commission which was influenced by the Freedom Rider protests and pressure brought upon them by RFK's Justice Department made Jim Crow practices illegal in interstate transportation.

His administration integrated the University of Mississippi by backing the admission of James Meredith in 1962. President Kennedy also ordered that the U.S Coast Guard recruit more minorities when he observed in the parade at his inauguration no black representation among their ranks. He also advocated for an anti-poll tax amendment which was approved by congress in 1962. This resulted in the ratification of the 24th Amendment in 1964.

This clearly was a more robust program than those supported by his predecessors. Nevertheless, his failure in the first two years to submit comprehensive legislation to ameliorate the injustices perpetrated by segregation in the south and discriminatory policies throughout the nation was disappointing. However, as Bernstein pointed out, "In my view this reasoning, while morally questionable, was politically unassailable."[97]

Kennedy after watching news footage of Commissioner Bull Connor's officers unleashing the dogs and the fire hoses on peaceful protestors in Birmingham, and after U.S. Marshalls backed by federalized national guardsmen had pushed aside Governor Wallace's last attempt to block the integration of the University of Alabama, had decided that he could not justify waiting any longer and submitted the most comprehensive civil rights bill to Congress since the Civil War. He addressed the nation from the Oval Office on June 11, 1963, and delivered one of the most eloquent speeches on Civil Rights that any president has ever given with exception to a speech orated by President Obama after a young racist named Dylann Roof had unleashed his fury on unsuspecting participants in a Bible class. Kennedy did this with the knowledge that this act could cost him his bid for reelection in 1964.

The March on Washington also fell victim to revisionism when it was routinely espoused by journalists and historians that the Kennedy brothers

The Hidden War

never supported it and had made a concerted effort to discourage Dr. King and his followers from organizing this event that was originally planned to be staged in front of the Capitol and then the Washington Monument. Once again this was an example of a half-truth that was distorting the factual record to fit their bias perspective. Although President Kennedy was concerned that this protest could alienate moderate congressmen, whose votes he desperately needed to pass his Civil Rights bill, he never expressed any threats to use his power as President to squash it. Once he and his brother realized that Dr. King and his inner circle would not be dissuaded, they decided to change gears and to make sure that the march was successful. The first thing they did was to convince King to relocate the event to the front steps of the Lincoln Memorial which was easier to provide adequate security, as well as providing a more relevant backdrop that was consistent with the messages that would be conveyed on that auspicious day.[98]

Robert Kennedy once the location was agreed upon began to work behind the scenes to beef up security, provide adequate food and refreshments and portable restrooms for what was anticipated to be a large crowd. He also invited as many Caucasian friends as he could to ensure that the spectators reflected a diverse gathering that would be present to hear the speeches scheduled that day. President Kennedy even read some of the initial drafts for their orations and provided cogent advice on language that could cost votes for the bill.

As the March on Washington bloomed into the magnificent event that history recorded, Kennedy stood while gripping the windowsill on the third-floor White House Solarium as he listened to the speeches through an open window when he exclaimed to the "Mansion's courtly black doorman" that, "Oh, Bruce, I wish I were out there with them!"[99] When the event had successfully ended, Kennedy had invited all those who were responsible for organizing the march to visit him in the Oval Office. Kennedy was incredibly pleased with how it turned out and was quite impressed by King's inspiring oration. He reached out and shook the preacher's hand while simultaneously stating that, "I have a dream!"[100]

Kennedy as a Senator from Massachusetts and while he was rehabilitating from back surgery had written his critically acclaimed book "Profiles in Courage" which was about leaders who "sailed with the wind until the decisive moment when their conscience, and events, propelled them into the center of

A Bitter Harvest (The Perfidious Manipulation of History)

the storm."[101] The Kennedy brothers were now fully in the vortex of the storm of civil rights and were determined to see it through until justice was done.

Kennedy's second tier of legislation was passed prior to his assassination. Many of these bills were to assist economic development in depressed areas such as Appalachia and to develop training programs to prepare American workers for the technological developments and challenges of the 1960s. He also signed legislation that promoted fair wage practices and supported collective bargaining rights for federal employees. The legislative bills he signed included the Area Redevelopment Act, The Manpower Development and Training Act, a minimum wage bill that extended coverage to millions of workers, and I would add The Equal Pay Act to this list as well.

This tier also included legislation to confront health care educational costs and the construction of facilities that permitted family members with mental health challenges to receive treatment in clinics closer to their home communities. The legislation that he signed that addressed the above issues encompassed The Health Profession Educational Act and The Mental Health Facilities and Community Health Centers Construction Act.

The Peace Corps legislation that provided for its funding was also part of this second tier.

Unemployment and welfare benefits were also enhanced and expanded by his administration to confront the social ills of poverty. For instance, the Aid for Dependent Children (ADC) created under the Social Security Act of 1935 was augmented financially and extended to adults caring for dependent children. The program was renamed Aid to Families with Dependent Children (AFDC) in 1962 to address concerns that the original program was unintentionally discouraging marriage. The recipients of AFDC benefits could extend as long as the family qualified under the act. Over the years the program grew as millions received financial support from this important program.

AFDC was a $24 billion-dollar program just prior to President Clinton's Personal Responsibility and Work Opportunity Act which was signed by him in 1996. This legislation is commonly referred to as The Welfare Reform Act. This new law drastically restructured how AFDC was administered and managed. For example, families with dependent children who qualified for benefits were limited to 5 years. He also cut substantially the amount of federal funds that were allocated to support the programs administered by the state governments. Millions of children were unceremoniously removed from this program whose families still needed it. This created a false impression that the numbers of people who qualified for it had decreased. The reality as reported in an article by Digital Journal was that a new study had concluded that 1 in 5 children in the U.S. live in poverty and millions are malnourished. They further asserted that more children were suffering from the degradation of poverty today than existed during the Great Recession of 2008. President Kennedy would surely have been appalled by the draconian restructuring of his once vital and robust program to assist children and their families from the ravages of poverty.

JFK's educational initiatives accounted for 33% of his bills that were debated in Congress. He was a staunch supporter in funding programs that modernized our academic infrastructure, enhanced our support for teachers and financially assisted those who wanted to pursue professional degrees. Scholarships and student loans were enlarged substantially during his administration. This included funds for libraries, school lunch programs, funds to teach the deaf, mentally ill and those that were handicapped. The Office of Education declared that the Kennedy years was "the most significant legislative period in its hundred-year history."[102]

Larry O'Brien, Kennedy's legislative liaison, in frustration over the media's failure to acknowledge the administration's legislative successes stated, "On balance I thought our 1961 record was a good one, even an outstanding one." Bernstein indicated that the President had submitted and backed 53 bills of which 33 had been enacted by Congress. Kennedy had signed more legislation than President Eisenhower had done in the final 6 years of his administration.[103] The major newspapers, however, continued to publish editorials that portrayed Kennedy's legislative agenda as a failure. It was true that his Medicare and his educational bill were defeated, but this was a myopic view of a much bigger story that was generally ignored. When Kennedy asked Theodore Sorensen his special assistant to brief the media on the inaccuracy of their reporting, the President was accused of attempting to manipulate and manage the press.[104]

This same disconnect with the media and reality as it related to Kennedy's legislative success occurred in 1962 and 1963. O'Brien opined that they had a very impressive record in 1962. He asserted that Congress passed 40 out of 54 bills that the administration had proposed. Once again, the failure to pass Medicare was the focus of the media. In 1963, 58 "must" bills were sent to Capitol Hill and 35 had been approved. O'Brien later wrote, "A myth had arisen

A Bitter Harvest (The Perfidious Manipulation of History)

that he (Kennedy) was uninterested in Congress, or that he 'failed' with Congress."[105]

The truth of the matter was that Kennedy had a very impressive record with the Congress. Each year as his knowledge of his office increased and as his confidence grew, his ability to persuade legislative leaders to champion his agenda improved. James L. Sundquist in his analysis of the 88th Congress stressed the legislative importance of the third year of any administration. The year of 1963 in his assessment of the Kennedy presidency is that all the major bills pending in Congress prior to Kennedy's assassination had significant support on Capitol Hill. This was the result of several factors. One of the more prominent reasons had been the consequence of Kennedy's successful campaign to get more liberal Democrats elected in the 1962 mid-term elections. Normally, the party in power suffer significant losses in these elections, but Kennedy's popularity and high approval rating gave a boost to his party that ushered in more Democrats who favored his agenda.

The President after the Cuban Missile Crisis was more confident and passionate in his support of his agenda that also had a positive impact on congressional leaders. Sundquist observed, "The considerable progress of the Kennedy program prior to November...suggests strongly that most of what happened would have happened – more slowly, perhaps, but ultimately – if Kennedy had lived."[106] This inference was also supported by legislators from both parties in a survey that was taken in the 1960s and in interviews that many had given over the years since Kennedy's death.

Donald Gibson who had a Ph. D. in sociology from the University of Delaware – whose research on economics and political power had spanned 15 years prior to publishing his authoritative book entitled "Battling Wall Street" (The Kennedy Presidency) in 1994 – opined that the primary objective of Kennedy's economic program was the advancement of the productive powers of the nation. This progress was to be achieved by expanding and improving human and technological capabilities of the country.[107] Gibson asserted that, "Throughout his presidency, Kennedy was committed, in words and action, to a higher level of sustained national economic growth."[108]

He further proffered that Kennedy's overall tax plan and reforms were "tactical measures to further economic investment and growth." His ultimate objective was to discourage the flow of money and credit from short-term, speculative, and non-productive investments and redirect them to long term capital and technological enhancements to augment production that would benefit the workers and the nation, not just a few investors and high-ranking executives. He intended to achieve this by eliminating tax advantages for those wealthy individuals and corporations that were diverting large sums of money to low-tax countries or other tax havens to avoid paying taxes that the nation needed. Kennedy also proposed to repeal all tax breaks for corporations that financed foreign investment companies abroad and to prevent wealthy individuals who were transferring large sums of money outside the U.S. to avoid paying estate taxes. In 1963, much to the consternation of the oil and gas industry, Kennedy proposed to terminate the oil depletion allowance that subsidized this sector of the economy with taxpayer money and provided tax credits that substantially reduced their tax burden. He also submitted the Tax Revenue Act that cut taxes across the board to stimulate economic expansion. In defense of his progressive tax cut that primarily benefitted the middle class he stated, "A rising tide lifts all the boats." The purpose of these reforms was to benefit the nation, as well as providing support for small businesses, underdeveloped countries and those trapped in poverty.

Kennedy's economic program was partially inspired by FDR's second bill of rights he proposed in a speech in 1944. President Roosevelt wanted to make it a right for every citizen to have a home, a job and health care and not be subject to the callous whims of the markets which caused the Great Depression of the 1930s. Gibson argued that, "Kennedy's program not only amended but went further than Roosevelt's statement of goals to an actual program to achieve these (laudable) goals."[109]

President Kennedy was an ardent admirer of the republic that our founders had created. He was intensely committed to the well-being of the nation over special interests that jeopardized the health of our democratic republic. He believed that our role in international affairs was as an exemplary nation that by its moral standing and innovative programs would lead the world by our example. As Gibson wrote, "His policies were intended to preserve and enhance the economic position of the U.S. in the world economy. He did not, however, view the progress of the United States as in any way at odds with the progress of other nations, nor did he seek such progress for the purpose of world domination." A view clearly at odds with those held today by neocons and neoliberals that support this concept of American exceptionalism which justifies U.S. exploitation and authority over other nations to benefit corporate and U.S. hegemonic power.

Gibson continued, "His goals for other nations and other peoples were completely consistent with his goals for the United States, even if his capacity to affect global trends was more limited...His foreign policy was an extension of his domestic policy, even though the ambiguities of particular situations rendered clear and consistent action difficult."[110]

Kennedy fervently believed that the president was the primary defender of "the public good and public interest against all the narrow private interests which operate in our society." Kennedy added, "Only a president who recognizes the true nature of this hard challenge can fulfill this historic function."[111]

A poignant example of this was his courageous stand to defend the interests of the nation in the Steel Crisis of 1962 against a handful of powerful steel executives whose desire for power and profit jeopardized the interests of 180 million Americans. It is hard to imagine any of our chief executives in recent decades confronting the corporate power that the steel industry represented in the early 1960s in the defense of the residents of Main Street America. For instance, in 2008, the Wall Street gurus crashed the economy and instead of prosecuting them we gave them hundreds of billions of dollars of taxpayer money to save them from their own avarice that contributed to the disaster.

Amongst the achievements of Kennedy's administration was the expansion of unemployment benefits, aid to our cities to improve housing and mass transit programs, investments in our national highway system, water pollution control act to protect the country's rivers and streams, and an act to augment farmer incomes. There were programs to ameliorate the effects of poverty and to increase Social Security benefits and an upsurge in our nation's minimum wage. In fact, workers were now permitted to seek early retirement at age 62. There was the passage of significant aid to depressed areas and food stamp programs were reintroduced. The pilot programs he authorized led to the modern food stamp program we have today.

Theodore White an American journalist and historian observed that during Kennedy's abbreviated administration there was more legislation approved and signed into law than any other time since the 1930s. In short, JFK's legislative record from 1961 through to November of 1963 was the best of any President since FDR's first term.

The legislation that was pending when he was assassinated comprised of the Civil Right Act, Medicare, Immigration Reform, the Tax Revenue Act, a major educational bill, and anti-poverty proposals. Most of the Great Society under

The Hidden War

President Johnson were Kennedy programs and initiatives. I cannot think of any administration since Kennedy that had a more progressive agenda and vision for our nation.

President Kennedy's foreign policy was also an anomaly not witnessed since his assassination. His overall objective was to end the Cold War, negotiate arms reduction accords with the ultimate objective of dismantling our nuclear arsenals, to support third world countries in their quest for independence, to seek rapprochement with Castro's Cuba, to pivot towards Nasser's Egypt and away from the dictatorship of Saudi Arabia, neutralize Laos and to withdraw from Vietnam. His goal was to build a world governed by law not power and a nation that was revered for its moral restraint and support of liberty. A nation that championed peace as our ultimate objective and by understanding our adversaries was willing to live peacefully in global diversity. Researcher Lisa Pease concluded in her article entitled "President Kennedy's Foreign Policy" in which she wrote for Progressive Historians in 2008, "Show me a better foreign policy than that."

While Ted Sorenson was organizing the final draft in what would become Kennedy's peace speech he would deliver on June 10, 1963, Kennedy and the first lady had decided to invite John Kenneth Galbraith back for another private dinner at the White House in May. Galbraith had returned to Washington as his last official duty as Ambassador to India. He had watched the young president grow in office and move in a direction he enthusiastically supported. Kennedy at dinner talked quite extensively about the contents of the speech that he intended to deliver at the commencement ceremony at American University just weeks away. He also talked about his vision for the future. Kennedy while discussing these matters asked if Galbraith would accept the Ambassadorship for the Soviet Union. Galbraith had declined in that he was looking forward to writing and teaching back at Harvard. Since that night and for the rest of his life, he reflected on that offer and had internally pondered whether he had made a mistake by rejecting Kennedy's proposition.[112]

Galbraith as he listened to the young President articulate his vision for peace thought to himself how pleased he was that Kennedy had rejected the advice of his national security team. He understood how powerful these groups were that would oppose the President's plan and solemnly remembered how Roosevelt's post war vision and domestic priorities were thwarted after his death. He, nevertheless, that night over dinner with cigars and brandy, thought of what could be achieved and how different the world could be if Kennedy's vision was realized. He thought to himself that this young vigorous President was only halfway through his first term and that he felt confident he would win in 1964. With 6 years ahead of him, Galbraith was full of hope that this would become the presidency he had longed for.[113]

Just several months later, Kennedy was dead and just like FDR before him his vision was shoved aside as we began to build up for war in Vietnam. Everything Kennedy had been planning was reversed with exception to his domestic agenda that would become Johnson's Great Society. All that remains is his memory and the eternal flame that flickers in the wind above the young President's permanent resting place, reminding anyone who knew the truth that relentlessly haunts them as they contemplated what might have been.

Jackie Kennedy after witnessing the horror of Dallas derided the "bitter old men" that wrote history by asserting that her husband should have his rightful place in American history. She stated to author Theodore White in earnest that, "History made Jack what he was." She continued, "This little boy, sick so much of the time, reading in bed." She affectionately added "Jack" believed that "History was full of heroes." His life, therefore, should be studied by "other little boys" seeking heroes amongst the stories that make history so readable and inspiring.[114]

Although President Kennedy had his faults, as all human beings do, he clearly was a good man that became a hero for our generation. And if the past can be accurately revised to reflect what Lincoln referred to as the "mystic chords of memory", he can be admired for what he accomplished and for what he stood for in all generations to come. And the Kennedy family should also be honored for what they exemplify which is a wealthy family with power that stood by the oppressed, the disadvantaged and the common worker even when it was not politically advantageous to do so or when powerful elements in our society opposed them. They have been over the decades devoted defenders of our Constitution and our republic even while elements of our government murdered members of their family.

The insidious nature of the perfidious lies and myths directed at President Kennedy to minimize his administration's accomplishments or the erasure of what he was striving for was a deliberate revision of our history. The objective was to paint Kennedy as a rabid cold warrior who used people to satisfy his lust and political ambitions, as well as to obfuscate the motive for his assassination. If Kennedy was all image and no substance, and his brothers and the origin of their family's wealth were just as corrupt as any affluent family with power,

The Hidden War

then politics surely could not be proclaimed as some honorable adventure as described by him. And just maybe the cynics were right that everyone is shady, and that politics is nothing more than pigs wallowing in the mud of their unmitigated deception. Just maybe, we should concede that we cannot make a difference by participating in social movements no matter how righteous their cause because in the end these movements are powerless to effectuate positive change in our nation. This is the inevitable conclusion many will discern if this history remains the narrative that is memorialized in our textbooks and taught to our children.

The veracity of our historical memory is not some utopian ideal but a living and working reality for any nation to accurately understand the values, the disasters and the triumphs that comprise their story. The leaders that were propelled into the center of the storm and when summoned rose to meet the challenges that faced their generation are to be revered by observing the truth - for their story is part of our national memory that should be sacred for all of us as a people.

The cumulative consequences for this menacing narrative are to portray JFK and RFK's assassinations, although admittedly tragic, as meaningless random events of two politicians that were irrelevant. And even if they were killed by conspiracies, it really doesn't matter. All of this encourages us to be further repulsed and alienated by the politics of our nation so that we leave it to the power elite who claim to know what is best. The real story of courage and hope for a better country and a more peaceful world that the Kennedys truly represented is buried by this false history so that we remain ignorant of our real past and discouraged by our lack of control over our future.

The seeds of deception that were planted on that tragic day when the glow of the New Frontier went dark has been a bitter harvest to say the least. We are no longer that nation that Kennedy so admired and risked his life for in World War II, nor are we the republic the founders created. The soil that could have given birth to a far better nation has been poisoned to such an extent that no matter what is grown in it will not sustain life, liberty, or the pursuit of happiness.

We can change this by reclaiming our history and by demanding the truth. We owe it to the Kennedys, our children, our nation and to our fellow human beings around the globe. As President Kennedy orated, "Our problems are manmade; Therefore, they can be solved by man. And man can be as big as he wants. No problem of human destiny is beyond human beings." If we desire to recapture that national spirit, we first need to get control of our present, so we can defend the integrity of our American narrative that should encompass the good and the bad, as well as the imperfect heroes that attempted to fulfill our national ideals in order to build a better country that we all could be proud of.

CHAPTER 14
Has Capitalism revealed its Innate Flaw?

We all have an instinctual impression that something is rotten in our political and economic national system. We can feel it in our gut and for most live the reality that many pundits in our corporate media minimize or have even denied. They spew out job numbers and an upsurge in our Gross Domestic Product (GDP) or the rising stock market as though these numbers have relevance to the average worker. The stock market for example reached historic highs in (2019) until losses due to poor economic news caused significant drops. And yet, all this had minimal impact on wages.

These market fluctuations are financial indicators that the wizards of Wall Street use as a guide to determine market trends and our national economic stability. These markets that are nothing more than sanctioned gambling casinos that capitalists and some of our citizens risk everything to enhance their financial portfolios. For most, it is cost prohibitive to participate in because of the potential risks involved. A major drop in the market for instance could financially ruin a small investor while major players hold their own, and in some cases increase their wealth, benefitting from their diverse investments.

The Trump administration tout increased job creation numbers much the same way President Obama did as proof that their policies are working, and our economy is growing. They of course do not discuss the limitations of these numbers, and the reality they fail to capture for those who reside on Main Street. These numbers for instance do not reveal the quality of those jobs or whether most of them provided a livable wage with benefits.

The statistics for example may indicate that 100,000 jobs were created that prior month which would appear to be a positive development until you get down into the weeds and examine these numbers. The ugly reality that would be uncovered is that many of these jobs were part time and that most were unskilled jobs with poor wages and no benefits. This examination would also reveal that many who were hired had taken jobs that paid much less than the job that was outsourced to another country.

The Gross Domestic Product (GDP) is also a misleading economic indicator if not coupled with other positive factors. For instance, the GDP may grow significantly while most wages remain stagnant and many are jobless. It, therefore, can be a poor measure of how well our nation is performing economically as pointed out by Senator Robert F. Kennedy in his 1968 campaign. He stated, "Too much and too long, we seem to have surrendered community excellence and community values in the mere accumulation of material things. Our gross national product (now referred to as GDP) ...if we should judge America by that – counts air pollution and cigarette advertising, and ambulances to clear our highways of carnage. It counts special locks for our doors and the jails for those who break them. It counts the destruction of our redwoods and the loss of our natural wonder in chaotic sprawl. It counts napalm and the cost of nuclear warheads, and armored cars for police who fight riots in our streets. It counts Whitman's rifle and Speck's knife, and the television programs which glorify violence in order to sell toys to our children." He then pointed out, "Yet the gross national product does not allow for the health of our children, the quality of their education, or the joy of their play. It does not include the beauty of our poetry or the strength of our marriages; the intelligence of our public debate or the integrity of our public officials. It measures neither our wit nor our courage; neither our wisdom nor our learning; neither our compassion nor our devotion to our country; it measures everything, in short, except that which makes life worthwhile. And it tells us everything about America except why we are proud that we are Americans."

We might laugh at the comment regarding the "intelligence of our public debate" and the "integrity of our public officials" when you reflect on what happened in the primaries and eventual fall campaign in 2016. Our current leadership for most of us could not be equated with "integrity" but of course Kennedy was speaking at a different time. He was also referring to those factors that measure the quality of our lives not just the quantity of our possessions. Nevertheless, the growth of our GDP is not a good measure when assessing the benefits those markets are producing for our citizens or the quality of our jobs.

What are the important numbers that tell the true story? The growth of our unions peaked in the late 1940s and the early 1950s. The percentage of workers that were members of private unions in 1948 was 37%. These numbers would remain roughly the same until the 1960s. In 1960 for instance, the percentage of workers that were in unions was 33%. It was not until the late 1970s that union membership began to significantly decline. By the 1980s, the Reagan administration's constant assault on unions, and his firing of all those members in PATCO that were on strike precipitously encouraged the decline of union membership.

The Hidden War

Today, there are only 6% of workers that are members of private unions and only 33% of government employees have joined public unions. The significance of this decline in the strength and influence of labor in relation to management has been disastrous to the average worker. For instance, the amount of income gains going to the top 1% was 10% between 1960 through to 1969 which was the height of the American middle class. From 2002 through to 2007, 68% of income gains went to the top and only 12% went to the middle class, according to statistics collected by the Center on Budget and Policy Priorities (CBPP – a progressive American think tank). In addition, wages for most Americans since 1978 have remained stagnant and have not kept up with inflation. This figure is astounding when considering that productivity per worker has increased during this period and that most fortune 500 companies are making record profits.

The CEOs and upper management salaries and benefit packages rose exponentially during this same period. When I was a teenager, CEOs earned 30Xs the average worker. Most corporate leaders now earn 200Xs the average worker and for some the gap is even larger than that. We presently have an economy that has the largest disparity between the rich and the poor in all western economies. This reality is more consistent with numbers that relate back to the Gilded Age as opposed to a modern healthy economy.

The decline of our once robust and confident middle class continues despite significant growth in our markets and our GDP. This is occurring while our public schools are defunded and consequently are producing mediocre students when compared to other economic powers. This is occurring while our infrastructure falls apart and our mass transit in most areas of our nation crumbles or is non-existent. We used to have the most modern trains and the best infrastructure in the world. Currently, our trains compared with Germany, China, England, France, and Japan are an embarrassment. And even more disturbing, a recent United Nation (UN) study (2018) had concluded that significant sectors of our society live in such squalor and destitution that it was consistent with standards in a third world nation. This is unacceptable and despicable when you consider we are the richest nation on earth.

To place this ugly reality in terms most can relate to, Donald Jeffries in his book entitled "Survival of the Richest" revealed that using 1950 as a base year, after adjusting for inflation and factoring in productivity rate, the minimum wage today should be $28.56. This means that over 90% of Americans earn less than minimum wage when you consider the purchasing power of the dollar and the cost of living in 1950.

We are presently arguing over whether workers should earn $15 an hour which still is much lower than what it should be. The CEO for Dunkin Donuts earns approximately $5,000 an hour, and yet he refused to raise the hourly wage of his workers to $15. The greed of these capitalists is beyond my comprehension. How is a guy managing a company that sells donuts worth $5,000 an hour? How is a basketball player worth $100 million over a 4-year contract? And yet, we fight over whether our teachers, police officers, firemen, treatment providers, case managers, carpenters, truck drivers, engineers and public servants should receive a modest raise as they struggle to maintain middle class status.

Capitalism in its purest form – without socialist influences and government regulations – descends into a Darwinist reality in which the most affluent and powerful live in opulence while all the rest struggle to live.

My economic professor at Pomfret School in 1979 described the difference between a developing nation and a highly advanced economy. He proffered that developing economies looked like a triangle that consisted of a very wealthy and powerful small elite with a large underclass. He added that the United States had a diamond shape economy with a small elite and group at the bottom with a large and influential middle class. I am not sure we are that nation today. If we want a robust and modern economy, we must legislate new laws that stimulate the rebirth of our unions which will result in the growth of our middle class.

The only thing we lead in is defense spending, weapon sales and the number of billionaires that exist in our nation. Justice Louis D. Brandeis, an eminent jurist on the Supreme Court, during another era of extreme inequity astutely observed, "We can have democracy in this country, or we can have great wealth concentrated in the hands of a few, but we can't have both."

CHAPTER 15
It is a Sin to Silence a Mockingbird

Harper Lee's beautifully descriptive book based on her childhood entitled "To Kill a Mockingbird" was required reading in my high school in the 1970s. Only three years after its publication, it was captured on the big screen in 1963 in a wonderfully done film that won Gregory Peck an Oscar for his portrayal of Atticus Finch.

This heartfelt story that takes place in a small town in the South during the 1930s is about innocence that is destroyed by evil. The innocence, literally and figuratively, of Tom Robinson who was falsely accused of sexually assaulting a white woman and the gentleness of Boo Radley that had been shunned by the community because of his mental disability that in many ways preserved the child within him. The mockingbird in the title and as briefly alluded to in her narrative represents this concept of innocence. Therefore, the killing of a mockingbird is to destroy the innocence of a person and a society.

Innocence is defined as the lack of guile or corruption. Other than young children, I do not think this term can be applied to most adults no matter how worthy and noble their actions. A hero for example is not some courageous saint who manifests their purity in everything they do but rather are human beings that rise above their frailties to do what is right in an opportune moment. Moral courage, however, is rarer and more significant than physical courage. For instance, it is natural to manifest physical courage in combat or even on the gridiron, but it is quite difficult to stand up for an outcast at risk of suffering the condemnation of your peers or even your community. Thus, the acts of Jesus to show compassion for those who were historically exiled from the inner social constructs of their societies or even the church as prostitutes, lepers and the indigent frequently were revealed virtuous courage.

Julian Assange has become one of those outcasts that has been silenced to prevent his voice from exposing truths that the establishment do not want the people to know. He remains (when I wrote this essay in 2018, it was several months prior to his arrest by British law enforcement) at the mercy of the Ecuadorian government who currently view him as an impediment for their desire to seek better relations with the United States (U.S.). Their goal to obtain an International Monetary Fund (IMF) loan is also enmeshed in their quest to make Assange's environment so unpalatable that he will willingly exit their embassy in London. Of course, his safe passage if he leaves the protected confines of his present imprisonment has not been agreed to by the British government. It is unequivocal that he would immediately be taken into custody by British authorities once he steps outside the protected boundaries of the embassy who will inevitably extradite him to the United States.

We now know because of an inadvertent disclosure contained in a legal document filed in an unrelated case that Assange has been secretly indicted by a grand jury convened by U.S. prosecutors. This occurred in a jurisdiction located in the eastern region of Virginia where a notorious national security court resides that has never ruled in favor of the defendant. The nature of the charges remain secret, but many have speculated that Assange has been charged under the Espionage Act of 1917 for his disclosure of classified documents that WikiLeaks received from Private Chelsea Manning in 2010 that exposed war crimes committed by U.S. military forces and their allies in Iraq and Afghanistan. At this point, there is no indication that these charges have any relationship with the DNC emails or the 2016 election. Because of this indictment, it is highly unlikely Assange will voluntarily leave the Ecuadorian Embassy and place his fate in the hands of U.S. officials that have openly expressed their yearning for his death.

To comprehend the severe predicament that Julian Assange and his creation WikiLeaks' face today, a review of Ecuadorian modern political history is necessary to appreciate the powerful forces that are guiding the events that will eventually decide the outcome for Assange and his media outlet.

On March 8, 1999, the Ecuadoreans started their day by being informed by the media that President Jamil Mahuad had declared a "banking holiday" that initially was to last only 24 hours but in fact continued for 5 days. The citizenry was outraged by the announcement that all the banks were closed and that they were prohibited from accessing their accounts. They stormed the banks and tried to open their doors by force which precipitated the need for Mahuad to deliver a nationally televised address to the nation. In that speech, he described the dramatic measures he had authorized to "save" the country's banking system. He indicated that all accounts of more than $500 U.S. dollars were to be frozen. The purpose of this emergency action was a concerted effort to rescue the private banks from a crisis they had created by their failure to maintain liquidity.

Mahuad transferred millions of dollars of government funds to private financial institutions to keep them solvent. This effort was in vain for 16 banks would eventually close because of the financial crisis. The major thrust of his

The Hidden War

policy prioritized the interests of the banks over the deposits of the Ecuadorian citizens. If this sounds familiar, it is because this is what the Bush and Obama administrations did a decade later to prevent private financial institutions and insurance giants that were determined to be too big to fail from dragging the U.S. economy off a cliff into another depression. Obama for instance gave significant support to large banks who were engaged in predatory lending practices while he condemned the homeowners for agreeing to loans that could conceivably become too expensive. Because of this, he permitted millions to be forced out of their homes as foreclosure actions were initiated by the banks. The most prudent and humane policy would have been to forgive the debts or at a minimum to restructure them consistent with what the mortgagee could afford.

The banking crisis and Mahuad's policies caused a severe recession that nearly destroyed Ecuador's economy. He then decided to end the currency of Ecuador and adopted the U.S. dollar as their national currency. He significantly deregulated their markets with the support of corrupt legislators who were in cahoots with the bankers. As an aside, these actions appear to be consistent with the confessions of an economic assassin named John Perkins. He asserted that the U.S. has three stages it implements to gain power over another nation's natural resources and their economy. Perkins was involved in the first phase which is to convince the nation's leaders to accept an IMF loan to create a debtor nation that can be easily manipulated when it has difficulty repaying the loan. The second phase is initiated when the leaders refuse the loan. At this point, they send in the jackals which are covert operators that assassinate leaders and foment coups against the government. If that fails, a pretext for using military force is then sought by the administration to forcefully remove the government. Perkins indicated that Hussein's Iraq is the perfect example of all three stages being implemented. As we will see, this operation is subtly being applied to Ecuador, as well as one of their neighbors, Venezuela.

Mahuad after ruining the economy and handing the financial strings to foreign interests left his native land to become a professor at Harvard University in Boston. After he exited, the Ecuadorian people suffered through 7 corrupt administrations in 10 years. When Rafael Correa was elected, everything began to change as he instituted reforms to regain control of the natural resources of the country and to restructure the economy much like Hugo Chavez did in Venezuela. Ecuadorian journalist Jose Riveria declared that he was the best president Ecuador has ever had. After he had completed his terms in office, he handpicked Lenin Moreno to succeed him. Moreno won a close election to maintain the reforms that Correa had so astutely instituted, as well as his humanitarian act to extend political asylum to Assange who sought refuge at their embassy in London.

Moreno so far has been a major disappointment to Correa and his party. He has fired judges in the provincial and the supreme courts, removing all those judges that supported Correa's reforms. He has consummated a referendum with the conservatives to handpick judges for the Constitutional Court that will uphold their austerity programs to enhance their chances in obtaining an IMF loan.

While this has been occurring, he has reached out to the U.S., seeking a more cordial relationship. He continues to pursue a loan to pay off Ecuadorian debts accumulated primarily with China and has met with Vice President Michael Pence to discuss their mutual interests which included the fate of Assange. In violation of international agreements and the 1959 UN Convention on Refugees, he has effectively isolated Assange by implementing draconian measures to prevent his access to the internet and his communication with the outside world. Only recently were these severe restriction's modified by Moreno's government that permitted family, friends, outside political leaders, and his legal team to meet with him. The UN has reissued their ruling that he is under international law being unlawfully detained. This was further buttressed by German parliamentarians who also gave a statement to the press after meeting with Assange.

These cries for justice fell on deaf ears for the Ecuadorian media is controlled by a powerful elite whose businesses have significant financial ties to the U.S. Thus, much of these statements by the international community are consistently ignored by their media. As a result of the anticipated IMF loan, Moreno is currently cutting social programs and firing government officials. His ultimate objective is to create a debtor nation that is no longer in control of its resources. A nation in which all its national wealth is funneled to the U.S. or seized by the Ecuadorian establishment, leaving little for the average citizen to survive on.

WikiLeaks has reported in documents it released that Moreno once he was elected was counting the days until he could leave office. Once he achieves the objectives on behest of the elite in his country, he plans to live abroad and take advantage of his new-found celebrity as Mahuad did. Thus, the situation

The Hidden War

appears very ominous for Assange because these same elites are intimately aligned with U.S. interests.

This in my opinion is what Assange may at some point be confronted with. Moreno's government will eventually find a way to relieve themselves of this diplomatic burden and blatant barrier to better relations with Trump's administration. He will be taken into custody by British law enforcement to resolve his bail violation. After the U.K. receives assurance from American officials that they will not seek the death penalty, he then will be extradited to the U.S. Once the U.S. has custody of him, he will be placed in solitary confinement in a maximum-security prison while waiting for his trial for charges filed under the Espionage Act of 1917. In order to avoid first amendment protections, as asserted in The New York Times vs. United States (1971) in which the court held that the Nixon administration did not have the authority to prevent a publisher from printing the Pentagon Papers given them by a third party, Assange will most likely be designated as an agent of a foreign government that disseminated classified documents in an attempt to damage the national security interests of the U.S, removing him from any protections that would be available to a journalist or a publisher. However, the Supreme court did leave open the possibility that a publisher could be prosecuted for disseminating classified materials to the public after publication.

His trial will be a farce for he will be unable to mount any legitimate defense for several reasons. Charges under this act are similar to strict-liability crimes such as statutory rape. For instance, it does not matter that the alleged victim lied about their age or that the sexual acts were consensual. The only relevant issue litigated is whether the act was committed and that the designated victim was a minor. Likewise, an espionage charge does not permit the defendant to enter evidence that he or she was serving a public interest or that the conduct that was revealed by the disclosure of classified materials were criminal acts. Additionally, his legal team in order to provide an adequate defense will eventually need access to classified materials that the government will most assuredly invoke the State Secrets Privilege as permitted under the Classified Information Procedures Act. The court after the privilege is asserted can conduct an in-camera examination of the information requested by the defense to evaluate the applicability of this protection to government secrets. Unfortunately, according to Wikipedia, the court rarely employs this right and as a result the veracity of the government's claim is not verified in a vast majority of the cases. This is what happened in John Kiriakou's case that compelled him to enter a plea bargain to mitigate his potential sentence which could have been life imprisonment. Consequently, his case, as well as Assange's, is not about justice but rather the prerogatives of those in power.

The government once they get a conviction will seek the maximum penalty available. Because of prior agreements with the British and possibly Ecuador, they will not seek the death penalty. Although, the court after Assange has been found guilty by the trier of fact has the final say in what sentence is imposed which could include the death penalty, regardless of prior agreements. The best legal mechanism to enforce the above agreements would be to incorporate them as part of a treaty. Otherwise, the only way to avoid this scenario is by negotiating a plea bargain that would include sentence recommendations to the court. The court has the discretion to accept or reject the agreement presented by the parties to the court. Nevertheless, he will most likely after a trial will be sentenced to life imprisonment in a maximum-security prison that will isolate him to limit his opportunities to communicate to other inmates or get messages to the outside world. He will be the primary example used by the government to discourage others from engaging in similar acts.

Chelsea Manning's experience I believe provides a good depiction of how Assange will be treated. She spent much of her time in solitary confinement and was brutally interrogated by federal authorities seeking further information on how WikiLeaks operates and if she had accomplices. She also was treated poorly by other inmates because of her transgender identity. Her experience while incarcerated was so traumatic that she attempted to commit suicide twice. It was because of these revelations that compelled Obama to commute her sentence as he was transitioning power to Trump.

Thus, the description of the judicial process so eloquently argued by Atticus Finch in his defense of Tom Robinson will not be the realty that Assange will be accorded in his case. Finch's closing argument so movingly performed by Gregory Peck in the movie observed that, "In our country the courts are the great levelers and in our courts all men are created equal" will not be evident in Assange's trial for the same reasons it was not in Robinson's case as exemplified by the jury's incongruous verdict. The government in an espionage prosecution holds all the cards and accordingly rarely loses this type of litigation. The social construct that ruled southern communities in the 1930s that mandated that Robinson be found guilty are comparable to the current

The Hidden War

prejudicial presumptions in favor of national security that will demand Assange's guilt as well.

The sad reality that history will record is that none of this is in the interest of the U.S., the international community or humanity. The corporate media by their egregious failures to challenge government officials or the narrative espoused by the agencies that they work for has permitted a political environment based on fear and hysteria buttressed by lies to infect our whole society. It is though reason and logic have been tossed aside in favor of revenge and retribution for a transgression that never occurred. As difficult as it is to admit, Trump won the election, and Clinton lost it. It was not the result of some mysterious and treasonous collusion between Trump, Assange, and Putin.

Ironically, one of the most egregious assaults on our democratic electoral process in our history occurred during the Democratic primaries in the winter and spring of 2016 when Clinton's campaign staff, their media allies and the DNC leadership conspired to surreptitiously derail Bernie Sanders' progressive campaign. A grass-roots movement that the national polls had indicated was in a better position to defeat Trump than the shockingly flawed candidacy of Hillary Clinton. All of this was revealed by WikiLeaks and ignored by the mainstream media in pursuit of the red herring promulgated by Clinton and her allies known as Russiagate.

In frustration of the media's false characterization of his cause, James Stewart in Frank Capra's inspiring film "Mr. Smith Goes to Washington" exclaimed, "Why don't you tell the truth for a change!" An indictment he rightfully announced as the media mocked his attempts to breach the walls of corruption in Congress to fight for "lost causes" as deemed by the establishment. This assertion was also acknowledged by progressive Eugene V. Debs over a century ago that "...the press and the pulpit have in every age and every nation has been on the side of the exploiting class and the ruling class." I guess the press of today desire to maintain their continuity for certainly no one could accuse them of being inconsistent.

The heart of the battle is between the reality that the power elite wants to prevail which affirms their supremacy through surreptitious alliances which are imminently entwined in their desire to maintain their secrets, and that reality beholden to the transparency of truth. WikiLeaks has breached their wall of secrecy and empowered the people by transferring knowledge to the masses on how the Oligarch's have rigged the political and economic structures in their countries to favor their interests to the detriment of the people that are cruelly sacrificed in their unnecessary wars. Assange and his courageous organization have effectively pulled back the curtain, revealing all the atrocities, corruption and destruction to those institutions that were initiated to benefit the governed. By capriciously dismissing Assange and WikiLeaks, you are not just supporting evil but are attacking truth to preserve the institutional structures of power insidiously transformed by the deep state that do not deserve your devoted faith. These institutions that have gained your allegiance based on perfidious narratives that manipulate your approbation for policies that are in effect slitting your own throats.

One of their central tactics is to solicit your patriotism by invoking God, duty, and country through symbols such as the American flag. By doing this, they beseech your support to discredit those that are seeking truth and justice. If you dismiss Russiagate or take Assange's or Putin's view, you are apologists that have been usurped by Russian memes to support treason. So, if the Russians do it, it is a flagrant violation of international law, and if we do the same it is in defense of democracy. Anyone privy to our real history knows this to be false, but nevertheless as the argument goes you must choose sides at some point. The question often posed to me is whose side are you on and my curt reply is "justice." As Malcolm X asserted, "I'm for truth, no matter who tells it. I'm for justice, no matter who it's for or against."

When Putin accurately describes an event or President Trump does the right thing, I support it. When they lie, I condemn it. I do not tolerate compromise when it comes to truth or justice. In my opinion, Assange has spoken the truth and if it hurts then so be it. The truth he has exposed by disseminating our government's secret documents has unveiled injustices on a massive scale and yet he is designated as the villain that needs to be incarcerated or even killed. A perversion beyond contemplation that the U.S. government and most of our corporate media are demanding that we assent to.

Atticus told his children at one of their family meals, "I'd rather you shot tin cans in the backyard, but I know you'll go after birds. Shoot all the blue jays you want, if you can hit'em, but remember it's a sin to kill a mockingbird." Scout recalled that this was the only time that she could remember Atticus asserting that it was a sin to do anything. Because of this she inquired of Miss Maudie – their friend and housekeeper – if this was true. Maudie graciously replied, "Your father's right. Mockingbirds don't do anything but make music for us to enjoy. They don't eat up people's gardens, don't nest in the corncribs, they

The Hidden War

don't do anything but sing their hearts out for us. That's why it's a sin to kill a mockingbird." The music for those who seek justice is truth. As James DiEugenio wrote, "Secrecy is not just the enemy of truth, but the enemy of democracy."

President Lincoln wisely noted, "Let the people know the facts, and the country will be safe." The preservation of liberty depends upon this important tenet of self-government. As President Franklin Roosevelt later affirmed, "The bulwark of continuing liberty is a government strong enough to protect the interests of the people, and a people strong enough and well enough informed to maintain its sovereign control over the government."

This all reminds me of a beautiful ballad sung by Don McLean when I was young called "Vincent." It is about the genius of Vincent Van Gogh and his tormented personal tribulations that culminated in his suicide at the young age of 37. His art, as with all great artists, was an interpretation of a world he wanted others to see that in his life was dismissed by their indifference to his suffering and their own ignorance of mental illness. The ending verse sadly concludes:

"Now I think I know
What you tried to say to me
How you suffered for your sanity
How you tried to set them free
They did not listen, they're not listening still
Perhaps they never will."

I hope we recognize that we need to listen more intently to block the noise that has been deliberately created to prevent us from hearing the message WikiLeaks is conveying to us through its disclosure of hidden truths. We need to appreciate the real threat to liberty, to justice and to truth which is power fueled by secrecy not the messenger who reveals their tyranny.

The innocence of Assange is his firm belief that in a world besieged in contrived propaganda masquerading as news that the bulk of civilization was yearning for truth. And because his mission was servicing this significant public interest, he would be shielded as a journalist and a publisher from the wrath of powerful agencies throughout the globe. My hope for humanity is that we will appreciate Assange and what he represents by demanding his liberty under international law and the protections allotted him as a journalist and a publisher be upheld before it is too late. For we all know in our hearts, it would be a sin to silence a mockingbird.

CHAPTER 16
WHY NOT?

Robert Kennedy in his 1968 campaign often paraphrased a quote by George Bernard Shaw that became not only his election theme but also his vision for a better future when he stated, "Some men see things as they are and ask, why: I dream things that never were and ask, why not." This quote was somberly recited by his younger sibling, Senator Edward Kennedy, in his eulogy of his fallen brother.

I was pondering the implications of this quote after I read an editorial on Antiwar.com that was supporting an approach towards foreign policy that was based primarily on pragmatic realism and was dismissive of paradigms that included universal principles that he proclaimed were advocated by sentimental idealists. He conceded in the article that some of our cultural values should be merged in our policy towards other nations, as well as our strategic goals that purportedly are supportive of our national security, but it could not become the dominant factor that formulates our ultimate policies.

He cited Henry Kissinger's political concepts that were significantly based on a Machiavellian perspective as an example of what we need to be cognizant of as we pursue our objectives in other regions of the world or when negotiating accords with other nations. He asserted further that history has unequivocally demonstrated that all powers had selfish policies. And when they could not negotiate treaties that accomplished their objectives, they seized what they wanted by force or at a minimum threatened military action. Consequently, the strong nations have been conquering weaker governments and subjecting their citizens to ruthless oppression that advanced the interests of the elite since the dawn of civilization.

Those nations that could project their power beyond their borders, or even their continent, colonized other nations by commandeering their sovereignty to control the people and all their natural resources. The British empire for example spanned the globe until the mid-twentieth century. To place this old argument into perspective, we essentially live in a violent and sometimes brutal world that makes it necessary to not only protect our borders but to project our power wherever we can to obtain the resources that can maintain and expand our wealth. In his view, and that of many others, this is what governs our reality and to think otherwise is to believe in a utopian vision that inevitably leads to disappointment and failure.

The Hidden War

Setting aside the fact that Henry Kissinger's policies primarily implemented during Nixon's administration in many cases were a disaster for our nation's long-term interests and were crimes committed against humanity, I accordingly will focus on the central premise asserted in this essay and many other orthodoxies that promote this notion that pragmatic realism and principled idealism are mutually exclusive concepts that naturally cannot be assimilated much like oil and water. Before I can confront this fallacious paradigm, I must review concepts related to international relations, organizations, and war itself, as well as the definition of "good government."

George Washington opined that any nation could not be trusted to fulfill obligations mandated by agreements that clearly were not in its interests to pursue.[115] With that in mind, we must seek our common interests which in many cases are the low hanging fruit that will enable two or more nations to build a bond that will permit the construction of a relationship that evolves into mutual respect and eventually a basic trust in each nation's ultimate motives. The advantages of this strategy were evident in the back-channel correspondences between Premier Khrushchev and President Kennedy in the early 1960s. Because of these communications, both leaders through their discussions on personal matters and politics of the Cold War had planted a tacit trust between them that permitted them the confidence in one another's character that empowered them to resolve the Cuban Missile Crisis peacefully. This trust once it is established, as shown in this poignant example, reveals that relationships can persevere through more contentious matters that formed the basis of their suspicions and past antipathies that historically was an impediment in achieving better relations.

This strategy is not unique or even a novel concept for this was used as a method of conflict resolution between nations for centuries, including political leaders such as Winston Churchill who was a major proponent of this strategy.[116] As previously cited, President Kennedy also utilized this strategy as he pursued the ratification of his Limited Test Ban Treaty in the summer of 1963 which was the initial step towards the laudable goal of ending the Cold War. This also is apparent in his rapprochement with Cuba that fall. He told his advisors not to impose conditions that Castro could not agree to. The initial goal was to consummate an agreement that would disavow his alliance with the Soviet Union and to get him to cease fomenting communist revolution throughout Latin and South America. In return, Kennedy would remove the travel ban and advocate for the termination of the economic embargo by the

Congress, as well as reestablishing formal diplomatic relations. The demands for democratic elections and other social and political reforms would have to be set aside until both governments could rebuild their relationship.

Likewise, this method was also employed by Mikhail Gorbachev to entice President Reagan to enter agreements that eventually ended the Cold War.[117]

The ultimate target for humanity in my opinion is a community of nations that are governed by international laws that establish the rules for conflict resolution to avoid war whenever possible. The rules of engagement as agreed upon in the Geneva Convention would be invoked when nations are not able to resolve their differences peacefully. The preferred goal to outlaw war as a means of resolving disputes between signatory nations as was attempted by the Kellogg- Briand Pact of 1928 is unfortunately – at least for now – an impracticable law to enforce as was demonstrated in the 1930s. Thus, we must instead try to make war a last resort and not an initial impulse as it is with some nations, including the United States (U.S.).

These laws would be enforced by international judicial courts that were formed and approved by all sovereign countries at the United Nations (UN). This requires that every nation large or small, weak, or powerful or wealthy or poor submit to the jurisdiction of these global entities. Consequently, nations would by necessity have to relinquish some of their sovereignty for this system to work effectively. The U.S. for instance could not ignore international law or refuse to submit to the jurisdiction of the International Court of Justice or another sanctioned international body simply to avoid consequences being imposed upon them for the sale of illegal cluster bombs to Saudi Arabia. This also would be true for other powers like Germany, Britain, Israel, China, and Russia.

The Security Council of the UN would also have to be amended such that the 5 permanent members would not have veto power that most often is used for political purposes not for the advancement of humanity. During the Cold War, the two superpowers made the UN irrelevant on many important issues because each power would veto anything that benefited its adversary. Therefore, a safeguard must be created to ensure that the majority within the Security Council were not supporting or sanctioning policies that harmed international relations or undermined the integrity of the United Nations.

This above goal may be too far advanced a political arrangement for most nations with power to accept much less ratify. For poor countries, as was contemplated by the formation of the UN and its operative charter, this organization granted them a voice in international relations that advanced human rights to every corner of the globe which naturally benefited them. This admirable goal has been diminished in recent decades and as a result the UN has less influence and power than it did in the 1950s and 1960s. Presidents for instance go there, or send their surrogates, to manipulate members with fictional intelligence to justify their wars or to threaten other nations, and not as a forum to build consensus for noble projects and programs as was done by President Kennedy in 1961 and 1963. His speeches to the Assembly of the UN were to challenge all nations to join in his quest to prevent the proliferation of nuclear weapon technology and to seek accords that permitted the reduction of these abhorrent weapons.

Most of our leaders today do not support the UN and deliberately fail to comply with their resolutions if they do not comport with their stated policies. The policy of Netanyahu's government towards the non-violent protesters in Gaza is a prime example of Israel ignoring international law and preventing UN investigations with the assistance of its allies to thwart official conclusions that condemn their current actions. John Bolton who was the National Security Advisor to President Trump has even advocated for the abolishment of the UN.

Our collective goals should be to construct a world of law and not a new balance of power that inevitably only benefits those nations who already have the means necessary to advance their national interests. Because most governments have convinced their people not to trust international organizations, the objectives listed above are not practical in our time. However, the U.S., as the richest and most powerful nation on earth, could set the example of good government at home and be a promoter of goodwill among nations if we had the will to do so as was done by Presidents Kennedy and Carter. William E. Gladstone, a British statesman in the 19th century, stated, "Here is my first principle of foreign policy: good government at home."

This leads us to the definition of "good government" and how it can be encouraged by the people. Our founders vehemently believed that government should derive their power from the people and that the instrument that ordained its creation must reflect that basic concept if we are to be a true republic. The Constitution, therefore, as stated by Patrick Henry "...is not an instrument for the government to restrain the people, it is an instrument for the people to restrain the government – lest it come to dominate our lives and interests."

This for a republic such as ours is crucial to understand because our Constitution, although not perfect by any standard, is constructed to provide checks and balances on the three branches of government. This is assured by dividing the responsibilities of each branch to ensure that one branch does not become too powerful as is the case in authoritarian governments. Consequently, the oath that all government officials take "to preserve and to protect the Constitution of the United States" is extremely important for the well-being of our nation. This oath that whistleblowers honor so deeply they risk their careers and their liberty ironically get smeared or imprisoned while those who mock and violate the Constitution are consistently rewarded. President Obama, a constitutional scholar from Harvard, did not seem to appreciate this irony as he prosecuted more whistleblowers during his administration than any of his predecessors.

As written by Thomas Jefferson, "The care of human life and happiness, and not their destruction, is the first and only object of good government." Thus, good government in my opinion is to promote the interests of the people and to prohibit policies that unnecessarily inhibit or diminish our fundamental liberty as enshrined in our Constitution. This requires an informed citizenry that can – with the assistance of a free press – hold the government accountable when it ignores or is diverted from that basic obligation by special interests. This requires a transparent government in which all its machinations are naked before the people. Those activities and programs related to national security that must be secret should be an extreme exception not the normal course of doing business as is now the case.

If we examine our present form of government, I think it is easy to discern that we are no longer the democratic republic we were taught about in school. We at best are an oligarchy dominated by corporate power that is permitted to influence our political leaders with unrestricted bribery that has perverted our policies domestically and abroad such that we are considered a threat to peace by the international community. In addition, we have allowed a disparity of wealth between the more affluent and the poor to reach levels not seen since the Gilded Age. And even though, we are still the wealthiest nation on earth we have gutted our safety net and have witnessed the growth of an underclass that reside in such destitution that their communities exemplify the standards of living in a third world nation. We are also privatizing our public schools and making a university education cost prohibitive to the working and middle classes. And even if they choose to avail their children of higher education, the

The Hidden War

students and their families must bear enormous debts that are not borne in other industrial nations, hindering the graduate's ability to compete in a global market.

Furthermore, we are witnessing the decline of our infrastructure that use to be the best in the world. We have mass transit systems that are underfunded and are an embarrassment when compared to other economic competitors. Most disturbingly our people are so uninformed on their history that many, even college students, do not know why the Civil War was fought or who were aligned to fight the Axis powers in World War II. Because of this historical illiteracy, or what might be described as national amnesia, we are refighting the same battles and trying to protect the same principles that prior generations had already successfully defended. As a result, we are re-fighting for clean air and water, attempting to protect and preserve our natural wonder, as well as voting and civil rights. It is also evident that there does not exist a legitimate oppositional party. Both political parties seem to be resisting progressive change in support of their donors' and sponsors' demands. There appears to be no major party that champions the causes of labor or the working and middle classes anymore.

Jim Gaffigan a well-known comedian has a very humorous parody on McDonald's in which he reveals the love-hate relationship we have with that American iconic company. He talks about how all his friends turn up their nose whenever he mentions the name. He observed that many he has spoken with in his travels claim that they would not be caught dead in one of their franchises. He then reminds his audience that every McDonald's sign asserts that they have served 99 billion. He then points out that there are only 300 million residing in our country. He conceded that he is not a mathematician, but "he thinks somebody is lying." Using the same logic, the U.S. spends trillions of dollars on our wars and is in the process of passing a $740 billion budget for defense (it passed with bi-partisan support). In addition, the Pentagon and the U.S. Department of Housing and Urban Development since 1998 cannot account for $21 trillion. When our elected officials arbitrarily dismiss programs such as Medicare for all or cut breakfast and lunch programs for children because we cannot afford them, I must concede I am not an accountant, but I think someone is lying.

We must always keep in mind what is realistic under the circumstances, but this understanding cannot become a rationalization for accepting our present predicament or realty, or for doing nothing. It is important that we continue to engage each other in a constructive dialogue that acknowledge our differences which in many ways are not barriers to progressive change but can enhance our lives and our interactions by appreciating the beauty of diversity.

The late Anthony Bourdain demonstrated this in his Travel Network show "No Reservations." The former chef in that format transported us to far off countries and unfamiliar cultures as he explored their natural beauty and their historical lineage, as he savored the native dishes on the streets and in their plush restaurants that comprised their contribution to the culinary arts. By doing this, he affirmed that we should not fear the diversity that exists all around us but rather embrace it. Our differences make our lives on this planet interesting and, therefore, are not natural impediments that must be overcome but understood. It is through understanding one another that will bring acceptance and cooperation among nations.

Nevertheless, we must initially focus on our basic common interests which Kennedy so eloquently expressed in his American University speech at their commencement ceremony in June of 1963. He orated that we all want to live in peace, that we all breathe the same air, that we all hope for a better future for our children and that "we are all mortal." These are common interests that we can build upon for a better future for ourselves, our children and humankind.

The realist advocates for the strategy we must pursue that usually reflects a compromise on our path to social, economic, and political justice or even peace. The universal principles, however, that underscore our objectives cannot be compromised or sacrificed for those fundamental values comprise those aspects of our reality that makes life on earth worth living. The inalienable rights of "life, liberty and the pursuit of happiness", including the principles that all men are equal under the law and that all nations have a right to their natural resources and to govern themselves, cannot be amended. This is not to grant a blank check to those who would oppress and brutalize their people, but rather the enforcement of international law and human rights should be imposed by a committed international community brought together by their common interests. As asserted by Robert Redford's character in the film "Brubaker", "I can compromise on strategy but not on principle."

While the realist recognizes our limitations in the moment, the idealist inspires us to act and never to tolerate injustice simply because of the age-old argument that it is everywhere and has existed throughout history. If we followed this flawed view, there never would have been a Civil Rights Act in

The Hidden War

1964 or a Voting Rights Act in 1965. The realist can negotiate the strategy, but the idealist will demand the observance of universal principles that are the foundation of our survival on this planet and the basic tenets of good government. Thus, realism and idealism are not just compatible but are intricately linked when aspiring for righteous objectives and progressive change to ameliorate the suffering of our fellow human beings at home and around the world.

The settling for what is considered a realistic Machiavellian approach to our foreign policy while ignoring our ideals led to the Syrian, Yemen, Vietnam and Iraq Wars, and the suppression of our civil liberties in the name of national security. Therefore, how we achieve our objectives are just as important as the objectives themselves. As Dr. Martin Luther King, Jr. observed, "Immoral means cannot bring moral ends." After all, as stated by libertarian author James Bovard, "Democracy must be more than two wolves and a sheep voting on what to have for dinner." Certainly, our nation is better than that.

Can we as a nation protect our natural wonder, support human rights, end poverty, promote public education, make our universities free and provide universal health care for our people or even aspire for a peaceful world? I think the more relevant question we should be asking ourselves is, "Why not?"

CHAPTER 17
The Enemy Within

The hypocrisy in our country is astounding. Trump talked about grabbing women while joking with a young journalist who lost his job over the incident. He was also accused of assaulting other women and girls. We all were justly outraged by these allegations and statements. Throughout the 2016 campaign, probably rightfully so, was labeled a misogynist.

Now we have the exact same circumstances with Biden in that he was accused of inappropriate conduct by multiple women throughout his long Senate career, including Tara Reade whose narrative recounts an incident in 1993 that has him not just talking about grabbing women, but penetrating her with his fingers. And when she refused to kiss him, he arrogantly scolded her by stating, "Come on man, I thought you liked me." And then paused and in a stern voice asserted, "You are nothing to me." She eventually was compelled to leave her position.

I recognize as a lawyer that her statement, as credible as I found her, is not absolute proof that he did this. However, I represented many clients as an attorney, and those I assisted in their release from jail as a pretrial case manager, who were initially arrested and incarcerated by less credible witnesses and evidence. The reason they were treated differently was that they had no power.

In Biden's case, as well as Justice Thomas', there is and was corroborating evidence. In Al Franken's case, he was accused of something far less egregious and yet he felt compelled to resign. The Democratic establishment are not only ignoring these allegations but are asking their party members, such as you and me, and the rest of the country to vote for him to the highest office in the land because he is a lesser evil that will rebuild our moral standing in the world. That of course is debatable on multiple levels. His voting record, his harassment of women and support for war are just as repugnant as Trump's record.

The problem from my vantage point is that we live in a corrupt system that caters to power. The two parties essentially fight over identity politics that are used as weapons, such as you must vote for Hillary Clinton because she is a woman. If you do not, you are a sexist and a misogynist.

A great analogy of how our duopoly party system works was made by Jesse Ventura on the Jimmy Dore Show. He asserted that the combative political

The Hidden War

rhetoric heaved at the opposing party are choreographed just like professional wrestling. He elaborated that the parties argue and protest in public, pretending to hate each other, while in private the political leadership agree to the outcomes of the legislation being debated in Congress.

This was quite transparent for those with objective eyes when Nancy Pelosi while standing behind President Trump at the end of his State of the Union address earlier this year (January of 2020) ripped up his speech. She did this after applauding the appearance of Juan Guaido who is a U.S. trained terrorist that is attempting to overthrow the legitimately elected government in Venezuela. She also did this staged symbolic act of defiance even though as Speaker of the House she helped guide Trump's entire legislative agenda through Congress.

This was evident in the Cares Act that was negotiated primarily by Speaker Pelosi, Senate Majority Leader McConnell, Senate Minority Leader Schumer and President Trump. This legislation essentially was the largest transfer of wealth to the aristocracy in this nation's history. The robber barons of the last Gilded Age would be in awe of the transparent temerity involved in such a rapacious act during one of the worst healthcare calamities since the Spanish Flu pandemic of 1919 and 1920 which caused the deaths of 50 million worldwide. The consequence of this act will impact generations well into the future.

Accordingly, Bernie Sanders' campaign was interpreted as a threat to that corrupt system and was smeared for challenging the preordained favorite of the Democratic establishment. His followers over time were pejoratively labelled "Bernie Bros." Another code word for misogynist.

For instance, it did not matter that I eventually voted for Jill Stein, a more compassionate progressive that sincerely cared about humanity and the perilous course this nation has embarked on over the last 5 decades. I was still accused of being a sexist and a Trump apologist. Fundamentally, when all this divisive rhetoric is removed, what is unveiled is that the two parties basically feed at the same trough and support the same militaristic and corporatist agenda.

Bernie Sanders, who I caucused for in 2016, was clearly - to use their language - the "lesser evil" who was not a dangerous radical but rather a New Deal Democrat. Furthermore, our horrible choices between Trump and Clinton were not the engineering of Putin, the Green Party or WikiLeaks. It was rather the corruption within the DNC to undermine Bernie's candidacy who in my opinion would have beaten Trump in 2016.

Bernie once again was robbed in 2020. The Iowa Caucus debacle was not a result of incompetence or a coincidence. We still do not have a final tally of the votes cast in that state. And of course, former President Obama promised to step in if it looked like Bernie might win the day with the voters. Just 24 hours prior to Super Tuesday when Biden's chances of winning the Democratic nomination appeared slim, Obama fulfilled his threat by reenergizing Biden's feeble campaign by convincing Pete Buttigieg and Amy Klobuchar to withdraw from the race and endorse Biden. Curiously, he did not make the same request of Senator Elizabeth Warren. He knew she would draw votes away from Bernie and thus wanted her to remain in contention.

However, this time Bernie contributed to his demise by continually calling Biden his friend while maintaining his silence on Biden's horrendous voting record in the Senate. He also was mute regarding the failures of Obama's administration that exacerbated the difficulties that confronted the nation in 2016 that contributed to the electorates growing apathy and righteous indignation of the political system. A corrupt system that inadvertently opened a path for Trump to deceptively, but nevertheless very effectively, campaign as a populist in support of the working class, so he could exploit this growing revolt against the establishment. Bernie by not accurately assessing the political dynamics of Trump's rise to power, and the motivations for the plutocrats revolt against him, cemented his demise by telling late night talk show hosts that he thought Biden could beat Trump, thereby forfeiting his candidacy.

The reason for this is that the hatred of Trump within the left is so intense that their myopic focus is beating Trump. Even though many liberal voters preferred Bernie's policy positions, he had successfully been labelled a "socialist" that was being propped up by Putin by Democratic establishment surrogates and their allies within the corporate media. These so-called political pundits and journalists that had conceded that if Bernie had won the nomination that they would consider voting for Trump. I surmise from their commentary that they perceived Trump as the "lesser evil" if those were the choices. I would also submit that the edict that you must "vote blue no matter who" as recounted by Chris Hedges only applies if that candidate is acceptable to the power elite.

The Hidden War

Thus, Biden was perceived as the safer more conventional candidate that even Bernie had conceded could beat Trump. A dubious statement at best considering Biden has the onset of dementia. Without a teleprompter, I have watched videos of him forgetting what state he was in, forgetting Obama's name and losing his train of thought that resulted in gibberish coming out of his mouth. Trump, I fear will mop the floor with him. He will not treat him as gently as Bernie.

All you must do is watch the 2016 debates, as pointed out by Jimmy Dore, that reveal how he destroyed the Republican establishment candidates such as Jeb Bush in the Republican primaries. In my opinion, Biden is not the candidate that will prevent a second term for Trump unless he unwittingly delivers to Biden an issue that contributes to his defeat such as his handling of COVID -19 and the outrage by the public over the brutal death of George Floyd by Minneapolis police. If his poll numbers continue to decline, Biden's chances for victory in November are still moderate at best. Although to be fair, his choice for his vice-presidential running mate could change the political optics considerably in his favor.

Tulsi Gabbard (Tulsi) was the candidate in my opinion we should have rallied behind. She served her nation in war and knew what it meant to send young men and women into harm's way. As she accurately assessed, "Foreign policy is domestic policy." She knew that unless we reigned in our militarism that we could not afford to confront the issues that were causing the decay of our democratic institutions, the suffering of our people and the decline of our society.

She had the toughness, the courage, and the fortitude to challenge the establishment - not only in our nation - but even within her party which Bernie in his feckless campaign refused to do. As Bernie told Chris Hedges in 2015, he did not want to become another Ralph Nadar. This is why, even though Clinton had won the nomination through deceit that amounted to cheating, he fell in line with the party elite's choice and campaigned for Clinton much to the chagrin of his supporters who were rightfully mystified by his decision to endorse his rival. In contrast, Tulsi's willingness to risk her career was unequivocally evident in her dismantling of the Democratic Party's initial favorite Kamala Harris in the first two debates. In her last debate, she did the same with Pete Buttigieg. She was telling the truth and thus had to have her platform taken away. She never was permitted to participate in another debate.

The Democratic leaders then went after Tulsi with their allies within the corporate media, labelling her Putin's preferred candidate as was done in an NBC hatchet story aired on their network.

Hillary Clinton (Clinton) even stated on October 17, 2019, in an interview on David Plouffe's podcast in which they were discussing the Trump presidency, his looming impeachment and the Democratic primaries scheduled for 2020 that, "I'm not making any predictions, but I think they've got their eye on somebody who's currently in the Democratic primary and are grooming her to be a third-party candidate. She's the favorite of the Russians...They have a bunch of sites and bots and other ways of supporting her so far. And that's assuming Jill Stein (Green Party presidential candidate in 2012 and 2016) will give it up, which she might not because she's also a Russian asset."

Of course, many Clinton supporters were quick to come to her defense by pointing out that she meant the "Republicans" not the "Russians" were grooming her. This of course may be about the multiple interviews Tulsi did on Fox News, including several on the Tucker Carlson Show. They also shamefully tried to assert that Clinton never mentioned Tulsi by name. However, this defense was completely obliterated when Nick Merrill, a Clinton spokesman, when asked if she was referring to the Hawaiian congresswoman replied, "If the nesting doll fits..." This resulted in Tulsi filing a defamation lawsuit, seeking $50 million in monetary damages for Clinton's reckless and false statement.

This Russiagate narrative, as Clinton's commentary clearly exemplifies, is now being weaponized against progressives as some journalists like Max Blumenthal, Glenn Greenwald, Aaron Mate', Chris Hedges and political commentator Jimmy Dore predicted.

Dr. King sagaciously observed that hate blinds the hater to right and wrong. It essentially destroys the character of the personality of the hater. The mission becomes so myopic that it contaminates and distorts the righteousness of the objective. Thus, he believed, as Jesus commanded, that you had to "love your enemy." He, therefore, attempted to love his adversaries through understanding while hating the system that had indoctrinated them with their flawed and immoral ideology. He would argue if he were present today that the hatred of Trump has diverted the attention of the movement for righteous change and focused instead on personalities that are trivial and ultimately irrelevant to the primary goals. Accordingly, his movement was attempting to radically transform the system in order to achieve genuine progressive structural changes, not token or symbolic reforms that are the usual

The Hidden War

prescriptions to severe systemic problems by timid leaders that have vested interests in not "rocking the boat" or disrupting the status quo. Such as Biden, who reassured Wall Street earlier in the campaign that "fundamentally nothing will change."

President Trump is a manifestation of how corrupt and sick our society has become. He is - as journalist Chris Hedges pointed out- is what a corrupt system "vomits up", but, nevertheless, is not the cause but rather a symptom. For example, many of us have purchased NyQuil or other similar products when we are inflicted with the flu. These products reduce our symptoms so that we feel better but are not addressing the core reason we are sick. The virus that infected us eventually goes away because our immune system over time destroys the contagion.

The exit of Trump may make the left feel better, but the pathogen that inflicts our nation will remain. Many have forgotten that most of us thought that George W. Bush was a horrendous President and that his removal would pave the way for a better future.

This is one of many explanations for the enthusiasm that Barack Obama's candidacy generated in 2008. He represented the "hope and change" most people were longing for. The hope eventually evaporated, and the change never manifested in ways that the electorate had anticipated. Although, McConnell and the tea party Republicans were clearly obstructionists and had no intention of working with Obama's administration, he through his own actions would reveal he was not the President that many, especially progressives, had envisioned.

He later conceded after he left office that he did not understand why his critics on the right so staunchly opposed him. He stated that if he were an elected official during the Reagan years he would have been considered "a moderate Republican." Essentially admitting, he had gaslighted all of us that had trusted him and read his book the "Audacity of Hope." It was all a facade.

Now with hindsight, we recognize how naïve those views were that the removal of Bush would solve our national despair, redeeming our nation's integrity and moral leadership in the world. Without the massive structural changes that were and are essential to prevent a climate calamity in our children's future and the evisceration of our democratic institutions and our liberty, the politics empowered by neoliberals and neoconservatives remain fundamentally the same.

Therefore, the serious problems that this generation must confront is systemic in nature. By voting for the lesser evil, as we have done over the last 40 years, has only made our predicament worse. We need a revolution is this country, hopefully a rebellion of ideas not violence.

President Lincoln once again appears as a prophet, as he does so often with his poignant observations, when he remarked, "America will never be destroyed from the outside. If we lose our freedoms, it will be because we destroyed ourselves."

In my opinion, we have over time witnessed this unraveling of our republic that has now imprisoned us within the structural impediments of a corporate Oligarchy masquerading as a democracy. A political and economic construct that is gradually denigrating our democratic institutions and sucking our liberty like a vampire into eternal tyranny. Thus, we must be able to see the enemy which is not at the gates but amongst us. It is a corrupt system that rots our national spirit from within that must be challenged not enabled. A malevolent possession that must be removed by an exorcism that liberates our nation from those demons that entice us by mendacious facades buttressed by empty slogans that encourage the electors to accept a reality that ultimately empowers the oppressors.

Bernie, and more significantly Tulsi, were our hope for that change. They represented the potential of what a populist progressive movement could accomplish if empowered by the people. Instead, the liberals capriciously dismissed them in their blind rage, while scorching everything in their path in a desperate quest for vengeance for the catastrophic election of 2016, led by a self-declared "moderate Republican", seeking anyone who could defeat Trump no matter how repugnant their record without realizing they had been manipulated by the power elite once again.

CHAPTER 18
The Shaming of our Discontent

Art in many ways reflects life in a form that allows us to observe it from an unorthodox perspective that does not alienate or threaten the sensibilities of its intended audience. For instance, great comedy is a revelation of paradoxes in a venue that permits us to laugh at ourselves, our professed cultural values, and the duplicity of our national leaders without provoking in most cases a reflexive visceral patriotic reaction. It unveils the absurd hypocrisies that are taught to us with such sincerity by credible sources of authority even though the foundation of their assertions is farcical. It is for many gifted comedians a vision of life rich in content that evolved in darkness, exposing a rational introspection through satire that seeks the light through laughter.

Robin Williams clearly was one of those troubled souls that pursued resolution and serenity through frivolity. He conceded this when he described the inspiration for his form of comedy. He observed, "For me, comedy starts as a spew, a kind of explosion, and then you sculpt it from there, if at all. It comes out of a deeper, darker side. Maybe it comes from anger, because I'm outraged by cruel absurdities, the hypocrisy that exists everywhere, even within yourself, where it is hardest to see."

The Democratic establishment, and most of the liberal elite, retort to Reade's allegations exposes that hypocrisy that Williams spoke of that I find even more appalling in many ways than President Trump's gross incompetence. Williams' humor would have discovered a treasure chest of material in their contorted rationalizations to redirect the narrative away from Biden's tabooed past as determined by the corporate media. This would also be true if John Stewart were still on the air doing his political satire on MTV. Can you imagine the fun he would have had comparing Pelosi's comments regarding the women who accused Trump of sexual harassment and even rape with her current dismissive statements regarding Reade?

Their insistence that the Democratic Party are progressive champions on issues of sexual harassment at the job, violence against women and the advocacy for victim rights rings hollow in their treatment of Reade and others that they have declared their enemy.

For instance, they were a significant component that joined the intelligence community in 2009 and 2010 to perpetuate this malicious mendacity that many still believe that Julian Assange was a misogynist and a rapist to divert the public's focus away from the truths that they wanted to remain hidden. Their insidious propaganda has very effectively smeared Assange's character that has significantly undermined his support and any empathy he might normally have received. Consequently, his present abhorrent conditions, as well as the psychological torture he has endured, continues with minimal notice or concern by the public and the mainstream media.

Katrin Axelsson and Lisa Longstaff of Women Against Rape in disgust exclaimed, "The allegations (against Assange) are a smokescreen behind which a number of governments are trying to clamp down on WikiLeaks for having audaciously revealed their secret planning of wars and occupations with their attendant rape, murder and destruction…The authorities care so little about violence against women that they manipulated rape allegations at will."

The origin of this lie was revealed in a 2008 classified Pentagon document prepared in the waning months of the Bush administration to undermine WikiLeaks' credibility, as well as Assange's public support. The mission of this insidious covert plan was to destroy the "trust" that was WikiLeaks "center of gravity" with threats of "exposure and criminal prosecution." When Obama entered the White House, he sanctioned and expanded this clandestine war on WikiLeaks and its founder.

This perfidious narrative has further been debunked by the alleged victims that were reportedly the source of these accusations. The two Swedish women in Assange's case indicated that the allegations were created by the police and that they had never accused Assange of rape. Additionally, the Stockholm chief prosecutor, Eva Finne, had concluded, after a thorough analysis in 2009 of the facts, that, "I don't believe there is any reason to suspect that he (Assange) committed rape." She later elaborated as she was closing the case, "There is no suspicion of any crime whatsoever."

The case was reopened by a colleague of hers in 2010 after Wikileaks published Chelsea Manning's classified documentation that disclosed war crimes being committed by the United States and its allies in Iraq and Afghanistan. The case would eventually be closed a second time when no evidence emerged to support a prosecution. John Pilger is one of the few journalists that has written about this abhorrent injustice.

When allegations are made against Republicans, or opponents of their agenda, the women must be believed and to not do so is to be a misogynist. When accusations, such as the ones being lodged against Biden are levied on their Democratic leadership, the women are treated like publicity seeking

The Hidden War

whores being manipulated by third parties to smear their honorable candidate which of course mirrors what the Republican Party does under similar circumstances. They and their media allies are implicitly in most cases, and explicitly in others, are calling Reade a liar.

How does this support victims? If she is telling the truth, and I believe she is, they are essentially revictimizing her. They are also discouraging others from coming forward, permitting men in positions of authority the opportunity to get away with this reprehensible abuse of their power in the future. In either case, whether rape is transformed into a weapon to assassinate a designated enemy's character, as was done to Assange, or whether credible allegations made against one of their members are casually dismissed, they are placing future women at risk and assuring that past victims remain silent.

There is a reasonable argument, even without the Reade allegations, that can be submitted that Joe Biden is not necessarily the "lesser of two evils." Biden has a horrible voting record when it comes to labor, the working class, criminal justice reform and the national security complex. As journalist Chris Hedges observed in his Rutgers University sponsored college course that he teaches to inmates at a maximum security prison in New Jersey, most of the participants in his class are poor, Black and Hispanic that have been convicted of non-violent crimes that are serving lengthy jail sentences because of President Clinton's 1994 Crime Bill that Joe Biden sponsored in the Senate and zealously advocated for its passage. A bill whose legacy is clearly evident by the overcrowding of our prisons that has scarred the American image as the "land of the free" as we have systematically incarcerated a larger percentage of our population than any other nation on Earth while we transform our prisons into private profit making machines.

He supported these insidious "free trade" accords that ripped the guts out of one of the remaining labor union strongholds in the manufacturing sector of our economy by outsourcing to other countries high paying jobs with significant benefit packages, such as the North American Free Trade Agreement (NAFTA), the Trans-Pacific Partnership (TPP) negotiated by the Obama administration in secret – which mercifully was rejected by President Trump - and was a major proponent that supported President Clinton's repeal of the Glass-Steagall Act of 1934. A crucial financial reform implemented as part of FDR's New Deal to prevent another Stock Market crash. Only a decade later, we had the financial collapse of 2008 under Bush.

He also asserted that even if both houses of Congress passed universal health care legislation that he would veto it, thereby going against what most of the citizenry need and want. A recent non-biased Yale University study (4/2020) concluded that Medicare for all or a universal healthcare program would save the United States $400 billion a year and prevent approximately 70,000 deaths of which the study indicated was a conservative number.

He has no problem spending trillions of dollars for bombs and wars but draws the line in providing healthcare to millions that desperately need it. Under the Affordable Care Act (ACA) that Obama signed into law in 2010 that he continues to stand by as the gold standard in healthcare legislation, even though 30 million remain without healthcare and 40 million more are underinsured, which according to a study conducted in 2018 had estimated that 45,000 people died that year because of a lack of healthcare coverage under their pro-pharma and pro-private insurance plan that whistleblower Wendell Potter, a former Cigna insurance executive, observed was prioritizing "profits over patients." Potter also asserted that ACA was a "windfall" for the insurance industry. He now is a zealous advocate for Medicare for all.

Just imagine if the government enacted a law which mandated that everyone purchase your product, or they would be compelled to pay financial penalties. I think we all would be doing Chubby Checker's "twist" as we anticipated the money train coming into the station. This anticipation of massive profits for private health insurance companies caused their stocks to rise exponentially after the passage of ACA. As this current COVID-19 pandemic has brutally revealed, private healthcare tied to employment during this type of crisis is a disaster that must be rectified in the future. Healthcare should be a right as FDR declared it in 1944 not a means for companies to profit from at the expense of their insureds and their country.

It is true that Biden is slightly better than President Trump on climate change and environmental issues but not by much. Earlier in his campaign when his chances for getting the Democratic nomination were slim, he scolded a potential supporter that if that person wanted a "ban on fracking" that he should vote for someone else.

He also, during Obama's presidency, agreed with opening the artic to drilling and did nothing to support the Native American's fighting to protect the Missouri River which was their major source of clean water by preventing the Dakota Access Pipeline. A pipeline that has subsequently, as they predicted, leaked thousands of gallons of oil since its completion. Although Obama issued

The Hidden War

an order that an environmental impact study should proceed prior to the completion of the pipeline, he did this as he was exiting the White House and transitioning power to Trump. Obama knew that because it was done in the form of an executive order that Trump would immediately repeal it upon entering the Oval Office.

In addition, the Paris Accords that Obama and Biden promote as a major positive component of their legacy fell far short of what environmental groups and ecological scientists were calling for. In fact, Obama demanded that the targets set forth in the agreement be non-binding. This all must be critiqued within the context that the Obama years, as a result of his policies and fervent encouragement for the development of widespread use of destructive fracking methods to extract energy resources underground, were responsible for more natural gas and oil being produced within the United States since the days of John D. Rockefeller's Standard Oil.

Obama's administration is riddled with so many contradictions that even liberal admirers have a difficult task rectifying his policies with his rhetoric. I voted for him in 2008 because I was conned into believing that he would be this generations Dr. King and Bobby Kennedy, representing "hope and change." In 2012, I supported him because I thought he would prevent another Cold War with Russia, avoiding an arms race and potential nuclear war. I wrongfully surmised from his policy positions that he would reenergize labor and support what former New Dealer, Henry Wallace, dubbed the "common man" in which he espoused was the backbone of this nation. Instead, at the behest of companies like Citigroup, he submitted most of his cabinet posts to the Senate from a list of recommendations from their company.

His cabinet as a result was filled with elite financial managers that through their greed and that of their organizations were partially responsible for the financial collapse of 2008. They were in essence the same men and women who had attempted to devour all the chickens that now had been put in charge of the chicken coop.

Obama wittingly - without any sense of irony or shame - appointed Lawrence Summers as the Director of the White House Economic Council. Summers prior to this had been a managing partner for a hedge fund, D.E. Shaw & Company, and had been a freelance speaker for other financial institutions which included Goldman Sachs, JPMorgan Chase, Citigroup, Merrill Lynch and Lehman Brothers. He also appointed Janet Yellen a former economist from the Brookings Institution as chairperson of the Federal Reserve, as well as appointed Timothy Geithner as Secretary of the Treasury who was the President of the Federal Reserve Bank of New York (2003 – 2009) and a former member of the Council on Foreign Relations.

These appointments as well as others clearly were contrary to a progressive administration that was to be the champion of structural changes that would create a more equitable society and a government that was "open and transparent." In fact, Obama would administer one of the most secretive presidencies in our history. He would also bail out the banks while permitting almost 6 million homeowners to be foreclosed on by these predatory financial institutions. In addition, he not only did not end the two Bush wars but expanded our warfare policies to 5 other nations. When he left office, we were involved in 7 wars.

Princeton Professor Cornel West appropriately labelled Obama in an interview with Truthdig.com in 2011 as "a black mascot of Wall Street and a black puppet of corporate plutocrats." In fact, the vast majority of Black Americans witnessed a decline in their wealth during his presidency, dissuading them of any illusions that a "brother" in the White House would be a catalyst for righteous change and justice to finally eviscerate the yoke of racism and the legacy of slavery. The resentment in many Black communities for Obama's failed promises and outright neglect, such as Flint, Michigan, caused thousands in key districts within battleground states to not vote. This contributed to Trump's narrow victories, coupled with Republican voter suppression tactics, in states such as Michigan and Wisconsin.

As to the national security complex, Biden voted for the largest defense budgets in history, voted for the AUMF and the Patriot Act in 2001, and in fact helped write and sponsor the bill, and advocated for its recent extension. He supported the invasion of Iraq, as did Hillary Clinton, managed with the CIA the overthrow of the pro-Russian government in Ukraine in 2014, supported the overthrow of Gaddafi in Libya, the creation of a civil war in Syria, the brutal war waged by Saudi Arabia against Yemen, the attempts to overthrow Maduro's government in Venezuela, the NSA and CIA's massive surveillance programs, the drone assassination program and was responsible – with Obama – for the new Cold War we are presently engaged in. He was also complicit, as was Nancy Pelosi, with the Bush/Cheney torture program implemented after 9/11.

The House and Senate Intelligence Committees were briefed by CIA and military personnel on what was called "enhanced interrogation techniques" in 2002 being used to obtain actionable intelligence to assist our war on terror. A

The Hidden War

war that was never declared by Congress as required in the U.S. Constitution. The Democratic leadership was essentially complicit in Bush's war crimes and that is the primary reason he was never investigated for these reprehensible violations of international law and the Geneva Convention by the Speaker of the House Nancy Pelosi.

Instead, President Obama directed us to forget the transgressions of the past and look forward. Thus, he decided to not prosecute the rapacious Wall Street elite who committed massive fraud that contributed to the financial collapse of 2008 and the Bush administration's war crimes but rather directed federal prosecutors to indict more whistleblowers than all his predecessors combined. Truthtellers who were revealing those egregious corruptions of our society that he shamefully argued we should ignore.

They are unequivocally a horde of corrupt liars. Is Trump a greater evil? The answer is probably "yes." But are we just becoming enablers for this corrupt system that Trump did not create but clearly represents when we continue to pledge our vote for a party that hold us, the working and middle class, as well as progressives, in contempt? As Lawrence O'Donnell admitted in an interview in 1995 when he worked as an aid in Congress, the Democratic leadership does not have to listen to liberals and/or progressives because they know "there is nowhere else to go." They focus, therefore, on appealing to Wall Street, moderate Republicans, and independents. This is one of many reasons the party has not nominated a true progressive since George McGovern in 1972.

They are all centrist corporatists that have imposed neoliberal programs, in coordination with conservatives, to deregulate the economy and privatize essential public services that traditionally were administered by the government while undermining labor by promoting free trade agreements to advance their globalization market model. They were complicit with Reagan and Bush for transferring trillions of dollars to the billionaire class and the fortune 500. In fact, Obama made the Bush tax cuts permanent. I recently read an article that Bill Clinton unraveled and repealed – as a so-called liberal Democrat – more of FDR's New Deal than Reagan could have ever done in his wildest dreams.

Chris Hedges accurately observed that Trump is what a corrupt and sick political system "vomits up". We need to stop enabling this system and recognize that Trump is not the problem, as George W. Bush was not the problem earlier this century. It is rather a systemic issue.

As Mark Twain purportedly quipped, "I don't vote because it only encourages them." I am not advocating to not vote, and neither was Twain who was a staunch advocate for the right of franchise, but you should exercise that right by voting for candidates that support real change; candidates that recognize the magnitude of the problems that inflict our society and threaten the survival of humanity. As John Quincy Adams, the eldest son of John Adams and a former Secretary of State and President, asserted, "Always vote for principle, though you may vote alone, and you may cherish the sweetest reflection that your vote is never lost."

Everyone that I know with exception to a few ridiculed me for voting for Jill Stein of the Green Party. Why not vote for her? She supported everything that I believed in and had written about. In my opinion, many liberals create self-fulfilling prophecies. They assert I am wasting my vote because Stein had no chance of winning. So, they follow the slogans like sheep. "Vote blue no matter who"; vote "the lesser evil"; vote for what is attainable not "pie in the sky" proposals; "Don't sacrifice the good for the great" or stop being a "purist". This is how the duopoly party elite maintain control. Hence, when Stein gets only 1% of the vote, they exclaim "we told you so." If they had all voted their conscience, she might have won.

Many forget that Abraham Lincoln in 1860 was a 4th party candidate. Believe it or not, there were 4 parties that had candidates seeking the presidency that year. Lincoln won because people voted for someone not just against someone. The other parties split their votes enabling him to garner just enough support for victory. Try to imagine our national history without Lincoln. I cannot.

The sad reality is there is no third-party candidate that inspires me in 2020, unless Jesse Ventura decides to enter the fray as the Green Party contender. Howie Hawkins who is currently their party's lead candidate for the nomination is even less known than Jill Stein. Their party needs to nominate someone with more name recognition who can motivate the electorate and tap into to that large block of voters who normally do not vote. Otherwise, I am being forced to choose between a war mongering elitist with the onset of dementia that is accused of sexually assaulting one of his young female staffers in 1993 or a lying narcissist that has also capriciously dismissed rape allegations against him.

Many liberals that I recently argued these issues with stated that they are "operating in realty" and dismissed me as a "purist" dreamer when I

The Hidden War

volunteered that I was probably voting for a third-party candidate. In anger, some have blurted out rhetorically "Why don't you just vote for Trump?"

The reality they patronizingly refer to is a lie masquerading as a truth that has been empowered by their silence. Their failure to stand up for what they genuinely believe in and have supported all their lives has contributed to the wretched choices we will all be confronted with this fall, unless something happens to change this dilemma facing progressive voters.

We as Democrats - in my opinion - should be outraged that after the disastrous election of 2016 that the candidate that the Democratic leaders want to shove down our throats is even more flawed than Hillary Clinton. They had 4 years to prepare for this election, and this is the solution they are proposing as the path to prevent another term for President Trump. As a progressive, after observing their attack dogs smash Tulsi's and Bernie's campaigns, my guarded delusions of reforming the Democratic Party from within have been rudely proven absurdly naïve.

One of my favorite quotes orated by Dr. Martin Luther King, Jr. was "It's not the repression of the bad people that hurts, it's the silence of the good." If we wish for progressive change, we must demand it. As Frederick Douglass sagaciously observed, "Power concedes nothing without a demand. It never has and it never will." The only real leverage we have is our vote. They – the Democratic Party – must earn my vote and the rest of you should compel them to earn yours as well. This also applies to Republican and independent voters.

The party elites cannot ignore us if we all stand together and demand change. They fear our solidarity and that is why they have exerted so much effort in dividing us with cultural and identity politics while insidiously dissuading the people from voicing their discontent with false choices imposed on the electorate with catchy slogans that shame us into voting for their candidate. And if we do not, we - the dissenters – invite chaos by permitting a more egregious evil to take over the reins of power in our nation. Hence, Ralph Nadar, Jill Stein, Tulsi Gabbard and Julian Assange are the enemy not the rapacious plutocrats and their corporate allies that dominate and control both parties.

As President Kennedy stated, "One man can make a difference and every person should try." It is true we may lose, but that should not be the justification for doing nothing. If we do not stand up for our national ideals, we will be relegated, as ardently asserted by Theodore Roosevelt, with "…those cold and timid souls who know neither victory nor defeat." After all, no worthy cause was assured of its success simply because of its righteousness. We must embark on this path of justice with confident anticipations of triumph but coupled with the awareness that we may fail.

    We, therefore, must begin to organize a third party such as a Progressive Party or support vigorously the People's Party and/or the Green Party. We also should return to paper ballots, increase the number of locations people can vote, reinstate section 4 of the 1965 Voting Rights Act, repeal Citizens United, shorten our election cycles, impose term limits on the House of Representatives, eliminate political financial contributions by federally funding campaigns for Congress and the presidency, as well as enact rank choice voting across the nation, as we have in Maine.

CHAPTER 19
Specifying the Targets of Hatred

The Cheyenne and Arapahoe encampments were set up in what was described as a "horseshoe bend" of Sand Creek just north of a stream that snaked through the landscape. The U.S. military had guaranteed their safety which prompted Chief Black Kettle to bed down for the winter at that location. Their intention was to continue to travel south in the spring away from U.S. military forts and activities to avoid further conflict and threats to his tribe. Black Kettle's tepee was situated near the center of their village while Chiefs White Antelope's and War Bonnet's tribes were to the west while the Arapaho camp was adjacent to the Cheyenne to the east. All in all, there were a total of 600 Native Indians of which two-thirds of them were women and children.[118]

Black Kettle was informed by Colonel Greenwood that if soldiers encountered his tribe that he was to raise the U.S. flag up a pole stationed by his tepee and stand by it as the cavalry approached. He was assured that this would prevent any misunderstanding that could lead to his tribe being designated as hostile Indians.

On the evening of November 28, 1864, Colonel John Milton Chivington's Colorado regiments began to assemble for their mission in search of renegade tribes. They were joined by Major Anthony's troops. Their army totaled 700 men, and four twelve-pounder mountain howitzers which were escorted by cavalry. His men were guided to the Cheyenne and Arapahoe encampments by James Beckwourth who was a mulatto that had lived with the Indians for most of his life.[119]

Colonel Chivington's tactics were brutal as he pursued his assignment to control the plains of Colorado. He was attributed with this vile quote that prophetically described the horror that was to befall the Indians at Sand Creek. He exclaimed, "Damn any man who sympathizes with Indians! I have come to kill Indians, and believe it is right and honorable to use any means under God's heaven to kill Indians...Kill and scalp all, big and little; nits make lice."[120] His means of course had nothing to do with heaven and everything that was emblematic of a hellish fire below.

So confident were the tribal leaders that they were safe that no watchmen were assigned that night to warn them of potential hazards. It was early in the morning of November 29th when Chivington's patrol saw the tepees of Black Kettle's tribe in the distance. The sun peeked over the horizon when the silence was broken by "the drumming of hooves on the sand flats." At first, those that were awake thought the sounds were created by Buffalo until it became evident it was the Army. Chief Black Kettle immediately brought out the stars and stripes and raised it on a pole as most of his tribe stood beside him as instructed by Colonel Greenwood in their prior discussions. They waited solemnly as the cavalry ominously approached their village. And then small blasts of firing carbines could be heard in the distance as the soldiers vigorously approached their camp.

Black kettle was so confident in what he had been told that he and hundreds of his people stood still at attention, hoping the soldiers would realize they posed no threat and would stop shooting. This of course did not happen as the sun rose higher into the sky revealing the horror of bodies scattered throughout their village that were laying on the ground, bleeding to death. Still they tried to convince the soldiers they wanted peace with their hands raised in the air. Only to be shot dead where they stood as the flag waved above them.[121]

As it became clear the army intended to slaughter them all, they began to scatter and hide wherever they could locate shelter. White Antelope ran out to the commanding officer holding up his hands while screaming for them to "Stop! Stop!" in English. "He then stopped and folded his arms until shot down." The Cheyenne survivors later observed that White Antelope stood in acceptance of death as he sang their death song, "Nothing lives long – only the earth and the mountains."[122]

The survivors were latter interviewed for posterity as they described what became known as the Sand Creek Massacre. They recalled, "When the troops came up to them, they ran out and showed their persons to let the soldiers know they were squaws and begged for mercy, but the soldiers shot them all." There was one squaw whose leg had been broken by a shell. "A soldier came up to her with a drawn saber; she raised her arm to protect herself, when he struck, breaking her arm; she rolled over and raised her other arm, when he struck, breaking it, and then left her without killing her. There seemed to be indiscriminate slaughter of men, women and children."[123]

A survivor continued to recount the horror he witnessed. "There were some thirty or forty squaws collected in a hole for protection; they sent out a little girl about 6 years old with a white flag on a stick; she had not proceeded but a few steps when she was shot and killed. All the squaws in that hole were afterwards killed, and four or five bucks outside. The squaws offered no

The Hidden War

resistance. Everyone I saw dead was scalped. I saw one squaw cut open with an unborn child, as I thought, lying by her side."[124]

When the shooting stopped, 105 Indian women and children, as well as 28 men were dead. In Chivington's official report, he wrote that 9 soldiers had been killed and 38 of his men had been wounded. Many of his men that had been listed as casualties had been hit by friendly fire because of the chaos and the intoxication of some of the soldiers who had been drinking the night before. He further claimed that 400 to 500 warriors had been killed that included Chiefs White Antelope, One-Eye and War Bonnet. Black Kettle had miraculously survived. Chivington's numbers, however, were disputed by all the witnesses in their testimony to Congress that uniformly recalled that most of those who were murdered were women and children.[125]

Why would the soldiers have committed such an atrocious act? Was it because they all were inherently evil? The answer is that they had been convinced by propaganda and by behavioral conditioning to view all Native Americans as a threat to their way of life. The goal of these malicious mendacities was to dehumanize their professed enemy to make it easier to kill them when ordered to do so by their commanding officers. The brutality of their killing and the lack of mercy displayed to the women and children by the soldiers confirmed the power of propaganda over the human psyche. The absurdities that they had internalized as truth made them susceptible to commit atrocities.

The reality is that the Cheyenne and Arapahoe tribes at Sand Creek, and most of the major tribes on the continent, were not a threat to the soldiers or their society. In fact, it was the opposite. We were the intruders that were threatening their way of life and the cultural heritage of all the indigenous people who lived on this continent long before we arrived.

But more importantly, this should not be interpreted as an American phenomenon, no more than the holocaust should be viewed as a genetic predisposition of the German people. In both cases, it was a learned social construct that had been imposed upon the citizenry by potent propaganda disseminated by the power elite. As Noam Chomsky has repeatedly observed, the elites in order to manufacture your consent for their wars need to first appeal to your fear by compelling the people to focus on a perceived threat. As Joseph Goebbels stated, "Propaganda must facilitate the displacement of aggression by specifying the targets of hatred."

Therefore, the primary conflict we all must recognize is not between good and evil, but rather between lies and truth. Human beings are born with a natural propensity to have empathy for others. We can see this manifested by the interactions of our young children at play prior to their socialization into societal norms. In addition, the universal principles that naturally exist are not the domain of one nation or a singular religion but can be found in all cultures and systems of faith. Humanity's failure to follow them is widespread because in all societies there are social constructs that are deliberately created to support the interests of the aristocracy to foment discord amongst the citizenry by directing their myopic focus on their differences and not their common humanity. Consequently, in countries such as the U.S., the whites are pitted against colored people, and the private workforce are pitted against the public workers, as well as union members and non-union employees, Catholics and Protestants, and Christians, Jews and Muslims. This is all done to blind us to all those common interests that would unite us. If we could see through their perfidious narratives and irrational social constructs, we as a result of our overwhelming numbers would know that the power was with us and not the few elites at the top. As Jefferson wrote, "When the people fear the government, there is tyranny. When the government fears the people, there is liberty."

There are many lineal attributes that we as Americans can be proud of but that does not mean we are unique or an exceptional nation, as my illustration above clearly demonstrates. Unfortunately, we have used our immense economic and military power to augment our wealth and supremacy to the detriment of others, as empires throughout history have done such as the British, the Spaniards, the Romans and the Egyptians. In all cases, the weaker societies were exploited for their labor and natural resources.

The focus that we - as citizens of the U.S. - should have is on creating an exemplary nation that encourages the observance of international law and respect for the sovereignty of other nations. As George Washington in his Farewell Address of 1796 asserted, our policy should be to "observe good faith and justice towards all nations" with the primary objective to "cultivate peace and harmony with all." Washington sagaciously added, "In the execution of such a plan, nothing is more essential than that permanent, inveterate antipathies against particular nations, and passionate attachments for others, should be excluded; and that, in place of them, just and amicable feelings towards all should be cultivated. The nation which indulges towards another a

The Hidden War

habitual hatred or a habitual fondness is in some degree a slave. It is a slave to its animosity or to its affection, either of which is sufficient to lead it astray from its duty and its interests."

If we are fully informed on the machinations of those in government, this knowledge endows us with power. This is the reason so much of what our government does is in secret. This permits government officials such as former Vice President Dick Cheney to assert that "you do not know what I know" in his dismissal of his critics. Secrecy, therefore, is an instrument that transfers power from the people to the power elite. Furthermore, this pervasive secrecy, except on rare occasion, is not to protect our national security but rather to shield those in power from embarrassment and prosecution for violating the Constitution they were sworn to protect or for breaching domestic and international laws that in many cases constituted crimes against humanity and in some instances war crimes.

The secrecy of their actions is also an attempt to prevent us from discerning the true objective of their policies. This is the primary reason the negotiations for the Trans-Pacific Partnership were conducted in secret with the assistance of 600 corporate lawyers and lobbyists while human right organizations, labor representatives and environmental groups were not permitted to participate. The goal was to promote corporate interests that would have inevitably over time have culminated in significant consequences for environmental regulations and labor rights. Accordingly, we must make our government more open and transparent by demanding that our national security laws be reformed and that those laws already on the books be vigorously enforced, as well as reestablishing a free and independent press to hold those in government accountable to the people.

With this knowledge, we also need to elect qualified candidates to Capitol Hill and the White House that champion those ideals that enhance our liberty, our security and are committed to promoting peace. We live in a time of rampant militarism in which the establishment, whether it be the intelligence community, the political leadership, the corporate media or the Pentagon, disparages anyone that pushes back against this common narrative, seeking progressive reforms in our economic and political structures while proposing a radical departure from our war economy that encourages these aggressive interventionist policies. As the only peace candidate running for president in 2020, Tulsi Gabbard has been subjected to reprehensible attacks by the corporate media, neoliberal Democrats and neocon Republicans that disseminate fictions to undermine her candidacy. Their vacuous smears have inadvertently unveiled the inefficacy of their political dogmas.

We also must shorten our elections and publicly fund federal campaigns to get special interests out of our politics. It is essential that Citizens United be repealed and that comprehensive election reforms be enacted that would include reactivating section 4 of the 1965 Voting Rights Act, reinstituting paper ballots and the abrogation of the electoral college.

We as a people must be more vigilantly skeptical of what we are told by the mainstream media and our government. For instance, the U.S. intelligence community has misinformed and has lied to us on so many occasions that they do not deserve your devoted allegiance or the benefit of the doubt. If you still do not believe me, this quote by former CIA Director William Casey made in February of 1981 when the Reagan administration was ratchetting up the Cold War narrative should awaken you to the dilemma we face as U.S. citizens. He surreptitiously assessed at a national security meeting that, "We'll know our disinformation program (against the Soviet Union) is complete when everything the American public believes is false."

You must confirm that the information you are receiving is from a credible source which in modern times is most often alternative media. Most importantly, before you decide to support regime changes or military interventions in other nations, it is imperative to demand that the government provides you with the evidence necessary to make an informed decision, as President Kennedy voluntarily did when his administration submitted classified photographs taken by U2 cameras to the international community at the United Nations that revealed Soviet missiles in Cuba.

And finally, do not be sucked into the vortex of identity politics being weaponized to compel your consent or labels that rarely are accurately defined by those that casually use them to promote myths and lies. In support of this premise, policies that are based on socialism are not all bad and those built upon capitalistic principles are not all good. For example, your local fire, police, and public schools are based on socialistic principles, as well as Medicare, Medicaid, and Social Security. I think most of us would agree that all these agencies, departments and programs promote the health, safety and welfare of our communities while making our society more humane.

For a democratic republic to not only survive but flourish, the citizenry must be well-armed with knowledge to participate in our national debates, serve our communities and responsibly exercise their right of franchise by voting for candidates that exemplify our ideals and promote good government. As President John F. Kennedy orated when being awarded an honorary degree at the University of Berlin on June 26, 1963, "Life is never easy. There's work to be done and obligations to be met – obligations to truth, to justice, and to liberty."[126]

CHAPTER 20
The Death of Russiagate

The year of 2019 began with leaks from those who were privy to the internal machinations within Mueller's investigation. The disclosures at the time appeared to be an attempt to lower expectations that the conclusions of this much anticipated report were to culminate in the end of Trump's presidency. Some journalists that had been staunch supporters of what had been dubbed Russiagate began to distance themselves from the controversy by preparing their readers, listeners, and viewers for disappointment.

This report that was to vindicate - if not rescue - the careers of those who spent over two years endorsing a conspiracy they had reported as an unmitigated fact had been sullied by other investigations that had ended their inquiries without a smoking gun or even a nugget that could reenergize their perfidious narrative. For instance, the Senate Intelligence Committee concluded that they could not find any "direct evidence" of collusion between Trump and Putin. There was also the famed investigative journalist of the Watergate scandal, Bob Woodward, who had conceded in an interview for his book on Trump that he could not find any evidence to support collusion in over two years of research. These were the ominous developments that proceeded Mueller's final assessment for those who had been stoking the flames of Russiagate since its inception.

The 448-page Mueller Report was finally completed on March 26, 2019. The media that had promoted this vast tale of Russian collusion with President Trump held their breath as they awaited the announcement of its finale conclusions that were disseminated by a summary prepared by Attorney General William Barr. The corporate newsrooms were stunned as they read Mueller's findings that cost the taxpayers tens of millions of dollars. This investigation that had issued 2,800 subpoenas, 500 search warrants, 230 orders for communication records, 50 orders for authorizing use of pen registers, made requests to 13 foreign governments for evidence and interviewed approximately 500 hundred witnesses could not substantiate what they all had endorsed as an incontrovertible fact.

After describing the extent of Mueller's efforts that included 16 lawyers and 40 FBI agents, Barr's summary asserted that Mueller did not find any evidence that the Trump campaign had colluded with the Russians in the theft of the DNC e-mails or in the general election. He also announced that there would be no more indictments. As to the obstruction of justice allegations, the Barr summary indicated that Mueller made no recommendations and deferred to the Department of Justice to make their own determination based on the evidence contained in his report.

This was the beginning of the end of a terrible display of media ineptitude and malfeasance not witnessed since the build-up to the Iraq War. The scramble to move goalposts and revise history was placed into high gear to salvage their reputations, their credibility, and their careers. Others – like Rachel Maddow - doubled down and continued to promote collusion, hoping that Mueller's investigation may have uncovered some evidence of perjury and obstruction of Justice by the President, as Special Prosecutor Ken Starr did that permitted a Republican House of Representatives to impeach President Clinton. The trial in the Senate, however, did not convict the President, but rather decided to censure him for his actions. The legal complaints that initiated all this was based on a false statement about Clinton's relationship with Monica Lewinski that he had made under oath in a deposition that was part of the Paula Jones case. This of course had nothing to do with the impetus that led to Starr's appointment which was to investigate an alleged corrupt real estate investment deal by the Clintons called Whitewater.

The other astounding developments that were gleaned from this investigation was that Mueller had never interviewed Julian Assange and Craig Murray who had been the recipients of the DNC e-mails and electronic communications that were published by WikiLeaks. His team had also not requested to have their own experts examine the DNC computers or their servers and instead relied on the dubious finding by a cyber-security company hired by the DNC named CrowdStrike. Incredulously, they had also failed to subpoena William Binney, Ray McGovern or any of the forensic experts that had examined the documents published by Guccifer 2.0 and WikiLeaks. They decided in lieu of investigating these matters to accept Guccifer 2.0's admission that this persona was responsible for the theft of the DNC e-mails that were subsequently published by WikiLeaks.

William Binney of the Veteran Intelligence Professionals for Sanity (VIPS) announced that same spring that forensic analysis of the DNC documents published by WikiLeaks further substantiated that they were locally downloaded onto a portable storage device and not hacked by an external entity and transported over the internet. Their findings were based on the examination of over 500 DNC documents on WikiLeaks' website. They found that all the documents they had examined were "date stamped" and rounded to the nearest even number. This is a method of organization used by a File Allocation Table (FAT) that is a system operated by a portable storage device, such as a thumb drive.[127]

The importance of this is that other programs randomly assign even and odd numbers to "the last modified times." If the e-mails were hacked, this should have been the method of organization used. The probability that all 500 documents would be randomly assigned even numbers is 1 chance in 2 to the 500th power.[128]

This unequivocally establishes that the data published on WikiLeaks' website "went through a storage device, like a thumb drive, …before WikiLeaks posted the e-mails on the World-Wide Web." All the forensic findings regarding Guccifer 2.0 and WikiLeaks' documents clearly would create "reasonable doubt" if the 12 Russian intelligence officers indicted by Mueller challenged his evidence in court.[129]

Former FBI Director James Comey, whose firing by Trump was the impetus for Congress to appoint a special prosecutor to investigate Russian collusion and obstruction of justice allegations, incredulously, after being one of the initiators of this Russiagate conspiracy theory, publicly conceded that the (DNC) emails were probably delivered to WikiLeaks by an intermediary. This is consistent with what Julian Assange has been saying for almost three years.

On April 11, 2019, news that Assange's asylum was revoked by the corrupt Moreno administration that permitted British law enforcement to breach Assange's legal sanctuary within the Ecuadorian Embassy and drag him unceremoniously out into a police van, as though they had just caught a sinister criminal such as Al Capone or perhaps Jack the Ripper, was announced by The Washington Post. He appeared to have aged decades with his white hair and beard and his pale complexion that was a result of not being able to walk outside because of his grotesque isolation. He was clearly squinting as his eyes were exposed to the sunlight for the first time in years and visibly weakened by his poor health. It was a sad sight of a once vibrant and self-assured man whose intelligence and core principles that motivated him were vividly evident in every interview that he participated in.

This reprehensible decision by Moreno occurred only one week prior to Ecuador's announced agreement with the U.S. to approve a $4.2 billion loan from the International Monetary Fund (IMF) that was to extend over a three-year period. It is anticipated that billions more are being contemplated to

The Hidden War

provide additional debt relief from creditors. The fact that the agreement was consummated on April 15th just several days after Assange's asylum was revoked by Ecuador was not a coincidence. They had offered to give up Assange for this IMF loan on several occasions in previous discussions with U.S. representatives.

He was held and eventually sentenced to 50 weeks of incarceration for breaching his bail at Belmarsh which is a notorious maximum-security prison in East London that houses serial killers and terrorists. Even after his sentence was satisfied, he remains in custody until the request by U.S. authorities to have him extradited pursuant to conspiracy charges that he allegedly aided and abetted Chelsea Manning's theft of classified documents is resolved. The charging instrument, however, has been conveniently misconstrued by the political establishment and the mainstream media. The actual allegations are that Assange encouraged Manning to get more classified documentation while assisting her to maintain her anonymity. This of course as pointed out by investigative journalist Glenn Greenwald is what real journalists do when doing their jobs. Hence, this complaint is criminalizing journalism not just Assange.

The Trump administration announced that spring that more charges would be filed. This all occurred while Manning remained incarcerated for failing to respond to questions posed to her by a grand jury seeking more evidence against Assange. To date, she has accepted full responsibility for the classified documents that WikiLeaks published that revealed war crimes being committed by U.S. military forces in Iraq and Afghanistan, including the Collateral Murder Video which captured U.S. personnel operating a helicopter killing 12 civilians. Two of the casualties were children and two others were identified as journalists who were employed by Reuters. This same video is where we learned the military euphemism for "double tap." This is defined as killing the alleged combatants and then also murdering the first responders sent to help them. Mercifully, Manning was eventually released from custody.

These events are an ominous development for free speech and a free press. If convicted and imprisoned by secret proceedings, this will have a chilling effect on any whistleblower who has witnessed violations of law or atrocities being perpetrated by the government to come forward with documentation and a publisher that is contemplating their publication. Of course, this is the point if you are a government that believes that secrecy and security trump liberty and our democratic ideals. They covet their secrets in most cases to protect themselves from ridicule, embarrassment, and possible prosecution for abuses of power that prior to WikiLeaks remained for the most part hidden from the public.

The voices of joy and satisfaction that Assange was now in custody was a bipartisan display that was repugnant to anyone who believes in liberty, in truth and in justice. Their gleeful manifestations in support of their national security state being granted the opportunity to torment a courageous journalist was revolting. This of course paled in comparison to the corporate media's condemnation of Assange and his organization WikiLeaks that further substantiated that they all had been co-opted by power and were no longer engaged in real journalism. They had no empathy for one of their colleagues as they parroted the intelligence community's narrative. They appeared oblivious that today it was Assange and that they were bolstering those powers that tomorrow maybe knocking on their door. It was assuredly a sad day that made me tremble for my country.

The only ray of hope came from Congresswoman Tulsi Gabbard who was the lone presidential candidate that defended Assange and condemned the actions of the British and U.S. governments to squash dissent and attack liberty. In fact, she asserted in an interview on Fox News that if she were elected president that she would drop the charges levied against Assange and pardon Edward Snowden. She would never be given the chance as her campaign was pummeled by accusations that she was a Russian asset by the mainstream media, Democratic Party leaders and the intelligence community. The same culprits, joined by neo-conservative Republicans, that have smeared Assange's character and credibility.

2019 thankfully ended only to usher in 2020 which to this point has been even worse. And for those who refused to concede that Russiagate was a hoax, it has been an utter disaster.

There are two major components of the Russiagate narrative. There is the allegation that Russian intelligence officers working for the GRU hacked into the DNC servers exfiltrating the emails over the internet to a Russian server that eventually transferred that metadata to Wikileaks who published it on July 22, 2016. And then there is the perfidious claims of collusion between the Trump campaign and Russian agents operating under the direct authority of Putin to coordinate their efforts that included the release of DNC emails to derail Clinton's bid for the presidency. In my volume "RETHINKING AMERICA", I primarily focused on the forensic evidence and testimony that established that the stolen emails had been leaked by an insider who had access to the DNC servers and was not a hacking operation conducted by an outside source.

The political aspects of Russiagate began inauspiciously by a conversation between George Papadopoulos (George) and an Australian diplomat, Alexander Downer, who was the Ambassador to the U.K. George at the time was a member of the foreign policy advisory panel for Trump's 2016 presidential campaign. Downer reported that on April 26, 2016, George indicated that he had spoken with a Maltese professor named Joseph Mifsud. He was unaware at the time that Mifsud had worked primarily with western intelligence agencies and accordingly had contacts with Russian agents. In that conversation, George explained that Mifsud had apprised him that the Russians were in possession of information that they planned to release that would be very damaging to Clinton.

After hearing this, Downer sent a cable to Australia's Ministry of Foreign Affairs in Canberra. He explained later, "There is no suggestion from Papadopoulos nor in the record of the meeting that we sent to Canberra … that there was collusion between Donald Trump or Donald Trump's campaign and the Russians." Downer added, "All we did is report what Papadopoulos said."

After the release of the DNC emails, this information was dispatched to the FBI whose counterintelligence unit initiated an investigation under the codename "Crossfire Hurricane." This covert operation was to seek any intelligence that confirmed collusion between Trump and Putin. A derivative investigation into Papadopoulos was named "Crossfire Typhoon." This investigation uncovered no evidence to support collusion allegations. For instance, the beautiful woman Olga Polonskaya that Mifsud had introduced falsely to George as the niece of Putin appeared to be a "honey trap" that Papadopoulos was immediately suspicious of and did not take the bait. In addition, they were unable to link Mifsud, WikiLeaks and the Russians. Curiously, even though Mifsud lied on three occasions to Robert Mueller's investigators no perjury charges were ever filed against him.

George would eventually plead guilty to giving false statements regarding the timing of these conversations and their significance. As we will see with Lt. General Michael Flynn, he was probably another victim of a "perjury trap" set up by FBI agents which is a common practice when they have no direct evidence for the underlining allegations that initiated their probe. The FBI knew after interviewing George that he was not involved in any scheme to acquire pilfered Russian emails on behalf of Trump's campaign.

Lt. General Michael Flynn was also scooped up in the nets as the FBI went trolling for any information that could damage, if not humiliate Trump. In classified documents released in April of this year, they revealed that in January of 2017, federal prosecutors wanted to close the case against him for lack of evidence.

Flynn, who briefly served as President Trump's national security advisor, because of a conversation he had with Soviet Ambassador Sergey Kislyak became a target of FBI's counterintelligence probe. The jest of the conversation had been about the sanctions and the expelling of 35 Russian diplomats by the Obama administration as a consequence of their alleged interference in our election process. He implored the Russian ambassador not to recommend a harsh response and that the Trump administration was planning to rebuild Russian-U.S. relations. This of course is a normal practice by the incoming administration as it prepares to assume power. As reported by the prosecutors, there was "no derogatory information" revealed against him in that conversation or the investigation in general. It was FBI agent Peter Strzok , who had been caught on tape indicating that he thought Trump was an "idiot" and that he wanted to do all he could to undermine his presidency, that intervened, demanding that the investigation remain open even though there was no evidence to support the allegations.

It was clear that the FBI mission as to Flynn was, as recounted by Strzok and as revealed in the documents, to "Get him to lie so we can prosecute him." Flynn while on vacation in the Caribbean was contacted by the FBI in which he was not totally forthright in the timing and content of his conversation with the Russian ambassador. The FBI got what they were hoping for and charged him with lying to federal agents in an ongoing investigation. The allegations had nothing to do with the theft of the DNC emails or collusion between Trump and Putin as reported by the mainstream media.

Flynn eventually pled guilty to perjury when prosecutors threatened to indict his son for matters that he was allegedly involved in. The Justice Department after the release of these FBI documents and other pertinent intelligence regarding Flynn's perjury conviction decided this spring to exonerate him. This instigated much dissent within the intelligence community and the corporate media but in the end it was not disputed that the plea had been obtained as a result of a threat which coupled with a lack of evidentiary support for any involvement in collusion with Russian officials was eventually allowed to be withdrawn by a federal judge.

The Hidden War

On the same day the Justice Department dropped the charges against him, the House Intelligence Committee (HIC) released further documentation that revealed that the FBI had no evidence that Russia pilfered the DNC emails by hacking into their servers in mid-2016. This could be conclusively stated because the FBI's investigation was solely based on CrowdStrike's assertion after they had examined the DNC servers that the Russians were the culprits for the alleged hacking operation.

This was debunked when classified testimony by CrowdStrike's President, Shawn Henry, was released by the committee. In that testimony provided under oath to the HIC, Henry admitted the following: "We have indicators that the data was exfiltrated from the DNC, but we have no indicators (direct evidence) that it was exfiltrated...There are at times when we can see data exfiltrated, and we can say conclusively. But in this case, it appears it was set up to be exfiltrated, but we just don't have any evidence that says it actually left." Essentially, they had circumstantial evidence that someone was preparing to pilfer the emails but had "no direct evidence" that this had occurred or that it was a leak or a hack, and certainly were not in possession of any evidence that established who the perpetrators were.

Ray McGovern of VIPS explained what this all meant. He indicated after consulting with former NSA Technical Director William Binney that the "preparation" referred to in Henry's testimony could be an individual getting ready to download the data onto a thumb drive which is what the forensic evidence indicates how it was done. In fact, Binney testified in the Roger Stone case that "WikiLeaks did not receive stolen data from the Russian government. Intrinsic metadata in the publicly available files on WikiLeaks demonstrates that the files acquired by WikiLeaks were delivered in a medium such as a thumb drive."

Furthermore, the report generated by Justice Department's Inspector General Michael Horwitz's on the FBI investigation of the Trump campaign unequivocally concluded that the only aid in Trump's campaign that had contact with Russian agents was Carter Page. These conversations, as established by the record, had taken place long before he had reported them voluntarily to the CIA. Essentially, the documental record established that he was working for the Agency. This was never reported by the FBI in the documents they filed with the FISA courts requesting permission to surveil Carter. In fact, they lied throughout the documents. When Chris Wallace of Fox News inquired about these fraudulent statements in his interview with former

FBI Director James Comey, he evasively replied that he was not aware of them. When asked if he had known about this would he have resigned? His response was that these false statements made to a secret federal court would not have resulted in his resignation. He arrogantly alluded to other FBI actions that were far worse than what was revealed by the FISA court documents, and it did not occur to him at the time to resign over those matters.

It also should be noted that after the "St. Petersburg defendant's" hired U.S. attorneys to file their appearance in court, seeking discovery from Mueller's investigation, all the indictments against the Internet Research Agency, the maligned Russian troll farm, were dropped.

And finally, the infamous Christopher Steele dossier that was initially funded by Clinton's campaign seeking dirt on Trump that was also used by the FBI to expand their investigation on Trump campaign personnel. This dossier that the mainstream media constantly referred to as proof of collusion that eventually to their consternation was revealed to the public as lacking in empirical evidence by the release of classified information that discredited its trustworthiness. The FBI had received multiple warnings about the lack of credibility of the dossier and its author, Christopher Steele. For instance, Robert Mueller was fully aware of a letter sent to Flynn's team in January of 2017 by the British government that totally disavowed any credibility of Christopher Steele that would have demolished the Russian collusion narrative if it had been made public at that time.

The FBI interviewed Steele's primary source on January 7, 2017, who denied any evidence of Russian collusion that was attributed to him in the dossier. The FBI also hid this information from the FISA court in its filings. More disturbingly, the FBI's own spreadsheets when commenting on the Steele dossier concluded that most of it was false and that other segments could not be substantiated. They further deduced that it contained internet-based rumors and was basically worthless as actionable intelligence. The FBI as revealed in Horwitz's report had even exonerated Michael Flynn on January 30 of 2017 as being part of a conspiracy to collude with Russia. These documents also revealed that Flynn had kept his former Defense Intelligence Agency (DIA) chief briefed on all his Russian contacts.

The question that should be asked is why with all this explicating evidence that essentially destroyed the Russiagate collusion narrative out of the gate did Mueller continue to pursue the matter for another two years? The other revelation is how much Democratic congressman Adam Schiff lied through his

The Hidden War

teeth when he had known that the Russia collusion allegations were groundless from the beginning. And yet, the corporate media without verifying anything continued to promote this vast conspiracy as though it was a proven fact. The sad reality of all this was that the intelligence community with the witting assistance of the media and DNC leadership had attempted a "bloodless coup" as described by Ray McGovern.

The fact that Trump is a repugnant figure to most and will probably be deemed to be one of our worst presidents in U.S. history is irrelevant. This vast conspiracy as alleged by the DNC, Hillary Clinton and her surrogates, the corporate media, James Clapper, James Comey, and former CIA director John Brennan was an affront and an attack on what is left of our fragile democratic republic. It is true that our electoral process has been significantly compromised over the last few decades but nevertheless working within that corrupted system Trump legitimately won the election. They all had common interests in endorsing this nonevidence-based conspiracy theory to obscure that fundamental fact even though they had different underlining reasons for its promotion.

The DNC leadership and the Clinton campaign conveniently used it as a diversion from the content of the emails that were published by WikiLeaks. The emails clearly revealed how the DNC electoral process was rigged against Bernie Sanders, and that Clinton was gaslighting voters with her "private" and "public" views that were explained in her infamous speech to financial giant Goldman Sachs and other Wall Street financial tycoons. In that speech, she basically told Wall Street that because of the publics anger over the financial collapse of 2008 and the vast financial inequities in our society that she would be compelled to support that rage using harsh political rhetoric (public views) to entice their votes, but this should be of no concern to them because she intended to bring them into her administration to assist her policy formation going forward (private views) after the election politics settle and the dusts clears. Additionally, the DNC did not want the public to focus on the substantive issues revealed in the emails because they had no intention of conducting an honest autopsy on the failures of Clinton's campaign or their leadership. A real autopsy would require major reforms that likely would alienate their wealthy and influential donors.

The intelligence community and defense contractors supported this conspiracy to intimidate Trump from pursuing some of his foreign policy agenda as espoused in the campaign that they vehemently opposed. They did not want him releasing FBI and CIA documents as required by the JFK Records Act of 1992 or withdrawing troops from Afghanistan and Syria. And they certainly had no interest in resolving the second Cold War initiated ironically by the Obama administration that had become a massive cash cow for the Department of Defense, as well as the intelligence community and the weapons industry.

The result of all this is that Russia has become once again the "boogeyman" for all our problems and anyone who articulates an interest in improving Russian relations or ridicules its underlining orthodoxy is attacked by McCarthyite tactics to smear their integrity and credibility as Russian assets or "useful idiots" that have been naïvely influenced by Russian memes. Essentially, militarism continues to flourish in this nation, dominating our foreign policy objectives and diverting most of our resources to military weaponry that is being used to continue our senseless and destructive wars.

Recently, the Congress with bi-partisan support rejected Sanders proposal to cut military spending by 10% to reinvest that money in our country and then, without shame, decided to overwhelmingly pass a $740 billion defense budget. They even had the gall to vote against a bill that would remove our troops from Afghanistan, advancing the interests of empire while incomprehensibly enabling our growing addiction to war.

The worst aspect of all this peddling of nonsense is that the truthtellers continue to be persecuted and hunted down like terrorists, as exemplified by Julian Assange's incarceration in a maximum-security prison. Meanwhile, the real traitors get promotions as they enrich themselves in this vast ocean of corruption that created the context for a narcissistic reality TV star and a demagogue like Trump to become the President of the United States.

CHAPTER 21
Water Most Foul
(How the decline of labor led to despair)

There was a time when Flint, Michigan, was a shining example of the triumph of labor and the capacity to improve the conditions in which people toiled through solidarity, through collective bargaining. The union became the legal mechanism to achieve those goals borne out of decency and fairness. Labor no longer could be divided and intimidated by the ruthless tactics of management. The dominance of corporate elites under the Gilded Age would fade into the mist of the past as labor proudly advanced its cause to sit at the negotiating table as equal partners in the company's financial wellbeing while rightfully sharing in the profits that their hard labor had help create.

The city of Flint is the birthplace of General Motors (GM). As the auto giant grew into the behemoth it would become in the 1950s, it became the largest employer in the area. Like most corporations of the 1920s and 1930s, workers were treated like cogs in a money generating machine that were expendable and easily replaced. The conditions in which GM employees endured were unsafe. They worked long hours with substandard wages and no benefits. They lived in hovels and shacks without heating and plumbing.[130] Management on the other hand were residing in large Victorian mansions on beautifully designed tree lined streets while sending their children to prestigious private schools as they sucked up the profits for themselves as the company expanded and prospered.

The Stock Market crash of 1929 that resulted in the Depression of the 1930s squeezed labor to the point that its anger and frustration could no longer be contained as employers such as GM continued to impose draconian policies on its employees. These policies included arduous work schedules that on occasion left workers unemployed for weeks and the arbitrary practice of firing employees when they turned 40 years old.[131] All of this culminated in a massive labor movement that compelled our leaders to respond to their demands to avoid further economic repercussions and violence. The period of 1935 up through 1947 witnessed the formation of unions in record numbers that rapidly empowered the rights of workers.

The Roosevelt administration - while attempting to save capitalism from its inherent selfish and rapacious tendencies - enacted programs that permitted economic and social progress that benefited the average worker. Under the umbrella of President Roosevelt's New Deal, the National Labor Relations Act (NLRA), commonly referred to as the Wagner Act which was named after Senator Robert F. Wagner from New York, was enacted in 1935. This created the legal framework that legitimized unions, transforming them from organizations that employers could ignore without penalty into legally binding structures that could practice collective bargaining. They could even strike if management refused to negotiate in good faith.[132]

The U.S. Supreme Court in 1937 upheld the NLRA as constitutional. I suspect this was done to avoid further conflict with the executive branch after President Roosevelt in frustration of prior court rulings that had determined much of his New Deal initiatives to be unconstitutional attempted to expand the court from 9 members to as many as 15, hoping to appoint liberal judges that would tip the balance in favor of New Deal legislation.

This became known as the "court packing" scandal of 1937 in which the media and the Republicans, including many Democrats, had declared was a blatant abuse of power by the Roosevelt administration. However, the court's conservative leanings resurfaced that same year in a schizophrenic ruling that partially stripped away what it had granted labor in its NLRA decision. In the Mackey Radio & Telegraph ruling, the Supreme Court held that striking workers could be replaced by "strikebreakers." Essentially, this decision permitted the firing of workers on strike by management. This little understood ruling at the time was referred to as the "Mackey rule."[133] However, the immediate growth of labor unions and their popularity deterred employers from using this obscure rule until the 1980s.

These laws that benefitted labor were tolerated by corporate management until they could mount their counteroffensive and augment their victory in the Mackey case. Wall Street and affluent companies sent scores of lobbyists to Congress to amend these laws and take back their historical advantages. These efforts culminated in a bill sponsored by Two prominent Republicans, Senator Robert Taft, and Representative Fred A. Hartley. This anti-labor legislation became known as the Taft-Hartley Act which was enacted over the veto of President Truman in June of 1947, amending much of the pro-union Wagner Act. This act enabled states and territories to ratify "Right to Work" laws that prohibited compulsory union membership as a condition of employment, even though they benefitted from the union's negotiated contracts with the employer. This resulted over time, as these laws became more prevalent in states dominated by conservative Republicans, and later neoliberal Democrats,

The Hidden War

in significant revenue reductions as a consequence of diminished membership dues collected to pay for administration costs and legal fees incurred by the union.

Prior to the above countervailing laws, labor had many triumphs – combined with the GI bill and other government programs – that contributed to the development of the largest middle class in history. The formation of labor friendly bureaucracies in Washington during FDR's administration for example encouraged 11,500 workers in GM's Guide Lamp plant in Anderson to join the sit-in strikes that were held in Flint that were initiated in late 1936. The demands of the strikers as asserted by the leaders of the United Auto Workers Union (UAW) were to provide a fair minimum wage, to establish a grievance system, and to improve safety standards to reduce assembly line injuries. This cooperative strike lasted for 44 days.

During the strike, GM had obtained a court order to evict the workers that had occupied the plants, preventing the company from bringing in replacements or what unions called "scabs." The Governor who owed his election to the unions was reluctant to authorize law enforcement to forcibly evict the sit-in workers and in fact never did give that order.[134] GM then decided that January when the temperatures hovered at 16 degrees to shut down the heating system in Fisher Body #2 that forced 100 strikers to huddle together in freezing temperatures, refusing to give in. After that failed, GM demanded that 22 local police officers armed with clubs and tear gas remove the workers to enforce the court order. This confrontation caused injuries to 16 strikers and 11 police officers but did not result in ending the strike.[135]

These aggressive actions by GM triggered further responses by the UAW that formed another sit-in strike at Flint Chevrolet No. 4 which was an engine factory. This takeover caused GM's monthly auto production to precipitously drop from 50,000 to 125 cars. GM finally relented and recognized the union. The first labor agreement was signed on February 11, 1937.[136]

The agreement included the recognition of collective bargaining and strikers as employees. It contained a promise by GM not to seek retribution to those workers who had participated in the strike and to provide for a 5% pay increase. It also permitted employees the right to talk to each other during lunch breaks.[137]

The success of Flint's inspired sit-in strikes proliferated across the country. The UAW triumph over the auto giant paved the path for future labor victories. The UAW's membership for instance jumped from 30,000 to 500,000 in the span of one year. Auto worker wages in general rose 300%, stimulating the growth of a large middle class that not only enhanced the wealth of the city of Flint but throughout the region. As union membership continued to grow, income inequality steadily decreased as the standard of living for many continued to improve in the 1940s up through the 1960s.[138]

The post war period for Flint that cultivated widespread prosperity that was not only reflected in its cultural community, its retailers downtown but also in its growing neighborhoods. There were plenty of jobs that provided a livable wage that benefitted everyone within the city. Families on weekends could visit the Sloan Museum, the Flint Institute of Arts, the Flint Institute of Music, and the Longway Planetarium. At the height of the city's prosperity in the 1950s, many were moving from faraway places, seeking work in their factories of which GM was one of many companies that operated in the region.

GM continued to manage its huge factories that employed tens of thousands of union workers. In fact, some families had multi-generational participation in the autos that were built in Chevrolet, Buick, and Pontiac plants, as well as engine and other parts manufactured by the company. It even had an engineering university that was funded by the auto giant.

By the 1970s, the economy began to incrementally decline. The energy shortage that created long lines, higher prices, and rationing at the pump coupled with stagflation deterred potential customers from purchasing gas hogs such as large sedans and wagons that Ford, Chrysler, and GM were producing at the time. This opened the market to foreign car manufactures that had many high mileage low cost models such as Volkswagen, Honda, and Datsun. This began an avalanche of criticism aimed at unions that blamed them for these downward market trends and the financial difficulties that the big three were managing.

President Ronald Reagan took advantage of the public's growing negative perceptions of unions and began his concerted efforts to deregulate the economy and eliminate the powerful unions that had been a vital financial resource of the Democrats. He fired all the air traffic controllers who were on strike as part of an initiative by their union, PATCO, seeking increased wages and improved working conditions, by using that long forgotten exception to labor regulations called the Mackey rule. By the end of his presidency, union membership had plummeted and their political and economic influence on the markets was in significant decline.

The Hidden War

The consequence of these national trends was devastating to Flint. GM would close its last plant within the city in 1987. Its footprint, however, would never completely cease from the city of its founding in that GM started building medium Chevy Kodiak and GMC Topkick trucks that employed 2000 hourly workers and 180 salaried employees.[139] This was miniscule compared to the 80,000 full time employees on its payrolls within Flint's metro region in 1978 that in 2010 was reduced to less than 8,000.[140]

This of course was not solely the consequence of Reaganomics but was most significantly the result of neoliberal free trade agreements that encouraged the outsourcing of millions of manufacturing jobs to other signatory countries that had no minimum wage, labor safety standards, or environmental regulations. The Huffington Post in an article in 2014 estimated that 1 million good paying manufacturing jobs were shipped abroad because of Clinton's North American Free Trade Agreement, as companies decided to cut costs and maximize their profits.

These companies did this fully appreciating the financial devastation that would befall the communities that had become dependent upon them and the desolation suffered by their former employees that had made it possible for them to grow into the powerful corporate entities they had become. The lack of loyalty to their faithful work force or any sense of economic patriotism was palpable as they relocated their enormous plants to southern states and other countries. They showed no remorse or mercy as they destroyed the financial wellbeing of tens of thousands of families, contributing to what is now called the "Rust Belt."

During this period, Flint's population dropped from 196,940 to 102,434. The city became one of the poorest in the country as good paying jobs vanished. Today 50% of Flint households earn less than $26,333 per year, and 41.2% of the population live below the poverty line. Most of those with the financial means moved to other regions of the country while those who could not were trapped. All of this contributed to an impoverished community with no jobs that became a breeding ground for violent crime and drug addiction.

The racial makeup of the city changed as well. It is now considered one of the "blackest cities" in the nation with the city of Detroit being number one. 59.5% of its residents are of African descent. This of course led to less attention being paid to its growing problems by State officials and national leaders that made it vulnerable to exploitive racial policies that targeted them to augment other revenue generated endeavors that ingratiated those with power.

Flint would eventually sink so low that it was on the verge of bankruptcy and was ordered to be under the auspices of a state appointed emergency management team by Republican Governor Richard Snyder. This action stripped Flint's residents of any rights to influence the policy that would be enacted by the city manager. The first impulse by this management team was to impose a policy of austerity that would cut and even eliminate city programs and services. One of those draconian measures was to significantly reduce the city's water budget. The water Flint residents were using came from Detroit which was pumped out of Lake Huron which was part of the largest body of fresh water in the world known as the Great Lakes. This was high quality water that came with a large price tag.

In April of 2014, Flint's water with a" simple flip of a switch" was transferred from the Great Lakes to the highly polluted Flint River.[141] The residents immediately noticed changes that included a brown color, a foul odor, and taste issues. They began to have rashes, hair loss and illnesses that appeared mysteriously. The residents were instructed by local authorities to boil the water prior to use which was the worst thing that could be done with water contaminated with lead. This only increased its concentration, creating severe health hazards. When the lead was discovered in the water in August of 2015, the State agencies in charge of health reversed themselves and published warnings not to boil the water.[142]

The next government response to deal with e coli and other bacteria was to elevate the levels of chlorine which also had consequences that could include carcinogen producing by products because of the chemicals being injected into the water.

According to Dr. Hanna-Attisha, a pediatrician at a local hospital, the problem was not exclusively the use of Flint River water. She indicated that if the water had been treated with anti-corrosive elements and other processes that the Detroit water was subjected to than the health issues listed above would have been significantly diminished, if not eliminated.

This of course was not done. This meant that the decades of toxic pollutants dumped into the river by companies, such as GM, began a corrosive process that caused the aging infrastructure that was contaminated with lead to leach into the water system, resulting in water that was exceedingly above the EPA's regulation which was 15 parts per billion.

The health hazards for lead poisoning are well documented. Children develop cognitive impairments that lead to severe learning deficits. For example, many

The Hidden War

school aged children in the city who had memorized the alphabet after drinking Flint water for months could not recite it any longer.[143] Lead poisoning can lead to cancer, liver, and kidney issues, as well as immune deficiencies that were exacerbated by environmental pollutants and poor nutrition in those neighborhoods.

In October of 2014, GM - eight months prior to the first newspaper editorials – stopped using Flint's water and switched to another source when they noticed the polluted water was corroding their engine parts. This change was not officially announced, nor did GM warn the residents of Flint or local health officials.[144]

This scandal was never properly addressed by state officials or overseen by the EPA. The Governor and his people kept telling city officials that the water crisis was resolved, and it was safe to drink and bathe in the water.

President Obama decided to visit the city on May 5th, 2016. Hundreds of Flint City residents flocked to the airport to greet the President. They cheered and waved American flags as his motorcade passed by them to attend an event scheduled in an auditorium with Governor Richard Snyder. A Flint citizen in relief stated, "We've been waiting (for him) to push this with urgency."

A thousand residents and representatives from the press crammed into the auditorium. They watched with anticipation that finally someone was going to confront this crisis in an honest and sincere way.

The event began with Governor Snyder making some opening remarks before he introduced the President. The crowd immediately booed him as he reached the podium. Snyder then stated in reaction to the crowd's response, "I understand why you are angry and frustrated. I wanted to come here to apologize." Someone in the audience shouted, "too late!" He then introduced Obama and the crowd's demeanor transformed immediately from anger to jubilation.

The President began to speak as everyone in the room listened for the words that they all had been longing for since the crisis began. Obama orated "Flint's recovery is everybody's responsibility." He then assured them that "I see you and hear you." The crowd cheered. Then without any prompting, the President asked for a glass of water while letting the audience know that this was not a stunt and that he was thirsty. The audience continued to applaud not knowing the purpose of this choreographed political moment. One of the residents exclaimed that you better make sure it is "bottled water."

Obama then sipped from the glass and placed it nonchalantly under the lectern. The crowd sensing something was not right became quiet. The President then patronized the audience with an example to demonstrate to them that a little lead was not harmful. He stated that he was sure that as a young child he had pulled lead paint off the wall and ate it. The audience sat stunned as their leader continued his commentary. The people that watched all this play out were utterly disgusted. Michael Moore who interviewed several of the residents that witnessed the event asked him rhetorically, "Why would you do that?"

The second event occurred backstage with the "criminal Governor" and the press. The President during his commentary asked for another glass of water and sipped from the cup. He later was filmed chatting with the Governor in the Presidential helicopter that would take him to the airport. When he reached the airport, he ran up the stairs as he always had done and waved to the crowd, as though he had done something noble. He then turned and entered Airforce 1 and flew up into the clouds never to return to Flint during his presidency.

The Governor followed up this Presidential visit with a statement to the press. He reaffirmed that the crisis was resolved and that the President had reinforced his contention that the filtered-Flint water was safe.

Moore interviewed black and white residents of Flint to get their reaction to what had transpired that day. They told him that they thought the calvary was coming to save them. They believed that Obama would declare the city of Flint a disaster area that would qualify them for healthcare and rebuild the city's water infrastructure. Instead, he mocked and minimized what they had been struggling with and the trauma they as a community had suffered at the hands of a corrupt Governor and his handpicked cronies. One woman in frustration sadly remarked "He was our hero, and we thought he had come to help us." Another young woman stated, "When he came, he was my President. When he left, he was not my President."

Jordan Chariton, formerly a journalist with The Young Turks, told Jimmy Dore in an interview that apparently without further investigation the Obama administration had accepted Governor Snyder's claims and state EPA official declarations on the matter.[145]

The Flint issue slowly faded from local and corporate media attention. And yet, the complaints by Flint residents continued.

The Hidden War

Chariton in that interview with Dore indicated that he decided to conduct his own investigation in 2019. They knocked on 450 doors and spoke with 150 residents, primarily, but not exclusively, in Black neighborhoods. What he discovered, as universally reported by residents, was that the State EPA representatives that conducted the tests that state officials used to declare that the water was now within State and federal guidelines had been fraudulently done. Each person they conversed with told Chariton and his crew that the officials would come in and run the water for 5 minutes prior to taking a sample that would later be tested in a lab. The officials were essentially flushing the lines before taking samples which is a violation of their written protocols and procedures. By doing this, they were dispensing with the stagnant water that would have higher concentrations of contaminants, such as lead, which is the water that you want to test to obtain accurate results.

Erin Brockovich, a well-known consumer advocate and environmental activist, when she heard how the study was conducted stated that this was "criminal" and was "one of the biggest coverups in the country."

This was only the tip of an exceptionally large iceberg. Chariton learned through documentation and interviews that Governor Snyder was warned one year before the water switch that the Flint River was full of bacteria, carcinogens and legionella which causes Legionnaire's disease. In fact, six months into the crisis people were developing and dying from Legionnaire's pneumonia. This was 16 months before he testified about the matter to Congress. His testimony of course did not accurately describe what he knew and when he knew it prior to his approval to switch Flint's water source. According to Chariton, the prosecutors who were investigating these matters were all fired by Snyder. Although some lower ranking officials were prosecuted, Snyder and his cohorts left office without any repercussions that resulted from this devastating human tragedy that he sanctioned, knowing the hazards that would befall an unsuspecting poor community.

As an aside, the statute of limitations for felony misconduct for public officials in Michigan is 6 years and that expired on April 25, 2020.

The resolution and prevention of this crisis would have been to never have switched from good water to bad. But after the corrosion of the pipes had occurred, the only way to have fixed the problem would have been to replace all the piping that would have cost $1.5 billion. Of course, the neighborhoods most impacted by the crisis were poor and black. If this had been in Greenwich, Connecticut or Beverly Hills, the pipes would have been replaced immediately.

Tulsi Gabbard was one of a very few that demanded an investigation based on Chariton's findings. The Justice Democrats, including Alexandria Ocasio-Cortez, were sent materials from Chariton, and not one of them has replied. Even Bernie Sanders has not responded to their investigation. In fact, Newsweek who was supposed to include an essay written by Chariton in their publication decided not to publish it because the study was "too complicated" for its subscribers. This caused Chariton in frustration to rhetorically blurt out during his interview with Dore, "What kind of country do we live in?"

The crisis still lingers and the residents who are trapped their still pay for contaminated water that they cannot safely use. Those that must use it are still getting rashes, losing hair and the children are still manifesting cognitive problems.[146]

The cancers that will afflict this population will eventually appear, killing many who were needlessly exposed to these toxins by their leaders. As expensive as replacing the piping infrastructure would have been, it is nothing compared to the healthcare costs that are and will be incurred by the residents of Flint for decades, not to mention the suffering that they have endured that has diminished the quality of life for many and has destroyed their children's future. These human costs are incalculable.

These victims of callous, if not criminal, decisions by public officials whose obligation was to protect them from these types of hazards are representative of what Dr. King referred to as the "unheard" that suffer in silence because they are poor, black and without power. It is one of many absurdities that exist in our society that we must remind ourselves that "Black Lives Matter."

CHAPTER 22
Broken Windows

The society in which we live is so fractured that it burdens segments of our government to ameliorate the growing despair and social unrest that structurally they were never designed to repair. It is a blatant representation of the failure of our leadership, and the policies they have implemented over the last few decades, that are unable, and in some cases unwilling, to make the systemic changes that would permit our democratic institutions to implement preventative programs to avert the severity of the social ills that plague this nation.

A primary example was observed by Judge Herbert Klein in Miami-Dade County in Florida in 1989 who stressed that his local jails were teeming with inmates who were mentally ill. The jail staff were not trained to address their needs which in some cases led to serious injuries, revictimization and even suicide. He also noted that many were suffering from serious withdraw from their drugs of choice. It was these observations that inspired the development of specialty courts, along with a task force's findings in Massachusetts that was organized by then Governor Michael Dukakis in the late 1980s. These courts were outside the box of standard practices in the judicial branch and initially were met with significant resistance. Judges on many occasions would blurt out in meetings and even while on the bench that "I was never trained to be a social worker."

The basic premise of Drug Courts – which are one of many problem solving courts – is that high risk non-violent defendants are admitted to a long term structured program administered by a multi-disciplinary team composed of treatment, case management, prosecutors, public defenders, law enforcement and a Judge who is the chairperson. The program has strict requirements that mandate treatment participation in which the team supports the goals of their treatment plan by imposing negative and positive reinforcement to change their behavior and achieve long term sobriety.

Today, there are thousands of drug courts throughout the nation helping addicts, veterans and those with co-occurring disorders reclaim their lives and become productive members of society. Although their success rates are much higher than voluntary treatment programs, incarceration or probation, many graduates unfortunately over time become complacent and slowly drift back into the thralls of their addiction. These are intensive and very time-consuming initiatives that are confronting long term maladies that if these defendants had been treated early on for their trauma or other mental health issues could have been prevented, resulting in significant reductions of expense to society.

New studies on trauma inducing events that can develop if untreated into other mental health syndromes, including Post-Traumatic Stress Disorder (PTSD,) have asserted that up to 80% of mental illness originated as a consequence of a single traumatic event or over a period of time, such as child sexual abuse or a domestic violent relationship. My observations over the last 30 years confirms their findings. As a lawyer, and most particularly as a case manager in a drug court and pretrial release, I have noted that 8 out of every 10 women I have worked with had a trauma history and at least 6 out of every 10 men. Some of them were veterans who served in our numerous wars.

The reality that confronted the criminal courts was that many were being brought before these judges not because they were dangerous criminals but were individuals with untreated mental health issues that resulted in severe addictions as witnessed by Judge Klein. They essentially got caught up in this declared war on drugs that the Nixon administration started in 1971. A war that has cost this nation trillions of dollars and yet the country's obsession with drugs as a tool to ameliorate the stress and emotional pain that many of our citizens are suffering from has become significantly worse.

Currently, most of our policies are geared towards confronting these problems in a reactionary way; problems that become monuments of our failed system and appear unsolvable to many. This is a consequence of several factors. In many cases, the national pathologies that are manifested by social unrest, violence, broken families, suicides, and severe addictions are masking far greater evils that continue to fester by the government's ongoing neglect. A distressing reality that the elite implicitly encourage because there are far greater profits to be realized in solving the problem once it has occurred than preventative measures that would have resolved the matter before it became a crisis. For instance, it is more profitable to build prisons, large courthouses and fund a vast network of law enforcement agencies than to implement policies to prevent childhood abuse and to support labor and provide universal healthcare. These factors have had severe negative impacts on the nation's courts and criminal justice system.

We also see this manifested in our nation's healthcare policies that inevitably promote profits over patients. There is more money to be made in developing treatments that include highly profitable pharmaceutical remedies than to engage in programs that prevent the factors that contribute to the ills that plague our national healthcare system, such as diabetes, obesity, cardiovascular pathologies, and cancer.

The remedies for many are cheap and easy to implement. They include a daily regimen of exercise, good nutrition, quality supplements, annual physicals, clean air and water, and the development of positive coping skills that mitigate environmental stress imposed on each individual as a result of the complexities inherent in this fast paced modern society in which we all must navigate.

This is also true for our overburdened criminal justice system. Because of the vast economic inequities, the lack of healthcare, lack of quality jobs that provide a livable wage, dilapidated and neglected neighborhoods, rampant injustice and corruption, lack of quality education and the numerous cases of untreated trauma that our children and adults have been subjected to all contribute to high crime rates, extensive addictions to alcohol and illicit drugs, and the neglect of our children.

The consequence for the courts are large child protection and criminal dockets and for prosecutors, assistant attorney generals and court appointed defense attorneys, or public defenders, are unmanageable caseloads that compel triage practices that in many cases unfairly impact the poor, creating a system that is prone to trampling on the defendant's fundamental constitutional rights while imposing on many unjust resolutions.

Hence, 97% of criminal cases are resolved by plea bargains or what many refer to as plea agreements. Most of those cases that defense counsel threatens to compel the prosecutors to fulfill their burdens of proof by vetting the evidence or going to trial are wealthy defendant's that can afford the legal fees associated with a zealous defense. In many cases, these affluent defendant's, who are predominantly white, get offers that provide an opportunity for the defendant to remedy the problem or participate in treatment in return for all charges being dropped. This is rarely, if ever, offered to a poor defendant, and almost never offered to poor citizens of color. In fact, Blacks and Hispanics are 25% more likely to be detained without bail and receive plea deals that include jail and/or prison sentences than white defendants. The consequence of these prosecutorial and structural biases is that 68% of inmates in our prison complex are people of color.

These structural issues also have consequences for the methods employed by law enforcement to confront the wave of crime they are mandated to deter and reduce, and the types of policing implemented to achieve those objectives. Many of the strategies that get applied unfortunately further alienate the individual officers with the communities that they are assigned to serve and protect. And for the residents of those communities, they do not perceive those officers as a support resource but rather as an occupational force that they fear.

This dynamic has created within many law enforcement agencies, particularly large municipality departments, an "us verse them" attitude that further entrenches an already corrupt culture within these departments that revile and feel threatened by the communities they are empowered to protect. And because of racial prejudices embedded in our society, this encourages racial profiling, over policing and aggressive tactics that further divide the residents of that community with the officers that patrol their districts that predictably leads to violence and tragedy. And because of the advent of smart phones, these violent injustices perpetrated by police have been captured on videos disseminated on the world-wide web for all to see. Confrontations that in the past were left to the integrity of the officers that reported on the events that led to the injury or death of the accused.

George Kelling was a criminologist that was employed at a large children's psychiatric facility in the late 1950s. He was appalled by the so-called Freudian methods used by the staff to treat the children. He resisted this policy by enforcing common-simple rules to diminish the chaos in which these children lived to achieve some stability. When things were broken by the children while manifesting their rebellious behaviors, instead of ignoring their destruction, he would immediately repair the damage. This all contributed to positive outcomes. His observations while at that facility would eventually be applied to the complex problem of crime and civil unrest in America's largest cities.[147]

He began to conduct studies on the effectiveness of foot patrols verse patrol cars in the 1960s. He surmised that policing was not just about enforcing the law but more importantly was about "maintaining order." He believed that the reduction of fear of crime was primary so that elderly for instance would feel safe to venture out at night in their neighborhoods. He felt that foot patrols were more effective at achieving that goal.[148]

His work was noticed by Harvard professor James Wilson who had invited him to co-author an article on law enforcement for a magazine called the "Atlantic." Professor Wilson also engaged Stanford professor Philip Zimbardo to implement an experiment in two distinct neighborhoods to study the

The Hidden War

reaction of the residents. Essentially, he left a car with its hood up and its license plate removed in a poor Bronx neighborhood and an affluent white community in Palo Alto. The automobile in the Bronx was immediately "skeletonized" in that its radio, battery and wheels were taken. The only thing left was the shell of the vehicle. In Palo Alto, the car was left untouched.[149]

Zimbardo then decided to go back to that vehicle and smash the windshield with a sledgehammer. The residents of the affluent neighborhood then "acted as though they were given permission to vandalize the vehicle."[150]

He was testing a theory long held by his peers that "If a window in a building was left unrepaired all of the rest of the windows will soon be broken." Hence, the title of their article became "Broken Windows."[151] This also became the name of a policy that would be adapted by large police departments in many of our cities in the 1980s up through the present.

Since the primary objective for police was maintaining order, a vague objective that is hard to define definitively that naturally would provide law enforcement a wide latitude to achieve it. Accordingly, Kelling argued that "Broken Windows" to work effectively on the scale that was required the police would be "given expanded leeway to enforce a nebulous and unwritten concept of law and order." Though it is not explicitly stated, it is implied by necessity that to achieve that laudable objective the cities would have to vigorously enforce "old vague vagrancy laws" and other petty crimes. It would also require senior officers to turn a blind eye to the occasional "ass kicking" by patrol officers of so-called troublemakers.[152] This was all required to prevent the "Broken Window" phenomenon. The elimination of numerous petty crimes would prevent the circumstances in which more serious crimes would be encouraged.

Kelling and Wilson were keenly cognizant of the fact of potential abuse and prospective racial profiling that might occur. He knew from examples he had read about in South Boston that maintaining order usually translated into keeping black people out of their neighborhoods. Nevertheless, he was hoping that stringent training, recruitment of qualified officers and constructive supervision would mitigate these potential abuses and would encourage officers to limit their discretion appropriately, knowing how it should be applied in each case.[153]

The problem with his presumptions would manifest in a very divisive and controversial policy first implemented in our most iconic metropolitan center, New York City. The two primary issues that hindered the overall effectiveness of his theory were that he underestimated how entrenched and prevalent racial biases were within these precincts. Secondly, he dismissed the destructive impact that the "code of silence" and other corruptive influences that permeated throughout the culture of each department could pose for the integrity of his program. The consequence in many cases, if not all, was that "bad cops" were protected by the system as opposed to being weeded out. It was not only frowned upon for any officer to report abuse or corruptive practices in these departments, but the loyalty demanded by their codes required absolute silence and those who violated them were labelled "rats" and in some cases subjected to rejection and violence, as was the case for New York Detective Frank Serpico that was depicted in a provocative movie released in 1973 in which Serpico was portrayed by Al Pacino.

Additionally, many police unions have blindly supported their members by providing rationalizations for the actions perpetrated by individual or groups of officers. Because of this, they have become part of the problem by wittingly reinforcing this counterproductive culture that eventually corrupts the good cops and protects the bad officers by not holding its members accountable for their biases and destructive behaviors.

Another contextual reality Kelling's new police strategy had to contend with in the 1970s was a weakening economy and growing crime rates in every city. Most major cities were in serious decline, and New York was the primary symbol of this pervasive trend.[154] Much of white America was migrating away from inner city life, bringing with them all the amenities of the city in the form of strip malls, large supermarkets, restaurants, and movie theaters, to obtain the tranquility of suburban life. They essentially were escaping the high crime rates and civil disorder that existed in many of our metropolitan centers. Much of this crime was associated with people of color as depicted in common stereotypes in cop shows on television and in the movies.

I vaguely remember as an adolescent reading about neighborhoods in the Bronx that even the police would not enter. These myths were reinforced and perpetuated in movies such as "Death Wish" and its many sequels that starred the iconic macho actor Charles Bronson who administered vigilante justice against powerful gangs and thugs that terrified the residents of these communities who were often portrayed by Hispanic and Black actors.

Kelling's reforms known as "Broken Windows" was first implemented in New York's extensive subway system that was plagued by vagrants and petty crime. New York's mayor brought in a seasoned and tough Irish cop from Boston

The Hidden War

named William Bratton who was appointed as the new chief of the Transit Police Department. His aggressive style of policing had some positive effects and was successful in reducing crime beneath the busy streets of New York. He was a "strong proponent" of Broken Windows. His primary objective was to take back the subway terminals from vagrants, drug addicts and criminals, restoring law and order. During his tenure, crime rates dropped 35% compared with a drop of only 17.9% at street level. His success was eventually rewarded by Mayor Rudy Giuliani when in 1994 Bratton was promoted to Chief of Police for all of New York City.[155]

Bratton's primary focus when implementing Broken Windows was "action and statistics" that were achieving positive outcomes. He was not interested in passive street patrolling in vehicles. He wanted officers on the ground and visible to the communities in which they patrolled. He wanted these officers to engage the residents and was less interested in solving crimes one at a time but rather wanted to prevent the circumstances that encouraged criminal behavior by a "goal setting culture" that produced outcomes that could be statistically measured.

The New York Police Department began to operate like a "giant corporation." Bratton's high-ranking officers would meet weekly in conference rooms reporting their precinct's statistics and discussing ongoing strategies. It was within these meetings that "stop and frisk" tactics were first discussed and then latter implemented under their Broken Window program.[156]

The focus then became the number of UF-250 police forms that were being filed each week that documented each stop by an officer. They were not interested in the number of felonies that were solved but were more focused on the amount of stops police in the streets were involved in.[157] Initially, the drop-in crime rates in these neighborhoods encouraged this type of policing and had aided the morale of the Department, but more importantly emboldened officers to rachet up their aggressive engagements in the neighborhoods they were targeting. Mind you, this police enforcement strategy was completely dependent upon each officer applying good discretionary judgment.

At the height of this stop and frisk tactic, 680,000 citizens a year were engaged by officers which resulted in millions of summons and arrests for petty crimes. Throughout the tenure of the program, Black and Hispanic residents accounted for 80% to 90% of all stops. This was occurring in a city in which they only comprised of 45% of the population. In addition, 90% to 95% imprisoned for non-violent drug offenses were citizens of color even though 72% of illegal drug users in the city were white.[158]

The reduction in crime rates, however, were widely reported by the media and politicians which led to this strategy spreading to other large cities. The only critics initially of Broken Windows and stop and frisk tactics were the minority neighborhoods that had been systematically targeted by police.

As the tidal wave of cases overwhelmed the court dockets, defense lawyers and public defenders began hearing all the horror stories being reported to them by their clients and colleagues. Scores of Black and Hispanic defendants told their lawyers that they were being assaulted and harrassed by officers who repeatedly "busted" them for "nonsense crimes" such as obstructing government administration, loitering, or obstructing pedestrian traffic. They even disclosed that some were being stripped searched on the street, humiliating them in front of neighbors and the public. Even judges knew that the charges were bogus and, in some cases, dismissed the charges while on the bench.[159]

During Mayor Bloomberg's reign of power, the stated goal was to change the psyche of young Black and Latino men by "instilling fear in them" every time they stepped out onto the street.[160]

Jesse Ventura described on the Jimmy Dore Show the effects it was having particularly on African American citizens. He revealed that a professional friend of his that resided in Minneapolis told him that every time he goes to the store at night that he places his license, registration, and insurance card on the dashboard of his vehicle. He stated that the purpose of this - as reported to him by his friend - is to prevent getting shot by an officer who mistakenly conflates his opening a glove compartment for reaching for a gun. Ventura added that throughout his life it never occurred to him as a white man to worry about the potential hazards of being pulled over by police.

The consequence of this police strategy was encapsulated in the unnecessary and tragic death of Eric Garner in 2014 that was not even committing the crime he was alleged to have done that day. It was true that on many prior occasions he had sold cigarettes without a stamp tax at that location but on that fateful day there were no customers. The police had essentially targeted a large conspicuous Black man that many of the Staten Island officers had become familiar with from prior interactions. Once the officers engaged him, they were determined to take him into custody and charge him with a petty crime. On this day, Garner decided that he was not going to compliantly go to jail as he

The Hidden War

had done so many times before. He argued with the officers that he had not committed a crime and inquired why they were doing this to him. This was to no avail. His plea for justice culminated in his death because of an illegal chokehold administered by one of their troubled officers who had upwards of 14 complaints for abusive and violent behavior in his relatively short career.

Matt Tiabbi in his fine book "I can't Breathe" wrote "Garner's death launched the career of the prosecutor who failed to indict a policeman who killed him. It even contributed to a national backlash political movement that eventually coalesced (around) a presidential candidate, Donald Trump, whose 'Make America Great Again' platform drew from an old well of white resentments." Once elected President, Trump appointed Jeff Session as the Attorney General who had a history of opposing civil rights. As Tiabbi noted, the nation clearly was moving back in time as it rejected the ideals of the long forgotten civil rights era.[161]

Tiabbi added, "But Eric Garner isn't a symbol. He was a flesh-and-blood person-interesting, imperfect, funny, ambitious, and alive – who just happened to stumble into the thresher of America's racist insanity at exactly the wrong time. But his story – about how ethnic resentments can be manipulated politically to leave us vulnerable to the lawless violence of our government – is not his alone. His bad luck has now become ours."[162]

He was not the first and certainly will not be the last victim of police bias and our nation's racist legacy. The latest victim is George Floyd soon to be followed by others.

This is a story that has a much larger relevance and meaning for us all. What is happening to our criminal justice system is a symptom of a much larger malady that is plaguing this nation and threatens the future of our children. A nation that has squandered its good fortune and promise to become another ethically bankrupt empire, imposing its will on the world by its weapons of war and its willingness to engage in violence no matter what the consequences for its citizens or for humanity to achieve the selfish objectives of rapacious plutocrats.

We have saddled our criminal justice system with the monumental task of solving our propensity as a culture for violence and to maintain order in a system that does not respect law nor the sanctity of human life, especially if they are black. A society that demands law and order for the poor and tolerates outrageous entitlements for the rich.

The whole approach of this misguided policy is irrational and ineffective because the underlining causes for crime, civil unrest and violence are triggered by the decay of our democratic institutions which have created circumstances in which our government is no longer capable of administering to the needs of its people or even representing them. Most of our representatives and senators, and even our presidents, are beholden to special interests and wittingly ignore the needs of the governed.

Hence, we reside in a nation that incarcerates a larger percentage of our citizens than any nation on earth. We consume 80% of the globe's opioids at a cost of $24 billion and 59,000 overdoses annually. We have more violent crime than any of our western competitors or allies. We have dozens of suicides every day. Our economy is based on the profits of predatory financial institutions and speculative investments that do not produce anything, not even good paying jobs. We are dependent on gambling casinos, pornography, pharmaceutical advances, weapon sales and war to sustain us.

Chris Hedges observed, "The radical left and the radical right, each made up of people who have been cast aside by the cruelty of corporate capitalism, have embraced holy war. Their marginalized lives, battered by economic misery, have been filled with meaning. They hold themselves up as the vanguard of the oppressed. They claim the right to use force to silence those defined as the enemy. They sanctify anger. They are consumed by the adrenaline driven urge for confrontation (much like our police departments). These groups are separated, as Sigmund Freud wrote of those who engage in fratricide, by the 'narcissism' of minor differences.'"[163]

He added that, "It was inevitable that we would reach this point. A paralyzed government, unable and unwilling to address the rudimentary needs of its citizens, as I saw in the former Yugoslavia and as was true in the Weimar Republic and Czarist Russia, empowers extremists. Extremism, as the social critic Christopher Lasch wrote, is 'a refuge from the terrors of inner life.'"[164]

The prescriptions for our social ills are conceptually simple but because of the nature of our current political system require courage and vigilance if these remedies are to be reenacted. I say reenacted because in my youth many of them were in place or were in the process of being implemented. These remedies consist of reenergizing labor to compel corporate conglomerates to provide livable wages with descent benefits. We need to bring good jobs into our inner-city neighborhoods by enacting regulations and programs that direct investment in these long-neglected areas of our nation. We need to rebuild our

The Hidden War

public schools, our infrastructure and develop new technologies that confront climate change and encourage the development of clean energy sources such as hydrogen and fusion technologies. The building of plants that remove toxins from our air and desalinate ocean water to mitigate water shortages in times of drought, as was done in Singapore.

We need to rebuild our manufacturing capacity by retooling our industrial base to build civilian products not the instruments of war, as we did at the end of World War II. And this nation must throw our illogical fears of socialism aside and provide a universal healthcare system that enables all our citizens access to quality healthcare. A system that encourages and invests heavily on preventative measures to avoid the serious diseases and maladies that are expensive to treat effectively.

This would also enable our nation to treat trauma at its inception to prevent the manifestation of maladaptive behaviors in adults that contribute to addiction, anti-social behaviors, suicides, and crime. And finally, we need to end this war on drugs and legalize or at a minimum decriminalize them. This would undercut and bankrupt the black markets controlled by ruthless drug cartels and other organized criminal entities just as the end of prohibition did in the 1930s. It would also unclog our court dockets and significantly reduce our prison populations, as well as saving the nation tens of billions of dollars each year.

The strategies of "Broken Windows", "Stop and Frisk", and the militarization of our police are not the solutions to crime or our social ills. These policies will only encourage over policing, officer abuse, racial profiling, and a disintegration of the relationship between the police departments and the communities they are mandated to protect and serve.

This will not be easy to achieve. Large amounts of political capital, investments, lobbying and violence have been invoked to create the corrupt system we have today. Hedges sagaciously observed, "The corporate state makes no pretense of addressing social inequality or white supremacy. It practices only the politics of vengeance. It uses coercion, fear, violence, police terror and mass incarceration as forms of social control while it cannibalizes the nation and the globe for profits. Our cells of resistance have to be rebuilt from scratch."[165]

The choice is ours, for like our forebears who engaged in sit in strikes or marched in the streets who paid the price, sometimes with their lives, to come together in a common cause to recapture what was stolen from us, or we can continue to enable this corrupt system administered by rapacious modern robber barons who are destroying the America we all love and the future of our children that we should be willing to fight for.

CHAPTER 23
The Need for Public Financial Banks and the Hazards of Incrementalism

The creation of Public Financial Institutions that were successfully used to fund and invest in New Deal programs could be highly effective in funding the policies we so desperately need in the present.

By merging the Treasury with the Federal Reserve as is being done to confront the financial crisis created by COVID-19, according to Ellen Brown, an author and founder of the think tank the Public Financial Institute, they are essentially creating the same mechanism that the Roosevelt administration utilized to pay for the programs that were enacted to ameliorate the suffering caused by the Great Depression that could potentially fund programs that benefit us all, such as Medicare for all, free state and community universities, provide universal basic income, invest in clean and bio-friendly technologies, massive infrastructure enhancements, repairs and new additions, as well as programs properly targeted to help the poor and provide shelter for the homeless.

The Reconstruction Finance Corporation (RFC) was created on January 22, 1932, by President Herbert Hoover to provide support and rebuild confidence in the financial sector as he was transferring power to the incoming Roosevelt Administration. The RFC was essentially a publicly owned credit-lending agency which invested in thousands of projects from 1932 through 1941, ranging from national infrastructure and small-business enterprises. It invested and paid for bridges, dams, post offices, electrical power, mortgages, farms and much more. Because of these initiatives, thousands of good jobs were saved and created that significantly reduced the unemployment rolls during the financial crisis. By 1941, it had loaned out over $9 billion.

The RFC also assisted in the war effort and in the post-war period. By the time it was totally disbanded by the Eisenhower administration, succumbing to the intense lobbying of private banks and Wall Street speculators, it had loaned out tens of billions of dollars and accomplished all of this while generating income for the government.

As I argued in my book "Rethinking America", the funding of large programs and projects are not "pie in the sky proposals" as asserted by former President Obama, Hillary Clinton, Nancy Pelosi, Chuck Schumer, Mitch McConnell, or their corporate media mouth pieces. They are essentially lying to us. It is all about reorienting our priorities.

The slogans such as "don't sacrifice the good for the great", or you must "vote blue no matter who" or labels meant to demean your objectives such as "purists", "socialists" or impractical "dreamers and idealists" are attempts by the political establishment and the power elite to convince you that you should accept that going back to normal, meaning beyond Trump and COVID 19, should be the objective.

The problem with this perspective is that what was considered normal prior to the 2016 election was a militaristic and inequitable system that was not sustainable and was placing our children's future in peril. It was a system based on crony capitalism; a corrupt political system focused on meeting the needs of special interests and not the governed. A system that was protecting an empire not a republic by the creation of a "Pax Americana" imposed on the rest of the world by our weapons of war; Which by the way is basically the same system we have under Trump.

The other argument, as framed by its proponents, is that we must achieve our objectives by taking one step at a time or what is commonly referred to as "incrementalism." Historically this approach was somewhat effective. However, since the 1980s, we have weakened our democratic institutions and eviscerated many of our fundamental rights to such an extent that change by this method has been made almost impossible as argued by Pulitzer prize winning journalist, Chris Hedges.

The task of rebuilding our republic requires thinking outside the proverbial box by implementing radical changes to our political, social, and economic structures. Some of these changes require re-instituting laws such as section 4 of the 1965 Voting Rights Act, the Glass-Steagall Act, the Fairness Doctrine, internet-neutrality and by repealing those segments of the Telecommunications Act of 1996 that enabled 6 giant corporations to own 95% of our media outlets and the overturning of Citizens United. Other changes should be inspired by new perspectives that confront the present ills that inflict our society and our rapidly contributing to our national decline.

What we need now are not words of caution and patience but rather words of urgency that empower our resolve to confront our national challenges with comprehensive solutions that concede the magnitude of the calamity that awaits us just over the horizon.

The Hidden War

In another time when liberty seemed too far to reach and yet there for the taking, Thomas Paine made his compelling plea to his neighbors and fellow countrymen to stand their ground and risk it all by reaching for freedom. He wrote, "These are the times that try men's souls. The summer soldier and the sunshine patriot will, in a crisis, shrink from the service of their country, but he who stands by it now, deserves the love and thanks of men and women. Tyranny, like hell, is not easily conquered; yet we have this consolation with us, that the harder the conflict, the more glorious the triumph..."

The change we seek will not be given to us. It must be earned. For as Frederick Douglass so passionately asserted, "Power concedes nothing without a demand. It never did and it never will."

This pandemic is an opportunity to demand not handouts, but rather fairness and justice. The context of our times should not be framed by movements in search of the lesser evil or what is less egregious. It should be about fulfilling our national ideals by saving our national soul in our quest for justice, liberty, and truth.

CONCLUSION
(Where are the Leaders?)

The first half of this volume set forth the circumstances that provided the contextual framework for what eventually culminated in another civil war in the 1960s. A conflict that for most remained hidden in the dark alcoves of our society and our government that would forever change the America that I knew as a child. The second half of my book unveiled the consequences to all those that were on the losing side of that hidden war that were unaware of this treacherous development. The victors of that battle immediately took advantage of our naïve ignorance and began to impose their ideological vision upon the rest of us that this nation has faithfully followed until the present.

This vision that manifested in a neo-colonial power whose foundation was skillfully erected in the 1970s and 1980s that over time transformed into a modern Gilded Age with a new set of rapacious robber barons. A nation that is currently viewed by the rest of the globe as a heartless empire that uses propaganda, coercion, and violence to sustain its hegemony at home and around the world. Consequently, over these five decades we have become financially addicted to manufacturing the weapons that are necessary to fight our perpetual wars to maintain that empire while the rest of the country slowly rots in austerity.

To perpetuate this political, economic and social construct that exacerbate the contradictions and hypocrisies that govern us, the power elite have captured both major parties such that they feed at the same trough and support the same corporatist and militaristic orthodoxy that justifies the desecration of our liberty and the republic it once nourished. It really does not matter anymore which party is in power. The real rulers are embedded in our national security complex whose alliance with Wall Street ensures that Congress and the president implement their desired policies that allegedly enhance our liberty and our security. In addition, they have coopted the mainstream media that spew out their insidious propaganda to manufacture our consent to maintain this political arrangement by voting for candidates and policies that reinforce the status quo while proposing token and symbolic reforms that create the illusion of change. Change that the gullible hope will advance the interest of the governed, but never do.

The consequences are in plain view for those who are willing to look. We now live in a nation in which approximately 80% of Americans live paycheck to paycheck. A society that has the largest disparity between the poor and the rich of all western nations. The wages for most as labor's influence has declined has been stagnant for decades. A healthcare system that condemns 70,000 each year to an early death because they cannot afford access to quality care or the 40 million who remain uninsured and millions more who are underinsured.

Although poor nations like Cuba have financed national healthcare systems that efficiently meet the needs of their people, we continue to accept the assertion of our national leaders that the richest nation on earth cannot afford such a program, even though as elected legislators they benefit from a comprehensive government financed healthcare program that they refuse to give to their constituents. Hence, they continue to support a market based system that enriches for profit hospitals, insurance carriers and pharmaceutical companies while providing outcomes consistent with a third world nation whose access to medical technology is drastically limited compared to what is available in the U.S. Simply because of our irrational aversion to that word "socialism", we continue to accept a failed healthcare system whose weaknesses have been further unveiled by the current pandemic facing the country.

We also have public schools that are dilapidated and in need of major repairs that are part of a national system that is underfunded and overwhelmed with the same social maladies that are negatively impacting our criminal justice system. Problems that they were never created to confront that are impacting the quality of education that can be delivered to their students. Of course, the affluent avoid these issues by sending their children to private preparatory schools whose reputations permit their children admission to the most prestigious colleges and universities in the nation. And even if a student from the working or middle class can obtain a college degree, they are saddled with huge student loans that generate significant disadvantages for them in the global marketplace.

The financial burden of these loans which are equivalent in many cases to a mortgage payment prevent many graduates from pursuing apprenticeships or volunteer positions that would assist their training for careers that are related to their degrees which are also entwined with their personal passions and interests. Instead, they must accept jobs that compensate them enough to pay their monthly loan payment with interest. We have so many languishing in jobs they were never trained to do, or were certainly not interested in, just to survive. This by the way does not happen in Europe and many nations around the globe who provide a free university education, such as Cuba.

While most Americans live in a constant state of survival mode with little hope of things getting better in the future, the plutocrats blatantly rape our society without concern for pushback or consequences for their reprehensible conduct and avarice. As Jimmy Dore pointed out that we live in a nation that promotes "rugged individualism for the working class and socialism for the rich."

A primary example of this was the Cares Act passed this spring with overwhelming bi-partisan support. Essentially, as asserted by congresswoman Alexandria Ocasio- Cortez, who inexplicably voted for the bill, the people in her district – which was true for the entire nation – received "breadcrumbs" while Wall Street was given trillions of dollars to bail them out and to survive this growing health crisis. One independent journalist pointed out that the amount of money given to the richest corporations and individuals could have been redirected to the people that would have resulted in a stimulus check that could have enabled all our citizens to survive the shutdown of our economy. This money ironically would have ended up in Wall Street pockets anyway as people used this stimulus to pay their bills.

This legislation has been described by economists as the largest transfer of wealth in human history. The committee that was authorized to oversee these enormous disbursements to corporate America had no subpoena power and only could pursue investigations of possible fraud after the money had left the treasury. It was not a safeguard against abusive cronyism but was a façade created to appease progressive legislators so that they could claim to their constituents that it was being appropriately supervised.

Since the passage of the bill, $7 trillion dollars has been transferred to Wall Street by the U.S. treasury and the Federal Reserve. This included millions of dollars to bail Nancy Pelosi's husband out for a bad investment in a motel chain just prior to a pandemic, as well as Mitch McConnell's wife. Many of these plutocrats have reaped billions in profits while millions of Americans are losing their homes, their jobs, and their healthcare, during the worst epidemic since the Spanish Flu killed millions in 1919 and 1920.

The primary reason in my opinion that the first act by Congress to address the pandemic was focused on Wall Street was that the leaders in Washington wanted to prop up the markets to insure that their stock portfolios did not suffer from the anticipated financial consequences of shutting down the

The Hidden War

economy to avert the spread of COVID-19. They even delayed the announcement of this health crisis so that many legislators and other elites could sell off stock that would be negatively impacted by the pandemic and purchase stock in companies that were projected to benefit significantly at our expense. This blatant example of insider trading which is illegal has not resulted in any charges being filed to date. These are the actions of our so-called leaders from both parties that allegedly understand our pain and are looking out for our interests. It is all an illusion and a sham.

Chris Hedges in his chilling and raw book "America: The Farewell Tour" reveals the dark truth that compose our true reality. He focuses in Chapter two on the circumstances of the residents and what they must do to survive in one of our poorest cities, Camden, New Jersey. He could have been describing any number of neighborhoods in many of our metropolitan centers scattered throughout this nation, such as Baltimore, Chicago, Los Angeles, and Washington, D.C.

He penned, "The poor in America get only one chance…most will live, suffer, and die within the space of a few squalid city blocks. No jobs. No hope. No help. They blunt their despair through alcohol or drugs. And if they do get out, as did Pagano (a former prostitute he interviewed), they carry the chains of their past wrapped around them. Employers do not want them. Landlords will not rent them an apartment. Real Estate agents will not deal with them if they seek to buy a home. Banks and credit card companies will not give them credit. They never have enough money. They probably never will. They live one step away from hell. And they know what hell feels like. This is how the Wall Street gamblers, bankers, bond traders, and financial speculators, the ones with the packed wallets, the ones with the fancy cars and the multi-million dollar homes in New Jersey suburbs of Mendham, Chatham, and Short Hills, the ones who paid Pagano for sex during their nightly journey home to their wives and girlfriends, want it. The hell of the poor is their playground."

This is an example of the degradation of the residents of a city that must sell their bodies to support their children, but as I alluded to earlier this is what happens to whole countries dominated by corrupt dictators that we control like puppets, such as Baptista in Cuba. Some of the advertisements I read long ago promoted this playground of the 1950s as having the "best prostitutes" in the world. How would you like this to be the image of your nation?

This is the same predatory oppression that promotes sex trafficking of young girls and boys that make men like Jeffrey Epstein rich while socializing within the exclusive networks of high society and serving the depraved desires of the elite, exploiting the misery of the powerless and the poor for their own pleasure.

There was a time when our leaders would have prosecuted the scoundrels for their reprehensible and criminal actions to protect the naïve and defenseless youth that were being exploited and violated. They would not have shielded them from prosecution nor when caught offered plea deals that constituted a slap on the wrist. Of course, when the gig was up, they then incarcerated Epstein while his prosecution was pending. He obviously knew too much about too many in power and would conveniently be found in his jail cell lifeless allegedly because of a probable suicide. As the cliché goes, "dead men tell no tales."

These auspicious leaders that by the late 1960s were whittled down to one. As the late John Lewis reflected on the tragedy of Dr. King's assassination and how his sagacious and inspiring presence would be missed, he assuaged his grief at the time by reminding himself that, "We still have Bobby." All the hopes of a better country and a just future for many coalesced with the quixotic campaign for the presidency of one man.

On a warm night on June 5th, 1968, they gathered in a ballroom filled with the exhilaration of a momentary triumph for those seeking progressive systemic change. The exultation captured by that instant that lingered briefly in a time when we could still dream of the promised land that Dr. King had seen on the mountain top. At the apex of that joy, Senator Robert F. Kennedy stood on a podium at the Ambassador Hotel after winning the all-important California primary on that fateful night declared, "I think we can end the divisions in the United States. What I Think is quite clear is that we can work together in the last analysis. And what has been going on in the United States over the last three years, the division, the violence, the disenchantment with our society, divisions between blacks and whites, the poor and more affluent, between age groups or the war in Vietnam, that we can start to work together. We are a great country, a selfless country, and a compassionate country, and I intend to make that my basis for running in the period of the next few months."

And they did come together for him to make that victory possible. He had Cesar Chavez and the Mexican community, the Black Panthers who provided his security when he campaigned in Watts along with his private security made up of Olympian Rafer Johnson and former member of the Fearsome Foursome of the Los Angeles Rams Rosey Grier, the black community, and many

The Hidden War

members of the white working class and the labor unions that all contributed to his triumph that night.

This was one of the leaders of my youth that inspired a generation to build a better future. This is the nation that I thought of when asked by teachers to reflect on the meaning of growing up in the U.S.A.

His death ended the resistance or any tangible threat to the growing empire. For that generation, it was the last gasp for a peaceful revolution empowered by the ideals of liberty and justice for all that founded the nation. A promise that remains unfulfilled. A mountain top that has yet to be seen by the people.

The nation that I believed in at the time seems like a distant memory whose faint traces make it difficult to clearly imagine the affection we had of that America, living within the protected enclaves of a prosperous, sanguine, and influential middle class. Did this nation really exist or was it a hope, a vision, a mirage created by our heartfelt beliefs that we were a great and compassionate nation?

The policies of the Johnson administration did not reflect that image as we attempted to bomb a poor nation into another stone age. This of course was true then as it is now. And of course, the leaders that represented the best in all of us, and the promise of a nation, were all murdered so that we could claim our place among the dominant empires of history. An empire that would sadly replicate the same mistakes, the same horrors, the same oppressive strategies to maintain its supremacy.

Those courageous and compassionate leaders that championed the laudable goals of multiple movements seeking social progress and justice were casualties of that hidden war that were never replaced and to some degree were irreplaceable. Like our founders, Lincoln, and the Roosevelts, they only emerge every so often. Their absence has left us five decades later with feckless and heartless leaders that ignore our demands for the same universal principles that people were marching for in my youth. These rapacious plutocrats and war mongers that masquerade as visionaries such as Hillary and Bill Clinton, Dick Cheney, George W. Bush, Nancy Pelosi, Chuck Schumer, Mitch McConnell, Barack Obama, James Comey, Robert Mueller, John Brennan, Susan Rice, Kamala Harris, Gina Haspel, James Clapper, Michael Pompeo, Joe Biden, and of course President Donald Trump.

Where are the leaders that want to end the divisions in this nation and bring us together in a common cause to rebuild our republic and fulfill the promise that was once that of America. The promise to make all our citizens free and to end the wars. The leaders that normally emerge in time of crisis.

The nation struggles while marching in the streets, leaderless. There are no champions to unify the cause and inspire righteous change. It is as sung by Simon and Garfunkel in their theme song written for the movie "The Graduate" entitled "Mrs. Robinson" that won them an Academy Award for best song in 1970. A nation that even then was in search of heroes.

"Where have you gone, Joe DiMaggio?
A nation turns its lonely eyes to you.
What's that you say, Mrs. Robinson?
Joltin' Joe has left and gone away."

EPILOGUE

Chris Hedges persuasively argued in many of his editorials that Bernie Sanders is a social democrat not a radical thinker or a socialist or a communist as the elites in both parties, including the corporate media, are attempting to portray him as. He is essentially a modern-day proponent of the New Deal and the New Frontier. He is not an anarchist who is advancing extremist policies as his opponents have argued.

President Franklin Roosevelt signed the Social Security Act in 1935 to ameliorate the vast injustices and human suffering that the Great Depression had unveiled by removing the curtain that had hidden these unacceptable tribulations of the working class and the elderly. At the time, the elites in opposition to Social Security put forward the same arguments that are used today to scare the public into supporting a for profit health care system that primarily benefits the insurance and pharmaceutical giants, and the affluent in our society.

When President John F. Kennedy proposed Medicare - which was health care for the elderly - he too was bombarded with baseless assertions that it was cost prohibitive, too bureaucratic and was a socialistic program. He at the time dismissed these arguments as fear mongering to frighten and confuse the public on the actual merits of his program. He was unable to get it passed prior to his assassination. It was eventually signed by President Johnson in 1965.

Medicare by any standard has been a success that has benefited and extended the lives of tens of millions of Americans. It - just like Social Security - is one of the most efficient programs in the world. For instance, only 6% of Medicare's budget is diverted to administration costs while private insurance companies spend up to 24% on overhead. As to Social Security, it would have plenty of money to sustain its obligations if the Congress had not stolen trillions of dollars from its funds to pay for their pork barrel projects and their undeclared and unnecessary wars.

The U.S. today spends $32 million an hour on war. We spend $4 billion per month in Afghanistan alone. Since 9/11, the taxpayers of this nation have spent $7 trillion dollars on 7 wars and countless interventions that have netted no tangible benefits. It has simply been used as an excuse to enhance our defense budget which is now - with bi-partisan support - $740 billion.

The defense budget sucks up 57% of our entire discretionary budget. None of this has enhanced our security, promoted democracy abroad or has expanded our liberty at home. The paradox that I wrote about in my first book is that our national security complex in fact undermined and diminished those laudable objectives that justify our militaristic and interventionist policies.

We are being fooled again. Please do not fall for lies masquerading as truth. The arguments against universal health care, a livable minimum wage, free state universities and the rebuilding of our infrastructure are ideological arguments not factual dissertations. The power elite are essentially supporting a political and economic system that is not of, by or for the people. It is an inequitable structure that permitted over the last 4 decades the slow undoing of our once vibrant middle class and the political power of labor. When I was a young lad in the 1960s, only 10% of the generated wealth produced each year went to the top 1%. In 2017, 82% of the new wealth generated that year went to this superclass of capitalists. At some point this economic arrangement - like a Ponzi scheme - will collapse in on itself or be forcibly removed by the oppressed.

The ultimate question confronted by this generation of leaders is whether they will permit these changes by peaceful cooperation or force those that demand them to resort to violence as the founding fathers did against King George III.

The party conventions of 2020 have ended. Both were a dismal display of the disconnect between the political elites and the reality most of the citizens they allegedly represent are struggling to overcome. The Democrats brought in Republican speakers that belittled progressive ideals while asserting that Alexandria Ocasio-Cortez (AOC) and her views did not represent the party, even though she is one of their most popular members. They snubbed former President Jimmy Carter, whose health may have prevented his attendance, and congresswoman Tulsi Gabbard. They allotted a small slot of just one minute for AOC that was much less than what was given to the Republican speakers, Colin Powell, and John Kasich.

Many observed that this party that was once led by Presidents Franklin Delano Roosevelt and John F. Kennedy who championed the rights of the working class and supported labor where ignoring this legacy as they engaged in class warfare, shaming the dissent of progressives, minorities and the working class as they attempted to appeal to moderate Republicans.

The Republican convention was more of the same. Empty slogans and token reforms but elicited no specific programs that would ameliorate the social and economic maladies of our society. They unconscionably ignored climate change which remains a major threat to humanity. Additionally, both conventions

The Hidden War

ignored the national security complex that is bankrupting the future of our children. There was no peace message, demanding an end to our destructive and heartless wars.

It was also very illuminating that Joe Biden chose Kamara Harris as his running mate. A candidate whose draconian and cruel initiatives as District Attorney of San Francisco and as Attorney General for the state of California was highlighted so effectively by Tulsi in an early Democratic debate that not only knocked her off her front running status but out of the race. This infuriated the party leadership because she was one of their chosen prospects for the Democratic nomination.

She essentially is a centrist Democrat who on occasion supports programs on the left. Thus, she was a better choice than Clinton's Senator Tim Kaine who was a Democrat in name only.

Biden's choice obviously did not inspire the base. The party leadership basically were playing identity politics once again that would not alienate their donors. Harris was a black woman that will support the agenda of Wall Street just like Obama. This insidious strategy is to get women and blacks to support the ticket without offering them anything in return. They essentially with their token choice from their perspective were killing two birds with one stone.

The Democratic strategy so far has revealed that the party has learned nothing from 2016 or are wittingly ignoring what they know because they are just too addicted to the money flowing into the party by affluent donors and special interest groups. They are too corrupt to change even when their instincts tell them this is potentially a losing strategy. Thus, Trump erased Biden's 17-point lead over the summer as calculated by trusted polls and transformed this race into a dead heat.

After Trump's disastrous performance in the first debate, Biden regained lost ground. However, his lead in many critical states is within the margin of error. If the dynamics of the race do not change, Trump could pull off another upset and retain the presidency.

If Trump presides over a second term, it will not be because of Putin, Russian bots, Tulsi Gabbard, Bernie Sanders, Jill Stein, the Green Party, the People's Party, Jimmy Door, or disgruntled progressives. It will be a consequence of the entrenched corruptive ties to Wall Street money, the weapons industry and rapacious plutocrats that continue to influence the strategies, the policies, and the choices the Democratic leadership implements.

If Biden wins, his administration could go in two possible directions. The one that is most likely is that he will pursue similar policies abroad while not offending Wall Street domestically. He will rejoin the Paris Accords and attempt to repair the nuclear agreement with Iran. He will reimpose sanctions for those who do not have proof of healthcare when filing their income taxes and will attempt to augment Obama Care. He may also pursue a second stimulus package that hopefully will focus on Main Street not Wall Street. Other than that, nothing will fundamentally change.

The other more remote possibility is that he might have an epiphany as he stares into the eyes of history and contemplates his legacy. In this scenario, he decides to govern more like FDR and JFK, promoting policies that will ameliorate the suffering and the injustices that are rampant in our society, as well as reign in our militarism.

The worst aspect of his victory is that the establishment Democrats will perceive their triumph as an affirmation of their neoliberal programs and their aggressive interventionist foreign policy that has bi-partisan support. They will further smear progressives as part of a Russian subversive plot and continue to ignore the interests of their base who overwhelmingly support universal health care, a Green New Deal, and an end to our perpetual wars.

The ongoing disillusionment of the left in every election cycle in my opinion will not end until they refuse to tolerate these insidious slogans that shame their discontent and compel them to vote for candidates that offer them nothing. A perfidious narrative that manufactures their consent with the assistance of a vacuous and compliant media. Never really understanding how propaganda and power work to maintain a system that benefits the elites.

This is what I grappled with and revealed in both my prior books. How this perfidious narrative that power depends upon for its perpetuation is obediently accepted as reality by our society without any meaningful discussion that would unveil the absurdities on which this narrative is founded. The reason for this is that to understand and accept truth is a very stressful process for many because in order to see truth you must accept that the reality you have been living in was a lie. Those that dissent or that promote the counter narrative in our nation, as well as other countries, have faced, and to some degree have cognitively seen, what power is and how it subtly manipulates and reaffirms the political, economic, and social structures of which power derives its strength. A form of propaganda that diverts us from understanding or viewing the source of that power.

The Hidden War

It is time to break from the two-party duopoly and form a progressive third party that represents the interests of the people and is not beholden to special interest money. A party that has a reasonable chance for electing its members and whose poll numbers are high enough to influence the decision making of the two major parties. Until that happens, we will remain in this inequitable system that is slowly desecrating our liberty and our hope of ever reaching the mountain top, fulfilling the promise of America.

UPDATE: As I was finishing my final edits for this volume, Joe Biden and Kamara Harris were declared by major media outlets as the victors of this highly contentious 2020 election. The Democratic leaders and their media supporters immediately declared this victory as an affirmation of their leadership and neoliberal policies. Pelosi even audaciously proclaimed that the results of the election had given the Democrats a "mandate."

This spinning of the election narrative was advanced even though the Democrats had barely retaken the Senate and had lost significant ground in the House of Representatives. Trump in fact had more support and votes than he received in 2016. The reality is that the vast majority of the electorate that had voted for the Democratic ticket were casting their votes against Trump and not for Biden.

The only positive outcomes were the overwhelming numbers who supported the same progressive candidates that the establishment Democrats had been marginalizing and smearing for years.

In any event, the primary goal of the left was to defeat Trump. The question now becomes will they all go back to sleep and watch feel good videos on Facebook or will they continue the fight to rebuild our republic which Biden and Harris only rhetorically support. As former British Prime Minister Winston Churchill observed when allied forces finally triumphed over field marshal Rommel and his much-feared Africa Corp in Northern Africa, "Now this is not the end. It is not even the beginning of the end. But it is, perhaps, the end of the beginning."

I recite this quote not because I view Trump as another Hitler or fascist. He was in my opinion just another corrupt politician whose policies were not that much different than many of his predecessors. What made his administration incoherent and chaotic was that he had no core ideological positions and would issue tweets based on his emotional response to criticism or what he perceived to be in his family's interests. The reason I used this quote is that his removal means nothing unless the people continue their righteous demands for real structural changes within our political, economic and social arrangements and structures, so that the government fulfills its obligation to represent the interests of the govern and future generations.

ENDNOTE REFERENCES

1. Beware: The Douglas/Janney/Simkin Silver Bullets by James DiEugenio
2. 2019 JFK Conference presentation on FBI by James DiEugenio
3. NBC story discussed on Jimmy Dore Show in 2019
4. I Can't Breathe by Matt Tiabbi pgs. 112-115
5. Interview of Phil Donahue in 2013 by Democracy Now
6. The Paradox of our National Security Complex by Otto pg. 250
7. Mary Ferrell Foundation Website (ZR/RIFLE)
8. Remembering America by Goodwin pgs. 205-206
9. Ibid pg. 207
10. Brothers by Talbot pg. 398
11. Ibid pg. 399
12. The Paradox of our National Security Complex by Otto pgs. 336-337
13. Ibid pg. 337
14. The Secret History of the CIA by Trento pg. 344
15. Church Committee: Interim Report – Alleged Assassination Plots Involving Foreign Leaders pg. 173
16. Remembering America by Goodwin pg. 189
17. Church Committee: Interim Report…pgs. 324-325
18. The Paradox of our National Security Complex by Otto pg. 127
19. Ibid pgs. 9-10
20. Church Committee: Interim Report…pg. 174
21. Into the Darkness – Volume 2 by Newman pg. 227
22. The Brothers by Kinzer pgs. 292-293
23. Ibid pg. 293
24. Ibid pg. 293
25. The Paradox of our National Security Complex by Otto pg. 70
26. Why the CIA Killed JFK and Malcolm X by Koerner pgs. 60-61
27. Ibid pg. 62
28. Ibid pg. 62
29. Ibid pg. 63
30. Ibid pgs. 64-65
31. Ibid pg. 62
32. The Brothers by Kinzer pgs. 292-293
33. JFK & The Unspeakable by Douglass pg. 13
34. Ibid pgs. 14-15

ENDNOTE REFERENCES

35. Ibid pg. 14
36. The Paradox of our National Security Complex by Otto pg. 283
37. Ibid pg. 159
38. JFK & The Unspeakable by Douglass pg. 14
39. The Paradox of our National Security Complex by Otto pg. 285
40. Ibid pg. 285
41. Outgoing Soviet Ciphered Telegram N. 20076 (10/27/62)
42. Soviet Memo by Malinovsky & Zakharov (9/8/62)
43. The Paradox of our National Security Complex by Otto pg. 140
44. JFK & The Unspeakable by Douglass pg. 21-29
45. Ibid pg. 21
46. Ibid pg. 22
47. Ibid pg. 29 & 47b. Ibid pg. 30
48. National Security Action Memorandum 263
49. The Paradox of our National Security Complex by Otto pg. 288
50. Ibid pg. 161
51. Ibid pg. 201
52. Ibid pgs. 159-160, 201
53. Katzenbach Memorandum
54. The Paradox of our National Security Complex pgs. 159-160
55. Ibid. pg. 159
56. Ibid pg. 159
57. Ibid pg. 160
58. Ibid pgs. 157-158
59. Reclaiming Parkland by DiEugenio pgs. 69-70
60. The Paradox of our National Security Complex by Otto pgs. 201-202
61. Ibid pgs. 157-159
62. Tosh Plumlee video on Youtube
63. The Paradox of our National Security Complex by Otto pg. 187
64. Bury My Heart at Wounded Knee by Brown pg. 446
65. Ibid pg. 448
66. Buck v. Bell, Democracy Now, 5/17/16
67. Ibid
68. The Devil's Chessboard by Talbot pg. 16
69. The Paradox of our National Security Complex by Otto pg. 338
70. The Johnson Tapes- telephone conferences with Richard Nixon on 11/3/68 & 11/8/68

71. American Values by RFK, Jr. pg. 351
72. CIA Rogues and the Killing of the Kennedys by Nolan pg. 191
73. The Paradox of our National Security Complex by Otto pg. 335
74. CIA Rogues and the Killing of the Kennedys by Nolan pg. 268
75. The Paradox of our National Security Complex by Otto pg. 335
76. CIA Rogues and the Killing of the Kennedys by Nolan pg. 189
77. Ibid pg. 189
78. Ibid pg. 189
79. Ibid pgs. 262-265
80. Ibid pg. 265
81. Ibid pg. 267
82. A Lie too Big to Fail by Pease pg. 493
83. Ibid pg. 493
84. Ibid pg. 493
85. Ibid pg. 493
86. Ibid pg. 494
87. The Devil's Chessboard by Talbot pg. 567
88. Ibid pgs. 566-568
89. Ibid pg. 568
90. Mort Sahl: The Kennedy Years, YouTube
91. Ibid
92. Ibid
93. Interview with David Lifton by Brent Holland of Night Fright
94. American Values by RFK, Jr. pg.133
95. Ibid pg. 9
96. Giants by Stauffer pgs. 114-115
97. Promises Kept by Bernstein pg. 295
98. Presidential Courage by Beschloss pg. 275
99. Ibid pgs. 275-276
100. Ibid pg. 276
101. Ibid pg. 272
102. Kennedy by Sorensen pg. 359
103. Promises Kept by Bernstein pg. 287
104. Ibid pg. 287
105. Ibid pg. 287
106. Ibid pg. 288
107. Battling Wallstreet by Gibson pg. 19

ENDNOTE REFERENCES

108. Ibid pg. 21
109. Ibid pg. 31
110. Ibid pgs. 33-34
111. Ibid pg. 151
112. John Kenneth Galbraith by Parker pg. 406
113. Ibid pg. 406
114. Presidential Courage by Beschloss pg. 279
115. President George Washington's Farewell Address, 1796
116. The Education of a Statesman by Leaming pg. 363
117. The Paradox of our National Security Complex by Otto pg. 78-81
118. Bury My Heart at Wounded Knee by Brown pg. 87
119. Ibid pgs. 86-87
120. Ibid pg. 86
121. Ibid pgs. 87-89
122. Ibid pg. 89
123. Ibid pg. 89
124. Ibid pgs. 89-90
125. Ibid pgs. 90-91
126. The Letters of John F. Kennedy pg. X
127. William Binney, Unity4J, You Tube, 4/8/19
128. Ibid
129. Ibid
130. America: The Farewell Tour by Hedges pg. 95
131. Ibid pg. 95
132. A Collective Bargain by McAlevey pgs. 47-48
133. Ibid pg. 56
134. America: The Farewell Tour by Hedges pgs. 94-95
135. Ibid pg. 94
136. Ibid pg. 95
137. Ibid pg. 95
138. Ibid pgs. 95-96
139. Ibid pg. 95
140. Ibid pg. 95
141. Interview of Jordan Chariton (Flint Water Crimes) The Jimmy Dore Show (4/17/19)
142. Ibid

143.	Ibid
144.	Ibid
145.	Ibid
146.	Ibid
147.	I Can't Breathe by Tiabbi pgs. 57-60
148.	Ibid pg. 57
149.	Ibid pg. 58
150.	Ibid pgs. 58-59
151.	Ibid pgs. 58-59
152.	Ibid pg. 59
153.	Ibid pg. 60
154.	Wikipedia
155.	I Can't Breathe by Tiabbi pg. 64
156.	Ibid pgs. 64-65
157.	Ibid pgs. 64-68
158.	Ibid pg. 68
159.	Ibid pg. 69
160.	Ibid pgs. 69-70
161.	Ibid pg. 304
162.	Ibid pg. 305
163.	America: The Farewell Tour by Hedges pg. 197
164.	Ibid pg. 197
165.	Ibid pg. 308

BIBLIOGRAPHY

Bernstein, Irving, **Promises Kept: John F. Kennedy's New Frontier** (New York: Oxford University Press, 1991)

Beschloss, Michael, **Presidential Courage** (New York: Simon & Schuster, 2007)

Blaine, Gerald & McCubbin, Lisa, **The Kennedy Detail** (New York: Gallery Books, 2010)

Brown, Dee, **Bury my Heart at Wounded Knee** (Canada: Holt, Rinehart & Winston, 1970)

Cohen, Stephen F., **War with Russia? (From Putin & Ukraine to Trump & Russiagate)** (New York: Hot Books – Skyhorse Publishing, Inc., 2019)

Dallek, Robert, **An Unfinished Life: John F. Kennedy, 1917-1963** (New York: Little, Brown & Company, 2003)

DiEugenio, James, **Reclaiming Parkland** (New York: Skyhorse Publishing, 2013)

Douglass, James, **JFK and the Unspeakable** (Maryknoll, New York: Orbis Books, 2008)

Ellis, Joseph J., **American Sphinx (The Character of Thomas Jefferson)** (New York: Vintage Books, 1996)

Ellis, Joseph L., **Founding Brothers (The Revolutionary Generation)** (New York: Vintage Books, 2002)

Fiester, Sherry P., **Enemy of the Truth** (Southlake, TX: JFK Lancer Productions & Publications, Inc., 2012)

Gibson, Donald, **Battling Wallstreet: The Kennedy Presidency** (New York: Sheridan Square Press, 1994)

Goodwin, Richard N., **Remembering America (A voice from the sixties)** (Boston: Little, Brown & Company, 1988)

Hedges, Chris, **America: The Farewell Tour** (New York: Simon and Schuster Paperbacks, 2018)

Jeffries, Donald, **Survival of the Richest** (New York: Skyhorse Publishing, 2017)

Kennedy Jr., Robert F., **American Values** (New York: Harper Collins Publishers, 2018)

Kinzer, Stephen, **The Brothers (John Foster Dulles, Allen Dulles and their Secret World War)** (New York: Times Books, Henry Holt and Company LLC, 2013)

Koerner, John, **Why the CIA Killed JFK and Malcolm X: The Secret Drug Trade in Laos** (Winchester, UK: Chronos Books, 2014)

Leaming, Barbara, **Jack Kennedy (The Education of a Statesman)** (New York: W.W. Norton & Company, 2006)

Lee, Harper, **To Kill a Mockingbird** (New York: Popular Library, 1960)
McAlevey, Jane, **A Collective Bargain (Unions, Organizing, and the Fight for Democracy)** (New York: HarperCollins Publishers, 2020)
McCullough, David, **John Adams** (New York: Simon & Schuster, 2001)
Meacham, Jon, **Thomas Jefferson: The Art of Power** (New York: Random House, 2012)
Muehlenbeck, Philip E., **Betting on the Africans** (New York: Oxford University Press, 2012)
Newman, John M., **Countdown to Darkness: The Assassination of President Kennedy (Volume 2)** (North Charleston, SC: CreateSpace Independent Publishing Platform, 2017)
Nolan, Patrick, **CIA Rogues and the Killing of the Kennedys** (New York: Skyhorse Publishing, 2013)
Otto, Richard, **The Paradox of our National Security Complex (How secrecy and security diminish our liberty and threaten our democratic republic)** (Winchester, UK: Chronos Books, 2017)
Otto, Richard, **Rethinking America: Lies Masquerading as Truth** (Kindle Direct Publishing, 2019)
Pease, Lisa, **A Lie too Big to Fail (The Real History of the Assassination of Robert F. Kennedy)** (Port Townsend, WA: Feral House, 2018)
Parker, Richard, **John Kenneth Galbraith: His Life, His Politics, His Economics** (New York: Farrar, Straus & Giroux, 2005)
Pinsker, Matthew, **Lincoln's Sanctuary (Abraham Lincoln and the Soldier's Home)** (New York: Oxford University Press, Inc., 2003)
Sandler, Martin W., **The Letters of John F. Kennedy** (New York: Bloomsbury Press, 2013)
Sholtz, E. Martin, **History will not Absolve Us: Orwellian Control, Public Denial, & the Murder of President Kennedy** (Kurtz, Ulmer & Delucia, 1996)
Sorensen, Theodore C., **Kennedy** (New York: Harper & Row Publishers, 1965)
Stauffer, John, **Giants (The Parallel Lives of Frederick Douglass and Abraham Lincoln)** (New York: Twelve – The Hachette Book Group, 2008)
Talbot, David, **Brothers: The Hidden History of the Kennedy Years** (New York: Free Press, 2007)
Talbot, David, **The Devil's Chessboard** (New York: Harper Collins Publishers, 2016)
The Teachings of Jesus (The Holy Bible King James Version) (New York: Penguin Books, 1995)

BIBLIOGRAPHY

Tiabbi, Matt, **I Can't Breathe (A Killing on Bay Street)** (New York: Spiegel & Grau, an imprint of Random House, a division of Penguin Random House, 2017)

Trento, Joseph L., **The Secret History of the CIA** (New York: MJF Books, Fine Publications, 2001)

Wiencek, Henry, **An Imperfect God (George Washington: His Slaves and the Creation of America)** (New York: Farrar, Strauss and Giroux, 2003)

NEWS REPORTS/EDITORIALS

Becker, Deborah, The Women in Kennedy's White House, 11/15/13

Cohn, Marjorie, Will Congress Authorize Indefinite Detention for Americans? Truthout.com, 5/10/18

Conway, Debra, US-Cuba Relations: Castro Assassination Plots, JFK Lancer, 2007

DiEugenio, James, Part II: Sy Hersh and the Monroe/JFK Papers: The History of a Thirty-Year Hoax, Kennedys and King

Doyle, Kate and Kornbluh, Peter, CIA and Assassinations: The Guatemala 1954 Documents, National Security Archive Briefing Book No. 4, 1997

Greenwald, Glenn, Veteran NBC/MSNBC Journalist Blasts the Network for Being Captive to the National Security state and Reflexively Pro-War to Stop Trump, The Intercept, 1/3/19

Hedges, Chris, The Martyrdom of Julian Assange, Truthdig.com, 4/11/19

Lauria, Joe, A New Twist in Seth Rich Murder Case, Consortiumnews.com, 4/8/17

Lawrence, Patrick, See No Evil Phase of Russiagate, Consortiumnews.com, 5/11/20

McGovern, Ray, Memo to President ahead of Monday's Summit, Consortiumnews.com, 7/19/18

McGovern, Ray, Turn out the Lights, Russiagate is Over, Consortiumnews.com, 5/19/20

Moore, Mark H., The Police and Weapon Offenses (The Annals of the American Academy of Political and Social Sciences), Vol. 452, Nov. 1980

Parenti, Michael, The JFK Assassination: Defending the Gangster State, Political Archives, 1996

Parker, Greg, The Myth of "Fiddle" and "Faddle", 2012

Parker, Gareth, The New York Times' Insidious Ongoing Disinformation Campaign on Russia & Elections, Consortiumnews.com, 3/17/20

Pilger, John, Assange Arrest a Warning from History, Consortiumnews.com, 4/12/19

Pilger, John, Getting Julian Assange: The Untold Story, 6/5/17

Pilger, John, Alternet, 5/23/17

Ritter, Scott, As Another Perjury Trap is Exposed the FBI's Case Against Trump Collapses, Consortiumnews.com, 5/14/20

Schlesinger, Jr., Arthur, JFK: The Truth as I see it, Cigar Aficionado, Dec. 1998

Sjursen, Major Danny, 18 Years of War, Truthdig.com, 11/29/18

Telesur, The Banking Crisis that nearly Destroyed Ecuador's Economy, 3/8/16

NEWS REPORTS/EDITORIALS

The Housing Time Bomb, Wealth Disparities in U.S. Approaching 1920s Levels, 2/21/10

SPEECHES/DOCUMENTS/REPORTS/VIDEOS/INTERNET
Adolph Hitler's speech on Enabling Act to Reichstag, 1933
A Study of Assassination (CIA Assassination Manual – 1954 Guatemalan Documents)
Center on Budget and Policy Priorities' graph based on data from Piketty and Saez
Church Committee: Interim Report on Assassination Plots, 1975
FBI Crime Statistics for 2019
Fidel Castro's speech on JFK Assassination, 11/23/1963
Inspector General Report (CIA) on Bay of Pigs, 1961
Inspector General Report (CIA) on Castro Assassination Plots, 1967
James Garrison's interview by Playboy Magazine in 1967, JFK Lancer
Martin Luther King, Jr. speech at Riverside Church in NYC, 4/4/1967
Michael Moore, Fahrenheit 11/9/2018, YouTube
Pontier, Zac-Stuart, The RFK Tapes (10 Podcasts), 2018
President Abraham Lincoln's Cooper Union Address, 2/27/1860
President Abraham Lincoln's Gettysburg Address, 11/19/1863
President Abraham Lincoln's Second Inaugural Address, 3/4/1865
President Barack Obama's Eulogy for victims of Dylan Roof, 2015
President George Washington's Farewell Address, 1796
President John F. Kennedy's Inaugural Address, 1/20/1961
President John F. Kennedy's American University Address, 6/10/1963
President John F. Kennedy's Civil Rights Address, 6/11/1963
President John F. Kennedy's speech at Amherst College, 10/26/1963
President John F. Kennedy's speech at Washington University in Seattle, 11/16/1961
President John F. Kennedy's speech at University of Berlin, 6/26/1963
President Lyndon Johnson tapes – telephone conferences with Richard Nixon, 11/3/1968 & 11/8/1968
Ray McGovern of VIPS, Russia-gate: Can you handle the truth? YouTube, 8/7/2018
Sahl, Mort, The Kennedy Years, YouTube
Senator Robert F. Kennedy's speech at University of Kansas, 3/18/1968
The Confessions of an Economic Hitman - John Perkins, You Tube, 2014
The Jimmy Dore Show, Interview of former NSA Technical Director William Binney, 2018
The Jimmy Dore Show, Interview of Presidential Candidate Tulsi Gabbard, 2019

NEWS REPORTS/EDITORIALS

The Jimmy Dore Show, Interview of Chris Hedges, 2019
The Jimmy Dore Show, Interview of Aaron Mate', 2019
The Jimmy Dore Show, interview of Jordan Chariton, 2019
The Jimmy Dore Show, interview of Jesse Ventura, 2020
The Tucker Carlson Show, interview of Terry Turchie of FBI, 2016
The Tucker Carlson Show, interview of Glenn Greenwald, 4/2019
Tosh Plumlee video on South Knoll in Dealey Plaza, You Tube
Uniform Crime Report, U.S. Department of Justice – Federal Bureau of Investigation, 9/10/1980
William Binney, Unity4J, You Tube, 4/8/2019
Wikipedia

Made in the USA
Middletown, DE
26 January 2021